Thomas Mc

Classic Thinkers

Thomas More

Joanne Paul

polity

First published in 2017 by Polity Press

Polity Press
65 Bridge Street
Cambridge CB2 1UR, UK

Polity Press
350 Main Street
Malden, MA 02148, USA

ISBN-13: 978-0-7456-9216-6
ISBN-13: 978-0-7456-9217-3(pb)

A catalogue record for this book is available from the British Library.

Library of Congress Cataloging-in-Publication Data

Names: Paul, Joanne, author.
Title: Thomas More / Joanne Paul.
Description: Malden, MA : Polity, 2016. | Series: Classic thinkers | Includes
    bibliographical references and index.
Identifiers: LCCN 2016016386 (print) | LCCN 2016031201 (ebook) | ISBN
    9780745692166 (hardback) | ISBN 9780745692173 (pbk.) | ISBN 9780745692197
    (Mobi) | ISBN 9780745692203 (Epub)
Subjects: LCSH: More, Thomas, Saint, 1478-1535. | Philosophy, Renaissance.
Classification: LCC B785.M84 P38 2016 (print) | LCC B785.M84 (ebook) | DDC
    192–dc23
LC record available at https://lccn.loc.gov/2016016386

Typeset in 10.5 on 12 pt Palatino
by Toppan Best-set Premedia Limited
Printed and bound in Great Britain by CPI Group (UK) Ltd, Croydon.

For further information on Polity, visit our website: politybooks.com.

Contents

Preface

I had not originally intended to write a book about Thomas More. He is too controversial a figure. He evokes too many emotive responses. He has been declared a saint, denounced as a murderer. To write a book about More is to invite fierce backlash, no matter what it says. Even a book about More's ideas, his thought and works, could prove deeply contentious.

And yet not to try is to continue to let such controversy cloud our understanding of More as a thinker. Thus, when given the opportunity to write an introduction to his thought, I took it. The intention of this book is to engage only fleetingly with the more controversial aspects of More's life – such as whether or not he lived for a time as a monk or tortured 'heretics', or how the overwrought question of his sexual appetite might be settled. Instead I focus attention on his writing, all of his writing, in an attempt to grasp what More was trying to do in his own context and what legacy he may have bequeathed to future generations.

The year this book is published, 2016, marks 500 years since *Utopia* appeared in print. *Utopia* has not been out of print since, and is still read widely today; few books can boast such a popular history. More's neologism is now part of everyday language and has come to denote a genre as well as a way of thinking. All that being said, this is not a book about *Utopia* either. Although *Utopia* is More's most significant contribution to the world of ideas, it does little to help us understand him or his times. It is purposely opaque and invites more questions than it answers, which is almost certainly part of why it has remained so popular. In order to appreciate More's ideas and their relationship with the times in which he lived, we have to go beyond *Utopia* and explore his other writings. This will certainly give us a better insight into this monumental text. But it is my hope that it will also produce reflection on More's wider intentions, his context and some of the lessons that we can take from his work.

I have written this book with the intention of making More's ideas accessible to an audience that has not necessarily encountered his work before. Part of the reason why *Utopia* has emerged as More's most widely read text is that it has none of the complexity and verbiage of his other works. It is easily digestible in a matter of days (though it has been 500 years and no one can yet claim to fully understand it). This book attempts to treat More's other works, for the most part, in such a way that readers may not have to read them, though it should be noted that they are not as hard-going as many scholars would have you believe. More writes with a wit and a passion that are still apparent 500 years on. But, as he himself would tell you, life is short and university terms even shorter, and this book has been designed to present an introduction to More's context and ideas that can be the foundation to further study – whether of More himself, of his texts, or of various aspects of sixteenth-century literature, politics, religion or thought.

It is for this reason that I have dedicated this book to all students of Thomas More in the past 500 years and for another 500 years to come. I believe our task to be worthwhile, if difficult and, at times, controversial. More lived in an age of great upheaval, characterized by rapid technological changes, religious controversy and violence, political protest and questioning of traditional loyalties. Even at an interval of 500 years, students of More can surely relate to him. We may imagine ourselves to make up a community of scholars over time, just like the Renaissance republic of letters or More's vision of a transtemporal church: a community whose contributions to shared knowledge, I hope, bring us together.

It certainly took a community to produce this book, and so it is essential that I express my deep gratitude before going any further. My thanks must begin with Elliott Karstadt, who first approached me about this project, and to Ellen MacDonald-Kramer and Pascal Porcheron, who have been my contacts at Polity. I am also very grateful to those who read early drafts of the book, either in part or in full, including Antoni Balcerek, Matthew Champion, Signy Gutnick Allen, John-Erik Hansson, James Lancaster, Suzannah Lipscomb, Mathew Lyons, Katie McKeogh, Julia Nicholls, Marius

Ostrowski, Estelle Paranque, Quentin Skinner, James Snell, Miranda Stanyon, Miranda Fay Thomas and Sarah Wilford, and my anonymous reviewers. Helpful suggestions and assistance have also come from Adrian Blau, Annabel Brett, Chris Brooke, David Colclough, Hannah Dawson, Robin Douglass, John Dunn, James Harris, Bruno Leipold, Carole Levin, Noel Malcolm, Sarah Mortimer, Johan Olsthoorn, David Owen, Jon Parkin, Richard Rex, Richard Serjeantson, Edwin Shaw, Gareth Stedman Jones, Latré Stijn, Peter Wilson, as well as from the audiences at the Institute for the Historical Research Early Career Seminar in the History of Ideas, the Cambridge History of Political Thought Seminar and the Oxford History of Political Thought Seminar, and from friends, colleagues and acquaintances too numerous to name. I must also thank both students and colleagues at the New College of the Humanities for listening graciously to more about More than they might have liked over the past two years, and to the staff at the Institute for Historical Research and at the Russian State Archive of Socio-Political History. In addition, the patient and knowledgeable contributions of my copy-editor, Manuela Tecusan, have significantly improved this book, and her expertise in classical thought was especially invaluable. Finally, I am very grateful to my close friends, family and partner for their support and indulgence.

London
2016

Abbreviations

NOTE   I have modernized the spelling of More's English-language texts for ease of understanding, but I have kept all the original words and suffixes. I have added modern punctuation where necessary. I have retained Yale translations of Latin texts in most cases, noting the original Latin or my own translation where relevant.

CW   *Complete Works of Thomas More* (New Haven, CT: Yale University Press, 1963–97)

    APB   *Answer to a Poisoned Book*, Vol. 11 (1985)
    ATM   *The Apology of Thomas More*, Vol. 9 (1979)
    CTA   *The Confutation of Tyndale's Answer*, Vol. 8 (1973)
    DC   *Dialogue of Comfort against Tribulation*, Vol. 12 (1976)
    DCH   *Dialogue Concerning Heresies*, Vol. 6 (1981)
    DT   *De tristia*, Vol. 14 (1976)
    FLT   *The Four Last Things*, Vol. 1 (1997)
    FV   *Fortune Verses*, Vol. 1 (1997)
    HRT   *Historia Richardi Tertii*, Vol. 15 (1986)
    LB   *Letter to Bugenhagen*, Vol. 7 (1990)
    LD   *Letter to Dorp*, Vol. 15 (1986)
    LM   *Letter to a Monk*, Vol. 15 (1986)
    LO   *Letter to Oxford*, Vol. 15 (1986)
    LP   *Latin Poems*, Vol. 3 Pt. II (1984)
    LPM   *Life of Pico della Mirandola*, Vol. 1 (1997)
    LQE   *Lamentation of Queen Elizabeth*, Vol. 1 (1997)
    PV   *Pageant Verses*, Vol. 1 (1997)
    RL   *Responsio ad Lutherum*, Vol. 5 (1969)

RIII   *The History of King Richard the Third*, Vol. 2 (1963)
SB   *Debellation of Salem and Bizance*, Vol. 10 (1987)
SS   *Supplication of Souls*, Vol. 7 (1990)
TL   *Translation of Lucian*, Vol. 3 Pt. I (1974)
TP   *Treatise upon the Passion*, Vol. 13 (1976)
Ut   *Utopia*, Vol. 4 (1965)
ODNB   *Oxford Dictionary of National Biography* (online)
OED   *Oxford English Dictionary* (online)
SL   Thomas More, *Selected Letters*, ed. Elizabeth Frances Rogers
        (New Haven, CT: Yale University Press, 1961)

Key Dates

1478	7 February: Born to John and Agnes More in Cheapside, London.
1483	July: Richard III takes the throne from Edward V.
1485	Begins school at St Anthony's.
	August: Henry VII defeats Richard III at the Battle of Bosworth Field and becomes the first Tudor king of England.
1489	Leaves St Anthony's for the household of John Morton, formerly bishop of Ely, now Lord Chancellor and archbishop of Canterbury.
1492	Begins study at Canterbury College, Oxford.
1494	Returns to London and begins legal training at New Inn.
1496	Advances his legal training at Lincoln's Inn.
	Begins writing English poems.
1499	Meets Erasmus for the first time and is also introduced to Prince Henry, the future Henry VIII.
1501	Lectures on Augustine's *City of God* at St Lawrence Jewry, London.
	Called to the bar at Lincoln's Inn.
	Begins residing at the Charterhouse.
1502	April: Prince Arthur, Henry VII's heir, dies and Prince Henry becomes heir.
1503	Becomes reader at Furnivall's Inn.
	Writes the *Lamentation of Queen Elizabeth*.
1504	Possibly sits in parliament.
1505	January: Leaves the Charterhouse and marries Jane Colt, moving to Bucklersbury, London.

Erasmus visits and they begin their translations of
   Lucian.

Writes *Fortune Verses*.

1506   More and Erasmus' translations of Lucian are published.

1508   Makes his first visit to the continent, to see universities
   associated with humanism.

1509   April: Henry VII dies and Henry VIII becomes king.

August: Erasmus stays with the More family and writes
   his *Moriae encomium*.

Becomes a 'freeman' of the Mercers' Company and
   negotiates with Antwerp officials on their behalf.

Appointed justice of the peace for Middlesex.

1510   Sits as representative for London in parliament.

Appointed undersheriff for London.

Publishes *Life of Pico della Mirandola*.

1511   Jane Colt dies; marries Alice Middleton.

Reader at Lincoln's Inn.

1513   Begins writing *The History of King Richard the Third*.

1514   Elected to Doctors' Commons.

1515   May: Travels to Flanders as ambassador.

Resolves Erasmus' financial troubles.

July: Meets Peter Gillis and discusses Utopia.

Writes the *Letter to Dorp*.

1516   Autumn: Becomes a member of the Court of Star
   Chamber.

December: Publishes *Utopia*.

1517   30 April: Called to an emergency meeting at the
   Guildhall and sent out to try to calm London rioters.

1 May: The 'Evil May Day Riots' break out throughout
   the early morning hours.

September: Embarks on a three-month diplomatic
   mission to Calais.

2 November: Luther publishes *95 Theses* in Wittenberg.

December: Travels to Bruges to meet Richard Pace.

1518   March: Officially begins work as a king's councillor and
   as 'Master of Requests'.

Latin Poems published in second edition of *Utopia*.

1520   Henry VIII publishes *Assertio septem Sacramentorum
   adversus Martinum Lutherum*.

1521   Knighted and made undertreasurer.

Travels once again to Bruges and Calais as ambassador.

Moves his family to Chelsea.

1522	Writes *The Four Last Things*.
1523	Writes *Responsio ad Lutherum*.
	Appointed Speaker of the House of Commons.
1524	Named High Steward at the University of Oxford.
1525	Named High Steward at the University of Cambridge.
	Becomes chancellor of the duchy of Lancaster.
1526	Writes the *Letter to Bugenhagen*.
1527	Summer: Diplomatic mission to France.
	Autumn: Henry VIII takes him into his confidence about the marriage annulment.
1528	Cuthbert Tunstall asks him to write in defence of the church in English.
1529	June: Publishes *A Dialogue Concerning Heresies*.
	Summer: Travels to Cambrai as ambassador.
	September: Publishes *Supplication of Souls*.
	18 October: Wolsey removed from the position of Lord Chancellor.
	29 October: Becomes Lord Chancellor.
1530	February: First evangelical martyr burned in England.
1531	February: Henry VIII made 'Supreme Head of the Church of England'.
	November–December: Richard Bayfield and John Tewkesbury burned at Smithfield.
1532	Publishes first part of *The Confutation of Tyndale's Answer*.
	30 April: James Bainham burned at Smithfield.
	15 May: Submission of the clergy.
	16 May: Resigns from chancellorship.
	December: Writes the *Letter against Frith*.
1533	Publishes second part of *The Confutation of Tyndale's Answer*.
	1 June: Does not attend Anne Boleyn's coronation.
	April: Writes *The Apology of Sir Thomas More*.
	October: Writes *Debellation of Salem and Bizance*.
	December: Publishes the *Letter against Frith*.
	December: Writes *Answer to a Poisoned Book*.
1534	January: More's printer William Rastell interrogated by Thomas Cromwell.
	February: More's name appears on the Act of Attainder against Elizabeth Barton.
	March: The Act of Succession passed.
	April: Leaves *Treatise upon the Passion* unfinished.
	12 April: Summoned to take the Oath.

	17 April: Imprisoned in the Tower.
	Writes *A Treatise to Receive the Blessed Body, A Dialogue of Comfort against Tribulation*.
1535	Writes *De tristitia Christi*.
	1 July: Tried and convicted of treason, sentenced to death.
	6 July: Executed at Tower Hill.
1547	January: Henry VIII dies and Edward VI takes the throne.
1551	First English translation of *Utopia* published.
1553	July: Edward VI dies and, after a short struggle, Mary I becomes queen.
1557	Roper and Harpsfield complete their biographies of Thomas More, which circulate in manuscript.
	More's English works published.
1558	November: Mary I dies and Elizabeth I becomes queen.
1563	Foxe's *Acts and Monuments* published with stories of More's persecution of Protestants.
1565–6	Collection of More's Latin works published in Louvain.
1570	Expanded version of *Acts and Monuments* published.
1588	Stapleton's *Life of More* published.
1599	*Life of Sir Thomas More* by 'Ro. Ba.' (thought to be Robert Bassett) published.
c. 1592	*The Book of Sir Thomas More* written.
1626	Roper's biography of More published.
1630	Cresacre More's biography of More published.
1879	Moritz Kaufmann publishes *Utopias; or, Schemes of Social Improvements: From Thomas More to Karl Marx*.
1888	Karl Kautsky publishes *Thomas More and His Utopia*.
1935	Canonized as Saint Thomas More.

Introduction
The Thought of Thomas More

Few who qualify for the title of 'classic thinker' are as widely known as Thomas More. Thanks especially to his role at the court of the infamous Henry VIII, there are countless biographies and fictional portrayals of him in novels, in plays, on television and in film. More has truly become, as Erasmus called him, 'a man for all seasons', employed in a variety of contexts, and given every role from saint to villain.[1] There have been, however, few attempts to treat More as a thinker worthy of study five hundred years later. Whereas most thinkers are known for their work and ideas, which must then be placed in the context of their lives, the life of Thomas More is well known, and we must seek to recover his thought.

This book embarks on precisely such an enterprise. Through a comprehensive engagement with More's writing, this study explores the development of More's thought, noting both its rich variety and some of the fundamental consistencies that run throughout. Set in the context of one of the most transformative moments in European history, More's ideas are in many senses dynamic, shifting in audience, tone and purpose with changes in the wider political and intellectual context.

That being said, there are also some static, constant elements to More's thought.[2] Throughout, More is concerned with the destruction of what is held in 'common'. This means, for him, what is shared, what no one holds to the exclusion of others, and therefore also what is 'public' or belonging to the corporate community as a whole, such as religious truth, the meaning of words or the structure of the polity.[3] In an ideal world (such as Utopia), common custom would reflect a reorientation towards what is commonly held, as reflective of the truths held in common. For More, this arrangement would be more real than his lived reality, in which artificial customs underpin individual ownership. Such investment in what is one's own serves to break apart those things that are held in common. Consequently, authority – whether religious, political or intellectual – becomes fragmented, resulting in disputes which cannot be resolved. This outcome was More's biggest fear, and in his view it could be avoided by refocusing attention on what is held in 'common', often through a consideration of our common mortal fate.

In setting out his system of thought, More expands on themes relating to the importance of public opinion, the role of the intellectual and the establishment of political legitimacy. More consciously placed himself in dialogue with thinkers such as Plato, Cicero and Augustine, and his ideas, in turn, were read and discussed by subsequent writers such as Bacon, Bodin and Marx. By developing our understanding of More's thought, we build a better historical picture of his own time as well as of his legacy in the centuries that followed, and we open discussion regarding how his thought might provide new perspectives for us today.

Scholarship

There are a number of reasons why More has been little studied as a thinker. Because of his dramatic role in a transformative moment of English history, biographical accounts have often taken precedence over studies of his thought. There is no question that More is a fascinating figure who led a compelling life, and it is easy to prioritize this over attempting to analyse volumes of text. Second, when scholars do turn to More's writings, he frequently becomes a victim of his own success – or rather the victim of *Utopia*'s success – and his thought is often seen solely through a reading of this single text. It is hard to blame scholars on this account; there are reasons why *Utopia* has been so widely read. It is a brilliant, pithy, entertaining and enigmatic text, with a great deal to offer to a wide variety of disciplines. More's other writings, especially the polemic texts, are not usually considered such engaging reading and are deemed not to offer as much by way of intellectual content.

In addition to considering the polemics tedious and intellectually unimportant, scholars also often find them difficult to grapple with because of their weighty theological and religious content. The difficulty often is in the nature of this religious content, which presents intense and often vitriolic arguments against figures whom More considers to be 'heretics', such as Martin Luther (1483–1546) and William Tyndale (1494–1536). More can emerge from these texts as an irrational and violent zealot, an enemy to freedom of religion – and especially to any form of thought opposed to that of the Catholic Church. The project of attempting to understand the foundational arguments to these views has proved objectionable to many.

For this reason, many scholars have resorted to creating multiple Mores, in order to keep the respectable humanism of *Utopia* untouched by the religious zealotry of the polemics. This strategy has a long tradition. In 1935, the year More was canonized by the Catholic Church, R. W. Chambers's biography presented him as a synthesis of religious features deemed to be 'medieval' and ideas contained in *Utopia*, which were claimed as 'modern'. Chambers brought together saint and scholar to create a vibrant protagonist who transcended his context, in his fight for individual conscience. Unfortunately Chambers got More tragically wrong on this point: individual conscience in fact represented More's greatest fear, as we shall see. Nevertheless, Chambers's saintly scholar was extremely influential, dominating much of the scholarship on More in the first half of the twentieth century as well as being immortalized on stage and in film, in Robert Bolt's *A Man for All Seasons*.

In the 1960s three new sets of publications prompted fresh scholarship on More. The first was the publication of More's letters by Elizabeth Frances Rogers in 1961. The second was the establishment of a journal titled *Moreana* by the association Amici Thomae Mori (Friends of Thomas More) for the study of More and his works. And, finally, the first of the fifteen-volume Yale edition of the *Collected Works of Thomas More*, still the standard edition of More's texts, was published in 1963. As a result, the 1970s brought a flood of new work on More. In particular, *Essential Articles for the Study of Thomas More*, published in 1977, brought the work of forty scholars, including James McConica and C. S. Lewis, and even of Robert Bolt himself, into a single volume.

Although much of this work presented More in a largely positive light, the renewal of interest and the re-publication of his polemical works also generated a strongly opposed view, articulated in the work of Richard Marius, Jasper Ridley and G. R. Elton in the 1980s. Marius provided a Freudian account of More as a sex-driven fanatic, whose 'failure' to live a monastic life led to his torture and execution of Protestants. In this reading, much of More's anger towards Lutherans stemmed from their allowance of clerical marriage and from Luther's own marriage to a nun. Ridley and Elton likewise saw More as a violent extremist. Ridley presents this fanatic More in contrast to Thomas Wolsey, Elton in contrast to Thomas Cromwell. Whereas the Chambers–Bolt view of More had been inspired by the Catholic biographies of the sixteenth century, these revisionist accounts were furnished with details from Protestant writers such as John Foxe and arguably went on to form the basis of the portrayal of More in Hilary Mantel's widely read *Wolf Hall* (published in 2009).

Although many of these biographies used More's works to substantiate claims about his life and outlook, they were not intended as analyses of his thought. About the same time, however, shifts in the practice of the history of political thought began to have an effect on the nature of More scholarship. Intellectual historians, led by Quentin Skinner and J. G. A. Pocock, argued for placing emphasis on the context in which thinkers wrote, thereby drawing attention to lesser known contributors to the development of political thinking. This shift prompted a renewal of interest in More's writing, though one largely limited to *Utopia*. Historians of political thought have often had a blind spot when it comes to religious content; hence it is no surprise that, apart from a limited engagement with other writings from More's 'humanist' phase (such as the *Life of Pico*, *History of King Richard the Third* and the *Letters* – to Dorp, Lee, Oxford, etc.), *Utopia* received the most attention. Historians such as Paul Oskar Kristeller, Elizabeth McCutcheon and Quentin Skinner have re-evaluated More's humanism, placing him in the context of the rise of 'civic humanism' and Renaissance rhetoric, but this work does not touch on anything written after 1520. Even Anthony Kenny, whose 1983 *Thomas More* seeks to treat all of More's writings, and argues that More 'deserves a place in the intellectual history of Europe', does so largely on the back of *Utopia*.[4] Debates about these studies continue; Skinner's argument that More belongs in the tradition of neo-Roman thought has recently been opposed by the work of Eric Nelson, who suggests that More was actually arguing against this tradition and in favour of Greek thought; but both historians focus exclusively on *Utopia*.

There are, of course, exceptions. Alistair Fox's (1982) *Thomas More: History and Providence* seeks to present a comprehensive view of More and his ideas, focusing on the theme of providence (God's divine plan) in his works. Fox opposes those who try to draw a dividing line between More's humanist and More's polemical writings, suggesting that there is a 'steady progression in the evolution of his thought' rather than a disjunction and that all of More's works are linked by the themes of universal history and divine providence.[5] Recently two books have furthered the project of breaking down the dichotomy between More's humanism and his polemics and of providing a comprehensive account of More's thought. The first is *The One Thomas More*, written by Travis Curtright (2012). As implied by the title, Curtright's aim is to present More's thought as unified and constant, against the 'multiple Mores' thesis and against those who have a 'prejudice against him'.[6] Curtright's text seeks to uncover More's 'Christian humanism' through an engagement that puts his 1510 *Life of Pico* front and centre. Curtright touches on some important themes, which will also be explored below, especially the importance of the *sensus communis* (common sense), though perhaps the book goes a bit far in expressing his desire to produce a coherent, consistent account of More's thought.[7] The second, Thomas Betteridge's (2013) *Writing Faith and Telling Tales*, tackles, as Chambers's biography had, the medieval–modern divide, still extant in More scholarship. Betteridge attempts to demonstrate that More has a place in the same historical 'tradition' as medieval writers like Chaucer, but states that he does not wish to show that More had ever read these predecessors' texts. This makes his book useful for considering More's literary themes but less helpful in providing the intellectual background for his ideas.

It seems that, after five centuries of division and turbulence, scholarship is moving towards acquiring the ability to engage with More as a historical figure and thinker without attempting to hive off pieces or to pave over inconsistencies, in a desire to produce a comfortable, consistent narrative. As More himself would say about the practice of writing history: 'Let historians begin to show either prejudice or favoritism, and who will there be to lend any credence at all to histories?' (*LP*, 221).

Humanism and Common Usage

To understand More as a thinker, one has to appreciate the intellectual movements of which he was a part. More's work attempted to bring together a variety of ways of thinking about the world. His was a context of conflict and division, and his work aimed to provide a unifying remedy. As Richard Pace (1482–1536) said of More in

1517: 'There's no school of philosophy he doesn't approve of in part. Whatever each one particularly excels in, that's what he particularly admires about it.'[8]

More was one of the pioneers of humanism in England, which sought to revive the study of a wealth of classical – that is, Greek and Roman – texts.[9] The dominant intellectual paradigm in Europe in the medieval period was scholasticism, a mode of study that the humanists found to be elitist, arcane and dogmatic.[10] The scholastics were dedicated to the philosophy of Aristotle (fully rediscovered in the west only since the twelfth century) and constructed complex philosophical systems for understanding Aristotelian ideas and for making them consistent with Christian theology. The humanists objected to these systems as the puffed-up imaginings of an isolated class of scholars and sought instead to understand the ways in which language and ideas interacted with the world around them, thus escaping the scholastics' ivory tower.

From its very inception, humanism was designed as a curriculum for training the young for public life, rather than simply as an exercise in scholarly erudition. Although it was usually noble boys who received such an education, humanists believed in 'true nobility' (*vera nobilitas*) – a combination of virtue, honour and learning that had nothing to do with family or pedigree. Women, too, could be the recipients of such an education, but that had a different aim: domestic rather than public virtue. These educational beliefs and practices were related to the humanist view of politics. Most humanists were dedicated to classical republicanism, that is, to the idea that the people should be the source of power – particularly political power – and that citizens had a duty to serve the republic. Although there were many city republics in Europe at the time – such as the Italian city-states in which humanism began – for humanists in monarchical contexts this dedication to republicanism usually meant a dedication to counselling the ruler and supporting popular institutions like parliament.

To the medieval *trivium* – literally 'meeting point of three ways': a syllabus of three subjects, grammar, logic and rhetoric – the humanists added more 'practical' studies, such as moral–political philosophy and history, and redefined the all-important study of grammar.[11] In their eyes, the ordinary custom of speech was more important than the scholarly 'rules' that guided it.[12] When done in the humanist way, grammar, as More puts it, 'invents no laws of speech in defiance of custom; instead, it simply sees which constructions appear the most often in speech and points these out to those who are unschooled in speech so that their speech will not flout common usage' (*LD*, 35). In setting out this view, the humanists, most notably Lorenzo Valla (c. 1407–57), drew on the work of the great Roman rhetorician Quintilian (35–100 CE), who wrote: 'Usage is…the surest pilot in speaking and we should treat language as currency minted with the public stamp.'[13] As this remark exemplifies, the emphasis on usage means that what is commonly held becomes important over and above the rules generated and perpetuated by elites.

In a letter to a theologian, Martin van Dorp (1485–1525), written in 1515, the same year as *Utopia*, More remarks that words are 'public property' (*LD*, 35). Theologians who go beyond what is common 'crown themselves victors just because we do not know in what sense, against all common sense, they have secretly agreed to construe our own words' (*LD*, 37).[14] Such scholars, driven by pride, have gone beyond their right; only the people hold the ownership of the meaning of words. More exclaims: 'Damn it, since when can some rule slapped together in some corner by men who themselves barely know how to speak impose new laws of speech on the entire world?' (*LD*, 35). He maintained this position on the common ownership of meaning throughout his intellectual career. In the longest of his polemics, *Confutation of Tyndale's Answer*, first published in 1532, More writes, under the marginal note 'the common usage of speech', that the 'signification' of words is determined 'by the common custom' (*CTA*, 167). This common custom, he goes on to say, 'is the only thing, by which we know the right and proper signification of a word' (ibid.). Scholars should not attempt to thwart this common custom in order to show their knowledge, as doing so is to obstruct truth itself.

For More, the entire enterprise of humanism is designed to give access to the knowledge expressed through common custom, as a way to mitigate the pride that comes from overconfidence in one's own abilities. This knowledge, he says, counteracts those who are 'perversely convinced of their total omniscience' (*LD*, 49). This argument is clear in his writings against both scholastic theologians and evangelical reformers such as Martin Luther and William Tyndale.[15] For More, both exhibited the same problematic feature, namely a proud over-reliance on their own intellect, usually manifested in the idea that they could interpret scripture without the aid of outside sources. More first sets out this view in his *Life of Pico*, published in 1510. The subject of the biography, Pico della Mirandola, is presented as a 'mirror' for the reader to reflect upon 'in what points honour standeth' (*LPM*, 53). At no point, however, does More assert that Pico himself is wholly honourable. In fact the reader may be inclined to think he is not, because by the end of the text Pico is condemned to the fires of purgatory, not received into heaven. More notes that Pico, having come close to infamy by seeking out fame 'of his high mind and proud purpose' (*LPM*, 58), turned his study only to the Bible, despite the fact that 'common profit pricked him' when he thought of how his works were desired and looked after by others (*LPM*, 66).

More repeats this argument against those who opposed the scholarly programme of the northern humanists. Writing to Oxford University in response to opponents of humanism there, More reiterates a line from Seneca the Younger (4 BCE–65 CE) according to which 'secular learning...prepares the soul for virtue' as it teaches 'prudence in human affairs' (*LO*, 139), without which a teacher cannot hope to benefit the public. Lacking an understanding of the real world around him, he will be able to preach 'for his own pleasure' but will not be suited to do it 'for the people' (ibid.). Only a study of 'poets, orators, and histories' will inform the scholar about the world around him.[16] This knowledge is necessarily 'common' and will make the learning relevant to all (ibid.). Humanism is designed, in More's view, to counter the prideful and selfish learning of the scholastics by offering a curriculum that teaches what is common and does so for the benefit of the community.

Like scholastics, heretics demonstrate an 'arrogance before God' (*RL*, 205) and a self-serving nature in thinking that they can interpret scripture without the help of others who had written before. Although, as we shall see, More is usually referring to the writings of the church fathers, he also points to the importance of humanist studies in this context. For instance, in line with Augustine (354–430), he suggests that an understanding of rhetoric is especially important, because Christ used rhetorical figures in his speeches and therefore to 'neglect the figures of speech' is to 'miss the real sense of Scripture' (*DT*, 295–7).[17] This is especially the case, the humanists maintained, when it comes to *decorum* – the idea of suiting one's speech to the audience and circumstances at hand. Erasmus, for instance, suggests that Jesus and Paul tailored their speech to their audiences; to miss this central point would be to misunderstand scripture entirely. In short, a reading of scripture requires the central humanist principle of returning *ad fontes* – going back 'to the sources'.[18] The need for the liberal arts in a study of scripture, however, often goes deeper than this.

In the *Dialogue Concerning Heresies*, More's interlocutor ignores topics such as logic and philosophy and studies only Holy Scripture. This desire comes, More writes, from a sense of pride; because the proper lessons of Holy Scripture are 'common', a proud man cannot distinguish himself by their study. Instead, focusing on scripture alone, he invents 'paradoxes and strange opinions against the common faith of Christ's whole church' (*DCH*, 123). The 'liberal arts' are the gift of God and serve as a 'handmaid' to the study of scripture, just as reason serves faith (*DCH*, 126). Philosophy, laws, history, and even poetry teach a man 'judgement' and 'wit', without which he cannot properly exercise the reason necessary for attaining a proper understanding of the scripture, or indeed of any element of faith.

Although More valued what was common knowledge, this did not mean that he thought that humanist ideas should be spread among the common people, as this could actually interfere with the expression of commonly held truth. Recall that, for the humanists, even Jesus suited his language to the common people. In the *Life of Pico* More details how Pico's works had to be kept from the public; for 'there were in them many things strange and not fully declared', which were 'more meet for secret communication of learned men than for open hearing of common people' (*LPM*, 58). The latter, 'for lack of cunning' – meaning intelligence – 'might take hurt thereby' (ibid.). When such ideas are disseminated publicly, this is usually done as a result of the scholar's pride and in the hope that they might 'win the favour of the common people & the commendation of fools' (*LPM*, 61).[19]

Even in Utopia, where people engage in scholarly disputations and elect political officials, 'to take counsel on matters of common interest outside the senate or the popular assembly is considered a capital offense' (*Ut*, 125). In other words, to discuss political ideas outside designated political institutions is punishable by death – a surprisingly severe policy. The Utopians fear the 'tyrannous oppression of the people' through the dissemination of political knowledge, though More does not say how these two things – the spread of information and tyranny – might be connected. It is probable that the situation the Utopians hope to prevent is the one that occurs in *The History of King Richard the Third*: a situation in which the consent of the people is fabricated through the manipulation of public opinion and the riotous participation of upstart youths. If there is no control over what knowledge is spread among the people, it may be possible to sway public opinion – in which case it no longer represents the truths that More contends common sense can hold.

The spread of dangerous ideas can also, More suggests, plant the seed of doubt, threatening political and religious authority. Even if merited, he writes, it 'were a lewd thing to suffer any prince, estate, or governor, to be brought in slander among the common people', because this would produce contempt for all ruling classes, whom the people ought to obey (*CTA*, 561). If a prince or governor is going astray, this ought to be communicated to him via the proper channels, 'confessors and counsellors', but not by spreading it abroad, 'whereof all the town may talk, & to their own harm defame the sovereign' (*CTA*, 590). As More writes in his *Apology*, it is only through 'secret advice and counsel' that suggestions regarding the reform of laws should be made, not in 'books in writing among the people' (*ATM*, 96). By 1532 matters were so bad that More even suggests that some of his own works ought to be censored. For, although they contain no 'harm therein, folk yet being (as they be) given to take harm of that that is good', he would rather they be burned, indeed would 'help to burn them both with my own hands', than anyone take harm of them, 'seeing that I see them likely in these days so to do' (*CTA*, 179).

Although censorship appears to be in contrast with More's emphasis on what is common, he sees it as essential to preserving common ideas and truths. For More, dangerous ideas are spread because of private, not because of common interest. When they take hold, they actually serve to obscure or get in the way of the truths that can be found in the community. The spread of such ideas can even tear apart the community itself, as More comes to believe towards the end of his life. Public opinion, then, becomes central to More's thought. He goes beyond the importance given it by the rhetorical theories of Cicero and Quintilian and makes it vital to the construction of a commonwealth – a *res publica*.[20] Taking the Ciceronian and Augustinian premise that justice and love hold a republic together, More seeks to understand how public opinion or common custom operates to maintain or break apart these bonds. Custom, likewise, demonstrates the legitimacy and uniformity of the church.

More's contribution to his divisive intellectual context, then, was not just to bring a variety of ideas together but to unify on a grander scale, by shifting attention to a nexus of ideas – public opinion, custom, consensus – that he considered central to the prioritization of what is held in common.

Outline

There are many elements of More's life and thought that contain apparent paradoxes but that can be understood in the framework of his central concerns and historical context. Chapter 1 begins with a description of More's early years, which had a profound effect on the course of his life and thought. More was born during the Wars of the Roses (1455–87) and spent his early teenage years surrounded by the politicians who had witnessed these civil wars first hand. It is perhaps no surprise, then, that More became preoccupied with threats of civil disunity and the fragmentation of authority. He received a medieval education and was introduced to the new humanist curriculum, establishing himself as a valued member of the European humanist network. He also developed important local connections, primarily with the London Inns of Court and with leading merchant guilds. More's familiarity with the workings of London politics would have an effect on his arguments for a corporate body politic.

This first chapter also details the foundations of More's thought, laid out in his earliest writings. More was heavily influenced by the *memento mori* medieval tradition, which sought to remind people of their death as a way of dissuading them from sinful living. For More, the fleeting nature of this life and of what it contains puts one in mind of what is eternal: notably, our equality and commonality. As we are all essentially the same before birth and after death, we should remember these lessons in our daily lives, avoiding the temptation to feel pride in worldly things; after all, our ownership of them doesn't last very long. Inspired by the work of the second-century writer Lucian of Samosata (125–80 CE). More plays with the line between reality and fiction to drive this point home. Reality as we know it – social hierarchies, property, politics – is artificial, in that it is fleeting and man-made. 'Real' reality can only be presented through fictions; but it is more real because it is eternal and set down by God. This is the reality of our equality and common humanity, which must take precedence over the fleeting artificiality of our world.

Chapter 2 examines More's use of these themes in *Utopia*, his most famous text. After a short overview of the main elements of *Utopia*, the 'dialogue of counsel' and the description of the island, the enigmatic nature of the text is considered in the light of More's other works. By describing a fictional island in which everything is held in common, as opposed to a 'reality' of private ownership, More reminds his readers that private ownership is in fact the fiction, while what is held in common is reality. In the same way in which it is a mark of pride and self-interest to cut off a piece of land from the commons and think yourself better for possessing it, More suggests that it is prideful to cut oneself off from worldly things, which is why his discussions of property and the active political life go hand in hand.

The issues of self-interest and pride are further played out in More's *History of King Richard the Third*, explored in Chapter 3. In this text More depicts a commonwealth gone wrong – which is the outcome of those who fail to prioritize what is common, in this case the commonwealth itself, over their own ambition. *Richard the Third* also picks up one of the themes of *Utopia*: the role of public opinion. In *Utopia*, the Utopians' use of public opinion to reflect 'truer' values – equality, commonality, reason – is contrasted with European public opinion, which has mistakenly attached value to valueless things such as gold and precious stones. In *Richard the Third*, More explores how public opinion can be manipulated, so that it no longer reflects the consent and consensus that legitimize political authority in the commonwealth. Without this basis for determining truth, no authority, political or intellectual, can be established.

The same fears about authority and consensus run throughout More's polemical texts, explored in Chapter 4. Responding to the works of evangelical writers such as Luther and Tyndale, More's extensive writing on the nature and authority of the Catholic Church provides our greatest insight into his thought. Here More lays out his view of the church as the embodiment of what is 'common'; it is the common corps of Christendom, the universal body of all believers and the source of all religious doctrinal authority. All those who seek to oppose this authority with their own – as Luther, Tyndale, or indeed Henry VIII did – exhibit the same sort of pride that More had condemned in his earliest writings; and they tear this common body apart, just as the nobles in *Richard the Third* had done.

More's opposition to Henry VIII's split with the 'Universal' Church ('universal' being the meaning of the Greek adjective *katholikos*, which has produced the word 'Catholic') would cost him his life, but it would also help immortalize him. Chapter 5 traces More's legacy and influence, beginning with the earliest attempts to portray him either as holy Catholic martyr or as zealous persecutor of Protestants – the same division we saw split interpretations of More into the twentieth century. These presentations of More coloured the interpretation of his thought and, despite the widespread dissemination of his works, many subsequent writers were reluctant to cite him. Nevertheless, his influence can be found in political thinkers such as Jean Bodin (1530–96) and in the utopian works of writers such as Francis Bacon (1561–1626) and James Harrington (1611–77). His greatest and most explicit influence comes about through the rise of socialism, and the chapter ends by considering More's presence in the nascent communist tradition of the late nineteenth century. I conclude by considering the ways in which More's intellectual contributions continue to have relevance today, especially in relation to the role of the intellectual, the tension between community and self-interest, and the study of public opinion.

When reading More, we have to keep in mind several differences between his work and that of others who might be considered classic thinkers. First, most of More's works are 'polemical' in the truest sense; it is difficult to identify any text of More that is not explicitly an answer to or an extension of another writer's work. This means that an attempt to understand More's thought has to begin with the sources he was engaging with. This is not always simple and leads us to a second point: More's intellectual eclecticism. More, like other Renaissance writers, took bits and pieces from a variety of sources, to construct what he considered to be useful to his argument. Finally, Renaissance writers did not always reference these sources clearly; sometimes they did so only through subtle allusion and sometimes not at all. Such allusions often formed a sort of code, which could unlock the meaning of the text. For these reasons some guidance is helpful for understanding Thomas More as a classic thinker: his ideas, legacy and contributions. It is with such an aim in mind that this book has been written.

1

Early Life, Education and Poetry

In his earliest works More develops a distinction between what is temporal, worldly and artificial and what is eternal, divine and 'real'. This was a division present in many of the authors whom More drew upon – perhaps most notably in Augustine's *City of God*, which makes a distinction between the city of mortals and the divine city, and in the works of More's friend Erasmus, who emphasized internal piety over outward ceremonies. More expresses this idea by drawing on the metaphor of the pageant or stage play of life, which implies that we are all just actors who play temporary roles here on earth. The play is short and, when it is concluded, we return to the natural equality whence we came. In using this metaphor, More combines a diversity of ideas on the notion of the stage play of life, including those of Lucian, who saw it as a reminder of death, those of Cicero, who saw it as a strategy for active citizenship, and those of early Renaissance humanists, who used it to express the temporary and equal nature of republican political leadership.[1] For More, all of these lessons come together to encourage people to turn away from self-oriented pride and to reflect on their commonality and equality.

Early Life and Education

Thomas More was born in London on the 7th of February 1478, during a relative lull in what we now know as the Wars of the Roses.[2] Edward IV (1442–83) had been on the throne for the previous seventeen years and, despite various uprisings and rebellions, had more or less managed to hold the throne. The period, however, remained tumultuous. Less than two weeks after More's birth, the king's brother, George, Duke of Clarence (1449–78), was executed for treason, allegedly by being drowned in a barrel of sweet malmsey wine – a story that More himself repeats in his *History of King Richard the Third*. When More was five Edward IV died and his young son Edward (1470–83) was declared king, as Edward V. Within months, the young king had disappeared into the depths of the Tower of London, along with his younger brother, and their uncle Richard (1452–85) took the throne as Richard III. Richard himself was overthrown just two years later by Henry VII (1457–1509), whose reign saw the end of the Wars of the Roses and established the Tudor dynasty.

This context of division and warfare is important, as it was the one in which More spent his formative years. His father, John More (1451–1530), a London lawyer, had ties to Edward IV; the usurpation of Richard III may have endangered his family's growing success. Nevertheless, after the accession of Henry VII the More family quickly ingratiated itself with the new Tudor monarch and by 1489 Thomas More had entered the household of the second most powerful man in the country, Cardinal John Morton (c. 1420–1500), then Lord Chancellor. More's education at Lambeth Palace included not only the standard medieval primers, but also a pragmatic understanding of the political world. Serving the Lord Chancellor and the visiting lords at mealtimes, More would have picked up information about the innermost workings of politics, perhaps reflections on the reign and overthrow of Richard III, debates over the rebellions of the 1490s and comments on Morton's influential but unpopular tax policies.

These years also furnished material for two of More's best known and most admired texts, *The History of King Richard the Third* and *Utopia*, both of which include the figure of Morton himself as a wise man and wily politician, committed to public order. Growing up in the unsettled world of the Wars of the Roses may also have played a role in fostering More's interest in the unity of the commonwealth.

Before entering Morton's household, More was enrolled at one of the best grammar schools in London, St Anthony's, not far from his home in Cheapside. There he learned the fundamentals of Latin grammar, rhetoric and literature as well as English literacy, music and public deliberation. These studies continued at Lambeth Palace, and after spending three years there More had impressed Morton enough to be sent to Oxford at the cardinal's expense.

At Oxford More joined other scholars in following the classical *trivium*, which consisted of grammar, rhetoric and logic.[3] Not only was he introduced to the major texts of a classical education; he was also able to hone the skills they taught him through scholarly debates. Like many students, More wrote during his time at school and university. His friend Erasmus (1466–1536) later suggested that some of More's poems dated from this period and that he participated in the composition and performance of plays, which unfortunately – if they ever existed – have not survived.

More's arrival at Oxford coincided with the growth of a movement that challenged the value of the curriculum in which he was enrolled. Humanism had emerged in the Italian city-states in the fourteenth century and arrived in England at the turn of the sixteenth, finding a place especially among scholars at Cambridge and Oxford. Those humanists with whom More would become most closely associated, the 'civic' humanists, were concerned to promote the 'active' life over the strictly 'contemplative' life. In other words, they believed that men (and, very rarely, women) had a duty to contribute their learning to the good of all, to the commonwealth or *res publica*. This tension between the active and the contemplative life would become one of More's recurrent themes.

More did not finish his degree at Oxford and returned to London, where he followed in his father's footsteps, studying the law. Such a path – interrupted university studies and then the law – was not uncommon for those preparing themselves for public life, and More certainly did not abandon his interest in humanism. Before the turn of the century, More had ingratiated himself with some of England's leading – and pioneering – humanists, such as John Colet (1467–1519), Thomas Linacre (1460–1524) and William Grocyn (1446–1519), who had travelled Europe, absorbed the central tenets of continental humanism in order to bring it to England on their return. Although this group is now generally known as the 'More circle', at the time More would have been one of its most junior and insignificant members: a young, albeit bright lawyer in a circle of esteemed scholars and politicians. In 1499 More was able to meet the rising star of the northern Renaissance, Erasmus, and they travelled together to meet young Prince Henry, then second in line to the throne, after his brother Arthur (who died in 1502). More's studies expanded exponentially during this period; in addition to acquiring a mastery of the law, he lectured on Augustine's *City of*

God, which would remain an influence for him throughout his life, and by 1505 he could read and translate ancient Greek. The larger European humanist network of which he had become a part, the 'republic of letters' (*respublica literarum*), was a close-knit community, bound together by the Renaissance ideal of *amicitia* – love and friendship – as well as by patronage and support.[4]

In all of this it is important, however, not to overlook the importance of More's life as a London lawyer. At the Inns of Court, More not only improved his knowledge of the complexities of English law, but also honed his skills as an orator, rhetorician and polemicist and forged valuable connections with the city elite. By 1500 London was a thriving metropolis, with long-established networks and institutions, many of which were at least nominally democratic.[5] The basic unit of government was the ward, in which all male householders could participate. There they elected the councilmen and debated matters that had to be determined by higher bodies, such as the Court of Common Council and the Court of Aldermen. Beyond the ward level, those participating in the government of the city were required to be 'freemen': they were given 'the freedom' by their respective guild or company, and this made them full voting citizens. This meant that it was essentially the guilds that had the power to decide citizenship in the city. Throughout the fifteenth and into the early sixteenth century, the guilds increasingly became the hubs of civil power within London. One of the most important and influential was the Mercers' Company, with which More began to forge profitable ties from at least 1505. By the start of sixteenth century, the Mercers had taken over much of the export market, largely with the Low Countries. It was on behalf of the Mercers that More mounted his first legal disputes and diplomatic negotiations.

Finally, More also built ties within the religious world of London. After being called to the bar in 1501, More appears to have spent three years living either in or beside the Charterhouse, the London home for Carthusian monks.[6] Although this arrangement may have been, as was later reported, More's 'testing' of the religious life, it might have simply presented him with the opportunity to live away from the business of the city, apart from his parents and close to an impressive library.

Regardless of his intentions in moving to the Charterhouse, for More the church was the ultimate community; those formed through bonds of friendship, family, profession or politics were all secondary to this all-encompassing corporation of believers. Although interested in classical sources, the humanists were still very much

Christian humanists. A focus on themes broadly consistent with Christianity – virtue–vice, the importance of the afterlife – was maintained even in their understanding of classical texts, and they used their study of ancient authors to inform their reading of scripture. As we've seen, for More – drawing on Augustine as he did – a reading of scripture *must* be accompanied by a thorough education in the 'liberal arts'; otherwise a scholar is likely to fall into the trap of pride by depending solely on his own interpretation.[7]

Pride and Fortune

More's earliest works uphold this Christian lens, focusing on the theme of the artificial and fleeting nature of worldly things and essential and eternal nature of our equality, as ways of combating pride. More takes the Augustinian view of pride: that it is the root of all sin. He adds to this the idea that pride is an essentially comparativist and competitive vice, which is only satisfied when it is superior to another. As he writes in *Utopia*: 'Pride [*superbia*] measures prosperity not by her own advantages but by others' disadvantages. Pride would not consent to be made even a goddess if no poor wretches were left for her to domineer over and scoff at' (*Ut*, 243). Pride will always be at another's expense.[8] For this reason, it is a vice that necessarily cuts across the bonds uniting people. Pride makes us interested in what is our own and asks us to focus on what separates us from other people. The inequality it draws on and fosters takes away from the common feeling that can be found in a recognition of essential equality. For More, it is the ultimate political, social and religious problem.

Fortune is also essential to More's understanding of pride. It is the fickle force that gives and takes away the worldly, personal goods and standing that found inequality and inspire pride. Describing Fortune, More draws on a rich tradition of classical, medieval and Renaissance thought and imagery, which places Fortune as an active force in people's lives, lifting them up and sending them hurtling down her 'wheel', without care or concern for their worthiness or pain. In More's view, nothing from Fortune is stable, and therefore nothing from Fortune ought to be valued. The world created by Fortune – the one that people live in – is one of inequality; and it is artificial because it is not lasting. The 'real' reality – the one that endures longer than our short lives – is one of essential equality – and thus, More suggests, commonality.

His first writings are a clear expression of this division between the artificial world we live in and a more real eternal world. These were a series of poems inspired by a collection of nine tapestries that hung in his father's home in London. The verses combine an English literary tradition of reflection on the stages of man's life with a humanist interest in iconographic representations of temporality. The first four tapestries present the stages of life: childhood, youth, love and old age. The four that follow are representations of abstract concepts – death, fame, time and eternity – and the series ends with a moral, communicated by 'the poet'. Each icon is overcome by its successor, who destroys it, and especially its pride. The first, the innocent child, is overcome by the vivacity of the young man, who tramples the boy beneath his horse's hooves. The 'goodly young man' is then tamed by 'Lady Venus' and 'the little God Cupid':

> By us subdued for all thy great pride,
> My fiery dart pierceth thy tender side. (*PV*, 4)

They are weakened, in turn, by 'old age', who in More's poem actually epitomizes the prime of man's life, 'the last and best part' (ibid.). It is he who 'help[s] to rule' the commonwealth because he has overcome Cupid, as well as the 'childish game and idle business' of childhood and youth (ibid.).

After the 'sage father', the poems move on to more explicitly Renaissance themes. The sequence of concepts that follows is drawn from Petrarch's *Triumphs*, written in the fourteenth century. In Petrarch's famous text, love is the first to triumph, followed by chastity, death, fame, time and eternity. More's version follows this example closely, with a few variations. First, the old man is overcome by Death, who tells him: 'set apart your pride' (*PV*, 5). Fame overcomes Death, because a noble man will be held in 'perpetual memory' (ibid.). Time destroys Fame, but divine Eternity overcomes even the 'pride and boasting' of Time (*PV*, 6). In the end, it is Eternity that stands triumphant, having thwarted the pride of every other stage.

Although the first nine stanzas are written in English, the final, called 'The Poet', is in Latin. The poet explains that the figures, although imaginary, represent reality. In fact they represent a truer reality than that of the world around us; for 'the elusive goods of this perishable world do not come so readily as they pass away', only the love of God endures forever (*LP*, 293). Thus mortals ought not to trust in such 'trivialities' and 'transitory advantage' but serve 'the everlasting God', who will grant 'eternal life' (ibid.). By acknowledging this succession of 'triumphs' and by focusing on the triumphant Eternity, who stands above them all, people can look past the pride that each stage inspires, allowing worldly things to pass away without attachment.

This theme is also clear in More's *Lamentation of Queen Elizabeth*, written on the death of Queen Elizabeth of York (1466–1503), wife of Henry VII. Written from Elizabeth's perspective, the poem opens with a warning to those who 'put your trust and confidence, / In worldly joy and frail prosperity' (*LQE*, 9). Elizabeth herself becomes a *memento mori* – 'remembrance of death' – a means by which others are reminded of impending death and the fickleness of worldly things. The lesson is, once again, about the folly of pride and also seems to include the equality that is achieved in death; as Elizabeth says:

Example I think there may no better be.
Yourself wote [know] well that in this realm was I,
Your queen but late, and lo now here I lie. (*LQE*, 9)

The poem continues in this vein, noting that, despite the 'richness, honour, wealth, and ancestry' she possessed, Elizabeth has found herself in the same position as all others: 'lo here I lie' (ibid.).

More also composed a series of *Fortune Verses* on this same topic, written around 1505, to accompany an unidentified 'book of fortune'.[9] In line with contemporary imagery, More portrays Fortune, the narrator of the first part of the text, as a callous and inconstant woman, who delights in raising up and destroying people according to her own whim. Fortune presents herself as a goddess who desires worship; those who do not look to her are destined for a life of misery and poverty. Fortune's nature is changing and variable, reminiscent of the series of conquests in the *Pageant Verses*. Sometimes she is 'as goodly Venus mother of Cupid', but then 'cometh a cloud, and farewell all our pride' (*FV*, 34–5). In the second half of the work More himself speaks, as Elizabeth had, to 'those that trust in fortune' (*FV*, 34). He identifies them as the 'proud', who pile 'up this wretched world's treasure' (ibid.).

Due to Fortune's capricious nature and arbitrary rule, those who trust in her are truly enslaved, even if they avoid worldly physical enslavement. More gives his readers a choice between 'stately fortune, or humble poverty' but notes that in the former lies 'bondage' and in the latter 'free liberty' (*FV*, 39). In worshipping Fortune, one must 'serve her day and night'; she keeps

> From every man some parcel of his will,
> That he may pray therefore and serve her still. (*FV*, 40)

But the reward will be fleeting, taken away without warning or cause. Instead, in turning away from Fortune, one has the stable rewards of 'manner' (meaning morals) and virtue, by which 'mayst thou boldly defy her turning chance: / She can thee neither hinder nor advance' (ibid.). True freedom – freedom of the mind and soul – comes from abandoning the desire for Fortune's worldly goods, even though doing so might leave one in material poverty or physical enslavement.

This is not to say that More thinks that one has to ignore or reject all worldly gifts of Fortune. He does not call on his readers to give away all they have and embrace an ascetic life. Instead, they should 'count [worldly goods] borrowed ware' and not desire more than what they are given:

> And take no thing at all, or be content,
> With such reward as fortune hath you sent. (*FV*, 40)

The most important point is not to worship or trust in Fortune, because of the fleeting nature of what she gives. This idea runs throughout More's works; as he writes much later in life, in his *Treatise on the Passion*, many souls burn in hell for 'the peevish pride of that borrowed ware' of this world (*TP*, 9). This is also a theme that, as we shall see, runs through the discussion of common property in *Utopia*.

Fortune also makes a crucial appearance in More's *Translations of Lucian*. In 1505 Erasmus returned to England, this time lodging at the More household in Cheapside. While there together, the two humanists collaborated on a translation of select dialogues by Lucian, a controversial ancient rhetorician known for his atheism and his biting wit, which disparaged philosophers of all stripes. His dialogues had been rediscovered by the humanists of the fifteenth century and he quickly became a Renaissance favourite.[10] More was responsible for three dialogues in particular, all of which he used to illustrate Christian humanist themes: *Cynicus* (*The Cynic*

Philosopher), which according to More denounces 'the enervating luxury of voluptuaries' and praises 'Christian simplicity, temperance, and frugality'; *Philopseudes* (*The Lover of Lies*), 'concerned ... with ridiculing and reproving the inordinate passion for lying'; and *Menippus sive Necyomantia* (*The Descent into Hades*), which 'rebukes the jugglery of magicians or the silly fictions of poets or the fruitless contentions of philosophers' (*TL*, 5).

It is this last dialogue that resonates most strongly with More's early interests and continued to influence his writing in the decades to come. In a central passage the main character travels to the Afterlife and is struck by what he sees. The bones of all those who have lived are piled 'one on top of another, ill-defined, unidentified, retaining no longer any trace of earthly beauty' (*TL*, 176). It is impossible for him to identify who had been a king or a hero and who had been a servant or a slave. He concludes that

> human life is like a long pageant, and that all its trappings are supplied and distributed by Fortune, who arrays the participants in various costumes of many colours. Taking one person, it may be, she attired him royally, placing a tiara upon his head, giving him bodyguards, and encircling his brow with the diadem; but upon another she puts the costume of a slave....And often, in the very middle of the pageant, she exchanges the costumes of several players; instead of allowing them to finish the pageant in the parts that had been assigned to them, she re-apparels them....For a brief space she lets them use their costumes, but when the time of the pageant is over, each gives back the properties and lays off the costume along with his body, becoming what he was before his birth, no different from his neighbour. (*TL*, 176)

The important lesson is that the trappings of life are just temporary costumes that do not belong to the wearer. Reality consists of equality and common fate, a remembrance of which is gained through reflection on death.

Lucian's metaphor of the pageant or stage play becomes one of More's most repeated images. He puts it to good use in his description of pride in the *Four Last Things*, which reflects on the importance of remembering the Christian four last things: death, judgement, heaven and hell. It was written around 1522, but remained unfinished and wasn't published until after More's death. More suggests that, in order to avoid sin, and especially pride, the 'root' of all sin, one should remember the nearness of death, which will take away all worldly trappings:

> If thou shouldst perceive that one were earnestly proud of the wearing of the gay golden gown, while the lorel [rogue] playeth the lord in a stage play, wouldst thou not laugh at his folly, considering that thou art very sure that when the play is done he shall go walk a knave in his old coat? Now thou thinkest thyself wise enough while thou art proud in thy player's garment, and forgettest that when thy play is done, thou shalt go forth as poor as he. Nor thou remembrest not that thy pageant may happen to be done as soon as his. (*FLT*, 156)

In other words, we would laugh at someone who took undue pride from the costume he wears playing a lord in a short stage play, knowing that when he was done he would have to go home in his ragged old coat. So we ought to remember that the roles we take pride in day after day are no more than costumes worn for a short time, which we will have to return for much humbler wear upon death.

Finding this example 'too merry' for the subject, More employs a second, also oft-used metaphor, that of life as a prison, with the same message: 'for, young, old, poor and rich, merry and sad, prince, page, pope and poor soul priest, now one, now other, sometimes a great rabble at once, without order, without respect of age or of estate, all stripped stark naked and shifted out in a sheet, be put to death' (ibid.; see also *LP*, 167 and *DCH*, 258–80). As the jailer says to the prisoners, 'all your pride is because you forget that it is a prison' (*FLT*, 157). In death the great and the lowly become 'matches', or equals.[11] This equality is the 'true figure', the 'very nature' of the world, which we take for 'fantasy' because of 'men's false opinion'; but, if we took it for reality, people would 'bear themselves not much higher in their hearts for any rule or authority that they bear in this world' (*FLT*, 158) – a theme he returns to in his *Dialogue of Comfort* (published in 1534). More is advocating a reversal of our understanding of what is reality and what is fantasy. The so-called real world is artificial, whereas the world we cannot see – the world beyond death – is the true reality. There we are equal.

This idea is most strongly and repeatedly stated in More's Latin poems, which he may have begun writing as early as 1496, and which were published in a collection known as *Epigramata* along-side his *Utopia*, in 1518. Some are translations or variations of Greek poems, others are of his own composition, and they address a vast array of themes. The most prominent of these is the inherent natural equality that exists beneath artificial worldly pageants and is revealed through the processes of time and the weakness of our physical forms. Death is the great equalizer in many of the poems:

'Though you conquer the world even to the pillars of Hercules, still the amount of earth which ultimately will be yours is the same as any man's. You will die as Irus's [the beggar's] equal, not a penny richer; and your land (yours no longer) will consume you' (*LP*, 125). All property and material possessions pass away in death: 'Just as surely as I came on earth naked, so surely naked shall I quit it. Why do I struggle in vain, knowing as I do that death is naked?' (*LP*, 85); and again: 'He is dreaming who thinks that in this life he is rich; and when death wakes him up, he sees at once how poor he is' (*LP*, 145). But other parts of life also draw attention to our essential humanity, which humbles us and makes us all equal. For instance, More writes about birth: 'Look here mortal, if you recall what your father did in engendering you, then pride will vanish from your spirit…if you want to hear the truth, you were born of coition amid shameful lust and of a pitiful droplet' (*LP*, 133). Sleep, as a prefiguration of death, also balances the worth of the richest and poorest: 'Almost half of life is sleep. During that period the rich and the poor lie equal. And so, Croesus, wealthiest of kings, for almost half a lifetime Irus the beggar was your equal' (*LP*, 161).

The pageantry motif from Lucian is recalled in a poem entitled 'On the King and the Peasant', which doesn't contain the reminder of death but still carries lessons of essential equality.[12] More tells the tale of a 'forest-bred peasant' who travels into town on the same day the king parades through. The crowd cheers the king, but the peasant is confused, remarking: 'Is that the king? I think you are making fun of me. To me he looks like a man in fancy dress' (*LP*, 233). In another poem More tells 'A Funny Story about a Courtier' who, upon dismounting from his horse, commanded a bystander to hold it. The bystander reluctantly asks: 'is one man enough then to hold this savage horse?' When the courtier replies that it is, the bystander retorts that, if so, 'then you can hold your horse yourself' (*LP*, 237–9). The lessons of the epigrams are the same as in More's other early works; life is a pageant of artificiality, which masks our inherent equality.

More makes standard humanist, Christian and republican assumptions in these poems, using them to mock the absurdity of contemporary social stratification. His most republican – and most enigmatic – poem is 'What Is the Best Form of Government' or '*Quis optimus reipublicae status*' – the same topic that forms the full title of *Utopia*: *On the Best State of a Commonwealth and on the New Island of Utopia*. More begins the poem by considering 'which governs better, a king or a senate' (*LP*, 229), going through each of the reasons why a senate would be better than a king. For instance, the 'greater good lies in numerous good men' and, because of the number of its members, a senate is more likely to 'occupy a position between good or bad' than to be wholly good or bad, like a single individual (ibid.). After listing several reasons, More breaks off his discussion suddenly, interjecting: 'but say, what started you on this inquiry anyway?' (*LP*, 231). Why, he asks, would anyone raise this question, as there is no place where 'you yourself, by your own decision, can impose either a king or a senate' (ibid.)? He tells his reader to 'stop considering to whom you may give power', as it is irrelevant. Instead, one ought to consider 'whether it would do any good [*expediat*]' (ibid.). On its own, this poem is difficult to understand, but, if we take it in the context of More's fuller treatment in *Utopia* – a 'no place' where he does indeed impose both king and senate – we begin to get an understanding of the sort of role an educated philosopher might be able to play in the commonwealth and of the ways in which the pessimistic lessons of More's early works can be overcome.

Conclusion

More's earliest works draw on common medieval tropes: the ages of man, the remembrance of death and the idea that this world is nothing more than a pageant or a stage play.[13] We can also find, in More's early writings, the influence of a number of classical and Renaissance writers. Lucian, popularized through More and Erasmus' translation, offered More his satirical reflection on pride and hierarchy and furnished him with the metaphor of the stage play or pageant of life. More would also have encountered this metaphor in Cicero, who uses it to remind readers not to disturb the pageant of life, and to do one's duty as a citizen serving the commonwealth, lessons we will see developed further in the next chapter.

The republican lessons of the stage play were also explored by the early Italian humanists, who used it to describe the short-lived nature of republican political offices. Of course, More was not writing in the context of a republican city-state, ruled by an elected senate, but rather in that of a hereditary monarchy. He resolved the issue primarily by positioning the king within this stage play metaphor: the king's term did not end, but his life would. This tension between republican sentiment and a monarchical context is expressed through More's enigmatic poem 'What Is the Best Form of Government', which asks readers to reflect on the nature of the context in which they find themselves.

More also adopts the definition and centrality of pride developed in Augustine, adding an element both of self-interest and of essential inequality, which sets it apart. This definition of pride can then be combined with More's recognition, drawn from Lucian, of the fictitious nature of worldly things such as social hierarchies built on material possessions. To avoid pride, then, is to focus on what is not one's own, and thus on what is held in common, feeding into the republicanism espoused by writers such as Cicero.

It is important to note that, for More, this focus on essential equality did not mean that all people are equal in every way. Part of his critique of the absurdity of social hierarchy was that it was based on the wrong qualities: birthright rather than merit. For More and his fellow humanists, virtue was what *should* distinguish people in the commonwealth. This was *vera nobilitas* – 'true nobility'. Inequality of social position, especially in political rule, *could* be justified, but not on the grounds of any material differences between people, such as the random circumstances of birth or the artificial value placed on gold.

For both More and Erasmus, true philosophers are able to see through the pageant of worldly things to the eternal truth of the matter. Erasmus explores these ideas in *Enchiridion militis Christiani* (*Handbook of the Christian Soldier*) and in *Encomium moriae* (*Praise of Folly*), the latter of which was written in More's home, was dedicated to More and contains a play on More's name.[14] Both of these texts, which Erasmus himself acknowledges were connected, advocate turning away from the transient and corporal to the divine.[15] This emphasis on inner faith over outward ceremony was part of the *devotio moderna* advocated by reformers like Erasmus and More; and it places their views in close proximity to that of later evangelicals.[16] However, whereas More placed emphasis on essential equality and, as we shall see, on active participation in the stage play of life, Erasmus advocated hierarchy and contemplation.[17] Both, nonetheless, embraced the essential nature of community.

Growing up in a context of warfare and division, More seems to have internalized the idea that unity is essential in the commonwealth. He would have seen this union expressed in the church, in the classical concept of the republic, in the restored English commonwealth and in the various smaller networks and institutions around him, such as the merchant guilds and the humanist republic of letters. Drawing on his understanding of Christian ideals and classical tropes, More took as foundational the idea that, beyond the artificial trappings of this world, we are all essentially equal. Social hierarchies might have their uses, but to put too much stock in them is to foster pride. This pride, as focused on inequality and self-interest, is the greatest sin, the most dangerous vice and the greatest threat to the unity of the commonwealth. This central lesson, expressed in varying contexts, to differing degrees and from different perspectives, would form the basis for much of More's work throughout his life.

2

Utopia *and 'Common Things'*

More's early works teach the reader that in the grand scheme of things all people are essentially equal, and thus we ought to be united by our common humanity, not torn apart by pride, which drives us to differentiate ourselves from others by concentrating on what is 'ours'. After all, it won't be ours for long anyway. This suggestion raises a fundamental question for the reader: How ought we to deal, then, with the worldly realities of property and luxury? How can we still value what is 'common' in a society that values what is private? This carries with it the question of how we can value republican ideals in the context of monarchical rule. These are the issues pondered in the course of *Utopia*, a book about 'no-place' that considers the 'best state of the commonwealth'. *Utopia* is a truly enigmatic book, but, by considering it in the context of More's influences and other works, we can begin to get at some of its central messages, especially the importance of *res publica* – 'public' affairs or 'common' things.

Diplomacy

By 1515 More was heavily involved in public affairs. In 1509 he became a member of the Company of Mercers and served on their behalf in international trade negotiations. Henry VIII acceded to the throne that same year, and More served as an MP for London in the reign's first parliament, in January to February 1510. Also in 1510, More was appointed justice of the peace for Middlesex and was selected as undersheriff of London, which gave him a role in presiding over court cases at the Guildhall as well as in overseeing city works. More was operating at the very heights of city power, with connections to the Inns of Court, merchant guilds, city administration and the court. Through all of this he retained his scholarly occupations and connections; Erasmus, for instance, visited him again in 1509.

In 1515 More received requests from the King's Council and the Company of Merchant Adventurers to travel to Flanders in order to resolve commercial disputes with England's most significant trading partner, the Low Countries. More was a natural choice for the merchants, who would have known his work for the Mercers. The fact that he was also the Council's selection suggests that, by that point, he may have come to the attention of some of Henry's most powerful ministers, perhaps even the Lord Chancellor, Cardinal Wolsey (1473–1530). This would not be surprising, as many of More's friends and contacts were at court.

Arriving in Bruges on 18 May 1515, this busy man of the world found himself in an odd and unfamiliar situation: he had nothing to do. It was two weeks until the representatives from Charles V arrived and, even when they did, progress was slow. In the meantime More had a visit from Erasmus, who needed his assistance in securing a post from Wolsey. More wrote to Wolsey about the position, even lying on Erasmus' behalf. This intervention was important, as it probably secured Erasmus' support for the publication of *Utopia* in the following year. Erasmus also took the opportunity of More's trip to introduce him to a local member of the republic of letters, Pieter Gillis (1486–1533), who was also chief secretary of Antwerp. As a close friend of the Antwerp printer Dirk Martens (1446 or 1447–1534), Gillis had helped to publish many of Erasmus' works.

It was in the company of Gillis, in the late summer of 1515, that More conceived of and began to write his best known text, *Utopia*. The book was written in two parts and placed in two different contexts. Book 1 is a dialogue that covers a variety of themes but, perhaps most importantly, is focused on the issue of how – or whether – a philosopher ought to engage with the world. It was almost certainly written upon More's return to England in the autumn of 1515. Book 2 is the description of the island of Utopia and appears to have been written while More was still in Antwerp.[1] It is important, however, not to overstress the differences between the two texts, as More saw their respective debates as two sides of the same coin. Both have to do with the question of placing the common before the individual, even if only in mindset. By avoiding the temptation to reverse these priorities, one can escape the enticements to pride that not only corrupt the individual, but also tear apart the commonwealth.

Inspiration

As in all of his works, in *Utopia* More combines insights from a variety of texts. His immediate inspiration for an imagined republic in which all things are held in common was probably the writings of his contemporaries, and most especially of Erasmus. In his *Adages*, written just after his first meeting with More in 1499, Erasmus gives first place to the adage 'Between friends all is common'. He writes that

> anyone who deeply and diligently considers that remark of Pythagoras 'Between friends all is common,' will certainly find the whole of human happiness included in this brief saying. What other purpose has Plato in so many volumes except to urge a community of living, and the factor which creates it, namely friendship?[2]

For Pythagoras (second half of the sixth century BCE), shared goods provide the foundation for a feeling of community. It is not possible to feel part of a community or to protect the common interest if one is concerned with one's own goods or property, a view repeated in *Utopia*. Erasmus goes on to explain that this was not only a dictate of pagan philosophers like Pythagoras, but also of Christ, who taught love above all things, and 'what else does love teach us, except that all things should be common to all?'[3] For Erasmus, it is knowledge, such as that contained in his *Adages*, that ought to be considered shared property in a community like the republic of letters.[4]

Although this connection, via Erasmus, to the Neoplatonist understanding of Pythagoras' ideas cannot be denied, the far more obvious parallel undoubtedly comes from Plato himself (429–347 BCE), whom Erasmus also includes in his discussion in the *Adages*.[5] Well known to More and his contemporaries, Plato's *Republic* is an extended dialogue that addresses the question of the best state of the commonwealth. More presents *Utopia*, with some irony, through a contrast with Plato's *Republic*: whereas Plato's perfect 'commonwealth' was imagined, Utopia is 'real'. In Book 9 of the *Republic*, Socrates, Plato's main character and spokesman, notes that the ideal state that he has been describing exists (in Latin translation) *nusquam*, or nowhere, which perhaps inspires More's original title for the text: *Nusquama*.[6] In the *Laws*, Plato returns to this theme, making the leading character, the Athenian, note that 'those laws are best, where there is observed as carefully as possible throughout the whole State the old saying that "friends have all things really in common"'; but the Athenian doubts that such a state 'in which there is a community of wives, children, and all chattels, and all that is called "private" is everywhere and by every means rooted out of our life...anywhere exists now, or ever will exist'.[7] Just as in Plato's text, More's discussion of the commonwealth in *Utopia* is a way of reflecting not only on contemporary political practice, but also about the individual and the good life. Thus in both works a connection is made between the choices of the individual and the well-being of the whole.

More also draws from Plato's student, Aristotle (384–322 BCE), and especially from his focus on philosophical happiness as the goal of political organization. Although the Utopians' view of pleasure has been thought to be influenced by Epicureanism – a school of philosophy known for its dedication to pleasure (understood, according to Epicurus, as the avoidance of pain) – it also accords with Aristotle's notion of happiness in the *Nicomachean Ethics*, especially the distinction between decent and indecent sources of happiness. Aristotle, unlike Plato in the *Republic*, was directly opposed to common property, as he argued that it served to stagnate the growth of the commonwealth – an argument that More himself repeats in his 1534 *Dialogue of Comfort* (*DC*, 179–80).

Roman writers such as Cicero (106–43 BCE) also condemned common property, yet maintained the idea that a free and ideal commonwealth must belong to everyone. For them, a free commonwealth in fact *necessitated* private property, as then every citizen, by owning land, had a stake in the governance of the commonwealth. It was through private property that the individual's interest could be turned into common interest, a view taken up again in the seventeenth and eighteenth centuries. Whereas, for the Renaissance Pythagoras, shared material goods were essential to the common feeling that supported the community, the Roman writers expanded on the progressive realism of Plato and Aristotle to support the idea that it was possible to have common feeling without common property; in fact common property may even get in the way of the cultivation of common feeling. This view is most clearly stated in Cicero's *De officiis* (*On Duties*): 'the chief purpose in the establishment of constitutional state and municipal governments was that individual property rights might be secured'.[8] It was for this reason alone that the first peoples founded polities, and it remained the purpose of politics. Although Cicero rejects the Pythagorean and Platonic sharing of goods, he and other Roman writers at the end of the republic retain the dedication to the community that it had underpinned, articulating it instead, as we'll see below, as a commitment to the active life of politics.

Also important to More's composition of *Utopia* was a very different and new genre: the travel writings of those exploring the 'New World'.[9] These works were often part fact, part fiction, intentionally sensationalized to sell the adventure, danger and exoticism of far-off lands. Notably, they were also often used to prompt reflection on conditions back home.[10] Particularly important were the writings of Amerigo Vespucci (1454–1512), mentioned by name in *Utopia*, whose descriptions of the native residents of the New World in some respects parallel those of the Utopians in More's text. These similarities include the principle of common property, the lack of property or trade, and disregard for the value of gold and gems. There are, however, many and extreme differences between Vespucci's description of native peoples and More's description of the Utopians, so we may not want to draw too close a comparison. Instead it can be said that, by using writings such as Vespucci's, More was able to place his *Utopia* within the context of the 'real world', blurring the lines between reality and fiction and prompting reflection on the state of sixteenth-century Europe.

Finally, in terms of More's inspiration, we must say something about his choice of the dialogue form in composing *Utopia*. The dialogue was much in vogue in the Renaissance, as it allowed the author to present views and argue *in utramque partem* – from both sides – and to involve the reader in the determination of the message of the text. Like travel writing, the dialogue has the effect of playing with the boundaries between fact and fiction, a theme important to More's argument.[11] Recall that, in the dialogues of Lucian translated by More, Lucian presents worldly reality as fleeting and artificial: a stage play that will one day end, revealing the eternal reality of equality and commonality.[12] Playing with the line between truth and fiction becomes a way of calling into question what we know to be 'reality', asking the reader to consider how we are to 'act' in this world, given that its conventions are artificial.

More brings these sources together in *Utopia*. Through his two books he presents what we might call a mirror for commonwealths, similar to the 'mirror for princes' genre of the Renaissance. As the theologian Jean Desmarez (also known as John Desmarais) writes to Gillis in a paratextual letter, published among the prefatory materials in the 1516 and 1517 editions of More's *Utopia*, 'whatever pertains to the good constitution of a commonwealth may be seen in [Utopia] as in a mirror' (*Ut*, 27).[13] In particular, *Utopia* shows the sources of good and evil in the commonwealth: 'the sources from which all evils actually arise in the commonwealth or from which all blessings possibly could arise' (*Ut*, 23). Although the island of Utopia is a fiction, its lessons are real and may even contain more truth than the so-called 'realities' of More's contemporary Europe.

Book 1

In Book 1 More sets the scene, anchoring it in the real world: he is on a diplomatic mission for Henry VIII that has stalled, and so he has journeyed to Antwerp to visit Pieter Gillis. Both More and Gillis become characters within the text, and much has been written about whether the character of More (hereafter Morus, as in the original Latin) represents More himself. After all, More and his humanist friends often used his Latin name as a pun on the Greek *mōros*, which means 'dull, sluggish, foolish, boring'.[14] So is Morus the author, or the 'fool'? We have to consider this question by examining his interlocutor in the dialogue, who constitutes the fictional element of *Utopia*. This is Raphael Hythloday, an experienced traveller who has thoroughly studied the writings of the ancients, primarily the Greeks; of the Romans he has only read a bit of Seneca and Cicero. This was precisely the curriculum for reading that More had recommended in his *Letter to Oxford* (*LO*, 143), so at a first glance Hythloday comes off as a well-read and experienced authority. But, once again, we must turn to the name. Hythloday – Hythlodaeus in More's original Latin – is a composite Greek name of disputed etymology and meaning. Its main part clearly derives from *hythlos*, which means 'idle talk, nonsense', but the second part is a matter of some scholarly debate. It could be for example the rare adjective *daios*, 'cunning, destructive', which would make Hythloday a 'destroyer of nonsense'. But a less strained interpretation, which gained wide acceptance, takes the second part of the name to be the neuter plural *hodaia*, 'merchandise'; on this reading

'Hythlodaeus' would be a 'purveyor' or 'pedlar of nonsense', which of course he is.[15] The island he describes is nonsense, as it does not exist. But what about the other arguments he makes? In the debate that Morus and Hythloday have in Book 1, with whom ought the reader to side? Morus, Hythloday, neither, or both?

The debate between Morus and Hythloday centres on precisely the problem raised by More's earlier works. If worldly things are fleeting and even corrupting, should the wise man engage with them? The dialogue considers these issues in the light of a re-emerging dispute over the relative merits of the contemplative and the active life.[16] Although drawn from the classical debates among Greeks (Plato, Aristotle, the Stoics) and Romans (Cicero, Seneca), in Renaissance monarchical contexts this subject had mutated into a discussion about whether or not, and how, one should give counsel to kings. There was no republic for humanists to take active political roles in, so their position would have to be that of adviser to a monarch. This idea spawned a wealth of literature that considered the role of the counsellor, *Utopia* being one of the first such texts written by an English scholar.

As monarchs weren't elected, it was a dangerous lottery whether or not they would have the skills and proclivity to govern well. If they would not govern according to virtue, then a virtuous philosopher would have to govern them. For writers such as Erasmus, this meant that all the attention was focused on the tutor to the prince. As Erasmus wrote in his *Education of a Christian Prince*, a draft of which More probably read as he was finishing *Utopia*: 'When there is no power to select the prince, then the man who is to educate the future prince must be selected with comparable care.'[17] For others, like More, the counsellor was the key figure, someone who could guide the prince's actions. Such a counsellor had to embrace rhetoric in order to persuade the monarch to virtue. That meant that they needed a combination of *parrhēsia* – willingness to speak the truth to power – and *decorum* – ability to frame one's speech according to the needs of the circumstances and audience.[18] To borrow a common sixteenth-century metaphor, they needed a combination of truth and compromise in order to navigate the stormy seas of the prince's temper and steer the ship of state towards virtue. It was precisely this difficult and dangerous balancing act that forms the basis of the debate in Book 1 of *Utopia*.

Gillis opens the dialogue by suggesting that Hythloday, given his experience and learning, ought to contribute to the good of the commonwealth by becoming counsellor to a prince. His reason, however, is easily dismantled: 'you would not only serve your own interests excellently, but be of great assistance in the advancement of all your friends and relatives' (*Ut*, 55). Hythloday objects that he has done his duty to his friends and family already and would not in fact be doing himself any benefit. In contrast to Gillis's suggestion that he 'serve' (*inservire*) kings, Hythloday observes that he would instead become a slave (*servire*) to them; after all, there is only 'one syllable less' between these options (ibid.). Thus the motive of self-interest is quickly done away with.

Morus then picks up the debate, accepting and even praising Hythloday's reluctance to be swayed by self-interest. He advances a view drawn from Cicero's *On Duties*, according to which, even if it is to one's disadvantage to serve the commonwealth, it remains a duty to do so: 'it seems to me you will do what is worthy of you and this generous and truly philosophic spirit of yours if you so order your life as to apply your talent and industry to the public interest [*publicis rebus*], even if it involves some personal disadvantages to yourself' (*Ut*, 57). This suggestion has more traction with Hythloday; but he still objects, and along strongly Platonic lines. First, Hythloday does not wish to leave the peace and freedom he enjoys independently of the court; second, he does not think that he would do any good if he did. Monarchs are only concerned with war and acquisition, and courtiers with personal profit and flattery. He would end up either speaking counsel that was too far from the interests and intentions of monarchs or being forced to repeat the corrupt advice of sycophantic counsellors.

Hythloday gives two examples to support this assertion, first demonstrating the flattery of courtiers and, second, showing the martial focus of kings. To begin with, he recounts an episode in the home of Cardinal Morton at Lambeth Palace, where More (and Morus) served as a boy. The discussion over dinner turns to the punishment of thieves, and Hythloday gives traditional humanist advice about equity and justice, observing that it is unjust to take someone's life for stealing money and that restitution should be made to the owner, not to the prince. In the end the cardinal remarks that an 'experiment' should be made in England, to see whether Hythloday's programme would go well or ill; and the listeners praise him for the idea. Hythloday takes this outcome as proving that, when it came from the cardinal, 'they all vied in praising . . . what they all had received with contempt when suggested by me' (*Ut*, 81). However, the cardinal's proposal was a compromise that took into account the realities of the situation. For instance, Morton suggests that, when a thief is sentenced to death, the king might postpone execution until Hythloday's proposals are tested and, if they do not work, carry out the execution as planned. The cardinal does, furthermore, take the given advice, contradicting Hythloday's second point – namely that princes are not interested in the advice he has to give.

For this second argument, Hythloday relates an imaginary scenario: sitting at the council table of the king of France. The councillors would debate strategies for war and accumulating money, and Hythloday wonders: 'In such a meeting...when such efforts are being made...what if an insignificant fellow like myself were to get up and advise going on another tack?' (*Ut*, 89). For instance, what if he were to say that peace and good governance should be the purview of the monarch, rather than war and wealth? 'To what deaf ears', he ends, 'should I tell the tale!' (*Ut*, 97).

Morus is forced to agree; Hythloday would indeed fail to persuade them. The issue is with how he delivers his counsel, for 'such ideas should [not] be thrust on people, or such advice given, as you are positive will never be listened to' (*Ut*, 99). Instead of 'this academic philosophy', which thinks that 'everything is suitable for every place', an adviser must adopt a 'more civil philosophy',[19] 'which knows its stage, adapts itself to the play in hand, and performs its role neatly and appropriately', or 'with decorum'[20] – an idea that runs closely alongside the humanist emphasis on common usage (ibid.). In this case, the speaker has to adjust high-minded or universal principles to realities particular to the situation. As Morus puts it: 'If you cannot pluck up wrongheaded opinion [*opinio*] by the root, if you cannot cure according to your heart's desire vices of long standing, yet you must not on that account desert the commonwealth' (ibid.). Furthermore, in order to change people's minds, you must use the 'indirect approach', doing the best one can with the situation: 'What you cannot turn to good you must make as little bad as you can. For it is impossible that all should be well unless all men were good, a situation which I do not expect for a great many years to come!' (*Ut*, 101).

Hythloday, however, persists, suggesting that to adopt this approach would be to become corrupt himself; by the 'evil companionship' of courtiers 'you will be seduced yourself or, keeping your own integrity and innocence, you will be made a screen for the wickedness and folly of others' (*Ut*, 103). There cannot possibly be any room for an 'indirect approach' when people remain greedy and proud, and people will always be greedy and proud where there is private property. Only common property will solve the problem of corruption in the commonwealth. And so the debate over counsel turns into the discussion of the commonwealth of Utopia in Book 2.

Book 2

As we've seen, in Book 1 Morus advances the view that a philosopher like Hythloday should give himself and his abilities to all, fulfilling his duty to the commonwealth – the *res publica* (literally the 'public thing', 'public interest' or 'public business'). To hold back from doing so, not to share the benefit of his wisdom, Morus claims, is selfish and prideful. It puts individual interests over the benefit of the whole. Philosophers should be concerned with common affairs.

This reorientation towards the common business is also the focus of the second book, which contains Hythloday's description of the island of Utopia. Hythloday's objection that his counsel would do no good at the courts of kings, for everyone there is self-serving, is supported by the idea that, 'wherever you have private property and all men measure all things by cash values, there it is scarcely possible for a commonwealth to have justice or prosperity'; and so he begins to 'ponder on the extremely wise and holy institutions of the Utopians', who hold all property in common (*Ut*, 103). Hythloday maintains that there can be no happiness where private property produces greed and inequality. Utopia is, for him, the best possible commonwealth, indeed the only one worthy of the name, because in all other polities there is no 'common' 'wealth', no 'public' (*publica*) 'thing' (*res*).

This lesson is introduced before Book 2, in the paratextual material – the letters and poems published in the same volume as *Utopia* – and in Hythloday's speeches in his examples in Book 1. The paratextual letters reinforce the idea that greed for personal gain separates one from one's neighbour, 'with whom he is joined by rights of citizenship' (*Ut*, 7). In Utopia, the 'common interest' is served because 'all men have all things in common', and thus 'every action, whether public or private, regards not the greed of the many or the caprice of the few' but 'is totally directed to the maintenance of one uniform justice, equality, and communion' (*Ut*, 35). Greed and personal interest are a fragmenting force, cutting through the communal bonds that should hold a polity in order.

This view of corporate society is one that we shall see again in More's theological works and, in negative form, in his *Richard the Third*. It is also an idea that More puts forward in one of his poems:

> A kingdom in all its parts is like a man; it is held together by natural affection [*amor*]. The king is the head; the people form the other parts. Every citizen the king has he considers a part of his own body (that is why he grieves at the loss of a single one). The people risk themselves to save the king and everyone thinks of him as the head of his own body. (*LP*, 164–5)[21]

This idea is drawn from Augustine, who wrote in *City of God* that Adam and Eve had 'lived in faithful and sincere fellowship' through 'the love of the pair for God and for one another'.[22] Such a love would be the only power strong enough to bind humanity into a political body once again.

Greed and self-interest cut these bonds apart. In discussing the punishment of thieves before Cardinal Morton, Hythloday finds himself on the topic of sheep, or rather on the topic of enclosing common land for sheep grazing. In the early sixteenth century the issue of enclosure was a highly controversial one.[23] It resulted in riots and in the impoverishment of families, and, as Hythloday argues, it wasn't clear that it had a beneficial effect on the wool trade itself. In an arresting image, Hythloday suggests that it has become common for sheep to eat people, as the wool trade had caused so many people to starve. In *Utopia* the problem of enclosure provides a useful example and an apt image of the way in which 'unscrupulous greed' damages the commonwealth. Self-interested landowners are cutting off bits of common land for themselves, ripping the commonwealth to pieces.

Land

In the first section of Book 2 Hythloday recounts the geographical situation of the island of Utopia, which bears a resemblance to England, recalling Utopia's role as a mirror of reality.[24] Like England, the island of Utopia is larger in the middle and tapers out at the ends, which makes it look a bit like a crescent moon. Although this crescent is difficult to discern in modern maps of England, sixteenth-century variants render this shape more clearly (Figures 2.1 and 2.2). Utopia's central breadth of 200 miles was equivalent to that given for England in a 1515 Chronicle, and is more or less a correct

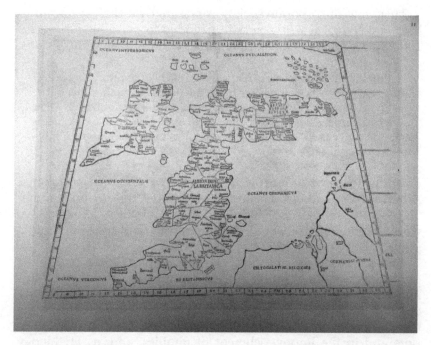

Figure 2.1 Ptolemaic map of the British Isles. Woodcut. From the Stras-
bourg 1513 *Geographia* of the renowned second-century Greek astronomer
and geographer Claudius Ptolemaeus, edited by J. Essler and G. Übelin.
As we can see, Scotland has been oriented the wrong way, to the east rather
than the west. If this were corrected, a clear crescent shape would be
apparent.
Source: Facsimile from G. R. Crone (1961), *Early Maps of the British Isles,
AD 1000–AD 1579*, London: Royal Geographical Society, plate 11.

calculation of the distance between the east coast of England at
Norfolk to its western border with Wales. The dimensions given,
however, remind the reader that no matter how much Utopia may
mirror reality it remains distant from it, as they defy laws of math-
ematics, and so Utopia cannot be properly mapped.

Beyond establishing Utopia as England's fantastic mirror image,
this section also exemplifies the proverbial idea that many hands
make light work – or, as it is noted in the margin, 'What Is Common
to All Is Borne Lightly' (*Ut*, 113).[25] The Utopians, working together,
have even managed to build a canal through the centre of their
island, a seemingly impossible task. And the harvest is also easier

Figure 2.2 Angliae figura / Map of the British Isles. MS on vellum. Anonymous, drawn between 1534 and 1546.
Source: British Museum, Cotton MS. Aug. i.i, f. 9. Facsimile from G. R. Crone (1961), *Early Maps of the British Isles, AD 1000–AD 1579*, London: Royal Geographical Society, plate 12.

through shared work: 'The Effectiveness of Cooperative Labor' (*Ut*, 117).

Not only can the Utopians, by sharing work, make the most of their small island, but they are also content with it. In this respect Utopia is in contrast with contemporary Europe, as noted in the margin: 'Today the Desire for Expansion is the Curse of All Commonwealths' (*Ut*, 113). In Book 1 Hythloday had wondered what the response from the French king and his courtiers would be if he 'argued that we should stay at home because the single kingdom of France by itself was almost too large to be governed well by a single man' and thus 'the king should not dream of adding other dominions under his sway' (*Ut*, 89). This was almost certainly a reflection upon the military ambitions of the young Henry VIII, who had his sights set on reconquering lands in France previously in England's possession. Humanists, however, rejected such expansionist policies. As More writes in his *Epigrams*: 'Among many kings there will be scarcely one, if there is one, who is satisfied to have one kingdom. And yet among many kings there will scarcely be one, if there is really one, who rules a single kingdom well' (*LP*, 257). The desire for expansion for the sake of personal gain, just like the desire for enclosure, pulls apart the bonds of the commonwealth.

Of course, there must be some division of land in Utopia, but none of it can be said to properly belong to anyone in particular. Utopian families have separate homes, but every effort is made to ensure that the allocation is done not only equitably, but in a way that does not allow people to believe that anything is their property rather than belonging to the community as a whole. Homes, for instance, just like the Utopians' fifty-four cities, are as identical as possible, and every decade families are relocated, a process taken care of through lottery. The doors to their homes are not locked and 'as a result nothing is private anywhere'.[26]

Politics

Political power, importantly, is also shared, mitigating the pernicious influence of personal interest that Hythloday had noted in Book 1. Most decisions are reached at the city level, where the basic unit is the household – that is, ten to sixteen adults; these elect 'phylarchs' or 'syphogrants' who represent them. Every ten syphogrants choose from the scholarly class one 'protophylarch' or 'tranibor' who in turn sits on the council to the *princeps* (usually translated as 'governor' or 'prince'). The *princeps* is elected by the syphogrants and holds the position for life, unless he is 'ousted on suspicion of aiming at tyranny' (*Ut*, 123). The tranibors consult with the *princeps* at least once every day. When a question comes before the city, the syphogrants first consult the families that elected them, before debating the matter together and then reporting a decision to the senate of tranibors, who counsel the prince on a final decision. Notably this structure is present just at the city level, and there is no *princeps* for the island as a whole.

Instead, the utopian General Council, comprised of 'three old and experienced citizens' from each city, is the ultimate authority for the entire island (*Ut*, 113). Thus the utopian system resembles city-state structures such as those of ancient Athens or Sparta or of

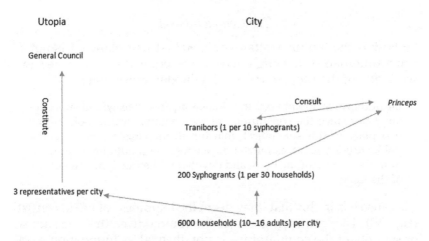

Figure 2.3 Utopia's political system.

Renaissance republican Venice or Florence, as well as being largely democratic and conciliar.[27] It is, in short, republican. Although the *princeps* is in place for life, he can be replaced if he becomes tyrannical, especially as there is a General Council that rules above him, much like in More's description of the relationship between the General Council and the pope (see Chapter 4). If we lay out the system in a diagram (Figure 2.3), one can see how directly the people are involved in the governance of their city and country.

More had titled one of his epigrams 'The Consent of the People Both Bestows and Withdraws Sovereignty' and written in it that a prince 'ought to have command not one instant longer than his subjects wish' (*LP*, 169). Likewise, in the *Confutation of Tyndale's Answer* he wrote: 'A governor of people is made for the people and not the people for the governor' (*CTA*, 75). In the utopian arrangement, this seems to be the case. Importantly, it is also a system in which affairs are discussed and deliberated, though not outside of official political institutions. Decisions are not made on the day when they are debated, so people will not vote obstinately and self-servingly, according to the opinion they voiced during the debate, but rather upon reflection on the good of the commonwealth as a whole; a person will not 'give more thought to defending his opinion than to supporting what is for the good of the commonwealth' (*Ut*, 125). Like much else in Utopia, the system is designed to place 'the public welfare' over individual interest (ibid.).

The Common Good

So how is the 'public welfare' defined? At first glance it is not as communitarian as one might have expected. In discussing the short work day of the utopian citizen, Hythloday notes that

> the authorities do not keep the citizens against their will at superfluous labor since the constitution of the commonwealth looks in the first place to this sole object: that for all the citizens, as far as the public needs permit, as much time as possible should be withdrawn from the service of the body and devoted to the freedom and culture of the mind

– because it is in this that 'they deem the happiness of life to consist' (*Ut*, 135). The 'common good' of the commonwealth – the success or stability of the community – is not, then, at its foundation a collectivist aim; instead the common good refers to the happiness (*felicitas*) of the individuals who make up the commonwealth. Importantly, although 'harmless pleasure [is] not to be spurned' (*Ut*, 145), this happiness, which Utopians value most, proceeds from the contemplation of higher things. Obeying the dictates of reason and living virtuously means to them following the guidance of nature, which tells us first to obey the divine majesty and, second, to lead a life full of joy and free from pain.

Some have suggested that the Utopians' views imply that they are modern 'Epicureans', that is, followers of Epicurus (341–270 BCE), leader of one of the five major Hellenistic 'schools', who put pleasure at the centre of his system of ethics by making it the supreme goal of human activity. This would appear, on the face of it, to put the Utopians at odds with Christian ideals of restraint and withdrawal, as these have far more to do with Stoic ethics, which the Utopians seem to reject. However, the desire for *felicitas* needn't be hedonistic (on the popular understanding of this term) or anti-Christian. More may have been drawing on the humanist writer Lorenzo Valla, who set up a contrast between Epicureanism and Stoicism in his dialogue *De vero bono* (*Of True Good*). There Valla seems to encourage his readers to find their own position between the two extremes of Epicureanism and Stoicism and to focus on 'heavenly pleasures' as a motivation to Christian behaviours and actions.[28]

Importantly, in Utopia individual happiness is placed in the context of the community. Nature calls people 'to help one another to a merrier life' (*Ut*, 165). Because all are equal by the grace and reckoning of nature – '[nature] equally favors all whom she endows

with the same form' (ibid.) – no one can claim that his or her right
to a happy life is more important than another's. In such circumstances, one's achievement of happiness must be bound by the
restriction that it does not threaten the achievement of happiness
by others: 'nature surely bids you take constant care not so to
further your own advantages as to cause disadvantages to your
fellows' (ibid.). The achievement of individual good is bound up
with the well-being of all within the community.

As all people have the right to pursue happiness, laws are necessary and should be given either by a good king (in the case of the
commonwealth's founding) or by the people, through common
consent. These laws ensure that each individual is given the same
opportunity to achieve the happy life. Where there is no law, the
Utopians recognize, most people will want to look after their own
interest. To look to the common interest instead of one's own is a
sign of pious devotion – and one much to be praised in Utopia. To
look to one's own interest instead, although expected, is looked
down upon. Where there is no law to govern a situation, to 'deprive
others of their pleasure to secure your own' is 'surely an injustice'
(ibid.). Because justice is defined as giving to each what he or she
deserves and all deserve the right to pursue this happy life, to
deprive them of that pursuit has to be an injustice. The community,
through its values, thus preserves and optimizes its citizens' ability
to achieve the good life, even where there is no law.

This sense of justice is the 'strongest sinew of the commonwealth'
(*Ut*, 197), which binds it together in a single whole. It is what keeps
the commonwealth together against the divisive effect of private
interests. Here More is drawing on the Ciceronian account of the
commonwealth. As Cicero writes, 'there is nothing more illustrious
nor of wider range than the bond between human beings and the
sort of fellowship and useful intercommunication and love among
human beings, which...is termed justice.'[29] For Utopians, this bond
is – importantly – natural. Utopians have no regard for treaties,
since surely 'nature herself' 'sufficiently bind[s] one man to another'
(ibid.). The Utopians object to the European penchant for treaties,
as they think it undermines the power of this natural bond. Treaty
making results in the emergence of two forms of justice: one for the
'common sort', which binds them 'in chains', and another for kings,
which is 'far freer so that everything is permissible to it – except
what it finds disagreeable' (*Ut*, 199). As a result, this natural bond
becomes broken, and every person conceives of himself or herself
as the enemy of another, except where a meaningless piece of paper

tells him or her otherwise. The Utopians believe 'that the fellowship created by nature takes the place of a treaty, and that men are better and more firmly joined together by good will than by pacts, by spirit than by words' (ibid.). To depend on treaties to keep people from each other's throats is actually to give people reason for war, against all natural inclinations to peace.

Public Opinion

Just as the Utopians prefer to have no treaties, they also have few laws. As we've seen, where no law arbitrates a situation, utopian public opinion motivates people to community-oriented just action. So in place of long and complex legal codes, in Utopia the citizens are 'trained': 'They have very few laws because very few are needed for persons so educated [sic institutis]' (Ut, 195). As a letter writer in the paratextual section, Jerome Busleyden, notes, Utopia 'has devoted its energies not so much to framing the laws as to training the most qualified officials' (Ut, 35). Hythloday repeats the same idea, but this time in reference to the citizens, noting that monsters and cannibals can be found all over the world, 'but well and wisely trained [sane ac sapienter institutos] citizens are not everywhere to be found' (Ut, 53). A reduced number of laws has the benefit of ensuring that every citizen can learn and know them, adding a level of transparency to the legal system in Utopia that is not achieved in Europe. But it also means that, in order to make sure that, in the copious silence of the laws, citizens do attend to the common good, emphasis has to be placed on these ideas of 'piety' and justice. In other words, public opinion and value systems have to be carefully constructed and maintained.

This arrangement is partly institutional. Utopians are given no opportunities for vice, for, as More writes in his *Richard the Third*, 'opportunity will often make even the lazy and peaceful do wrong' (RIII, 329). In Utopia there is 'no wine shop, no alehouse, no brothel anywhere, no opportunity for corruption' – a state of affairs that prompts the marginal note (most likely from Erasmus): 'O Holy Commonwealth – and Worthy of Imitation Even by Christians!' (Ut, 147). The secret to the Utopians' success is that there are no secrets: 'being under the eyes of all, people are bound either to be performing the usual labor or to be enjoying their leisure in a fashion not without decency' (ibid.). This 'universal behavior' ('universal' in the sense of 'adopted by the [entire] population': populi morem) 'must of necessity lead to an abundance of all commodities', which is then shared equally among all (ibid.).[30] Because everything is common, everything is observable by all, and thus subject to justified praise or blame. There can be no deception: 'Citizens Very Rightly are Invited to Well-Doing by Praise and Honor' (*Ut*, 143).[31] Unlike the kind of praise that leads to the vice of pride, this worthy praise encourages virtue. This is partly because these actions are praised as pious. The praise they warrant is really the praise of God, communicated by Utopians. We might compare this approach to the one that More takes in his account of pride in *The Four Last Things*: people ought to 'turn their appetites from the laud of silly, mortal men, and desire to deserve their thanks and commendation of God only, whose praise can never die' (*FLT*, 155). This is a higher sort of praise, which does not play upon the pernicious sort of pride that Hythloday condemns.

Society's values are decided through the consensus of its people, rightly or wrongly. As Hythloday notes, in Europe it is 'futile consensus' that determines things 'to be sweet to [the people] in spite of being against nature (as though they had the power to change the nature of things as they do their names)' (*Ut*, 167; here he may be alluding to the rhetorical figure of paradiastole, examined further in Chapter 3). For instance, people outside Utopia value clothes, false honours, nobility, gold, silver and gems, which have little or no value in and of themselves. It is this 'consensus' or 'opinion' that is at the heart of these values. There is a 'false idea of pleasure' (*falsa voluptatis opinio*) and a 'meaningless nobility' (*vana nobilitas*), which is created by those who have a 'belief (idea) of nobility' (*nobilitatis opinio*), in other words who 'imagine themselves to be noble' (*Ut*, 169). Because Utopians are committed to real and decent pleasures, they see through this façade of imagined pleasure generated by 'perverse habit' (*Ut*, 173). The greatest and most lasting example of this is in the Utopians' treatment of precious metals and gems: 'Human Imagination [*Opinio*] Gives Value to Gems or Takes It Away' (*Ut*, 169). Gold and silver they use for chamber pots and slaves' chains, and 'thus by every means in their power they make gold and silver a mark of ill fame' (*Ut*, 153). Gems are given to children to play with, so that when they grow older, 'they lay them aside, not by any order of their parents, but through their own feeling of shame' (ibid.). Such practices are also allegorical; Europeans are chained by their desire for such precious metals and rendered children in their love of gemstones. In a parallel to More's epigram about the peasant who thought the king was just a 'man in fancy dress', when ambassadors come to visit Utopia in their gold chains and gem-studded jewellery, children giggle and adults mistake them for fools and slaves. The Utopians, despite not valuing gold themselves, do keep a store of it, in case they need to use it for trade or defence, because other countries place value on it. They use these artificial trivialities without becoming corrupted by them, and in this way they provide an example for others. This is the power of the metaphor of the stage play. If one recognizes all such 'devices' of the 'conspiracy of the rich' (*Ut*, 241) as fictions, their power can be repurposed for the good of the commonwealth.

In Utopia one of the most important agents of public opinion is the priest. There is a strict line between the counsel of priests and the command or sovereignty of the government. Priests offer 'advice and admonition', as opposed to civil officials, who 'check and punish offenders' (*Ut*, 229). In part, this division is intended to restrict the potentially negative influence of priests; they are 'invested with no power except the influence of honor', and hence 'it need not be feared that they will cause any great harm to the state' (ibid.). But, more importantly, it ensures that there is a class of persons who are responsible precisely for this 'influence of honor', which holds such great importance in the cohesion of the utopian commonwealth. Priests are in charge of children's education and 'take the greatest pains from the very first to instil into children's minds, while still tender and pliable, good opinions which are also useful for the preservation of the commonwealth' (ibid.). These opinions, Hythloday reports, once 'firmly implanted in children…accompany them all through their adult lives and are of great help in watching over the condition of the commonwealth', which cannot decay, except 'from wrong attitudes' (*ex perversis opinionibus*, ibid.).

There is a civil religion in Utopia, and people are allowed to worship in private however they please. This toleration has several limits, all to do with religion's role in reinforcing what is 'common'. Anyone who does not believe in God and divine providence, which are thought to be the beliefs that separate humans from animals, is to be treated as a beast, because 'Who can doubt that [such a person] will strive either to evade by craft the public laws of his country or to break them by violence in order to serve his own private desires when he has nothing to fear but laws and no hope beyond the body?' (*Ut*, 221–3). Public worship includes only what can be shared by all – 'nothing is seen or heard in the temples which does not seem to agree with all in common' (*Ut*, 233) – and their prayers ask God to direct them towards the 'commonwealth which is the happiest' and 'the religion which... is the truest', if they have not found them already (*Ut*, 237). In short, they ask him to bring them all to the same 'way of living' (*instituta vivendi*) and to the same 'opinion of God', that is, belief about or notion of God (*de deo opinio*; ibid.).

Hythloday indicates that the Utopians have begun converting to Christianity, now that he has introduced them to it, as they found that it resonates with their already held beliefs. A religion like Christianity, the text seems to suggest, is already so consonant with the dictates of 'nature' to which the Utopians adhere that it will quickly become the dominant religion, without an enforced conversion. They will still not allow it, however, to threaten the unity of their commonwealth. When a utopian Christian convert begins preaching zealously, he is punished for disrupting public life. Utopians have good reason to fear zealotry and sectarianism: these forces caused the collapse of their commonwealth before, giving their founding prince, Utopus, the opportunity to conquer the island and make it his own. Utopus learned from this history and set up a limited amount of religious toleration, as well as the other institutions that hold Utopia together, orienting public opinion around what can be shared by all. Without this, their history makes clear, the commonwealth falls apart.

Mirror for Commonwealths

Hythloday concludes by restating the general lesson that we have uncovered so far: in Utopia what is *common* is upheld over what is *individual*, by means of institutions and the norms they generate. Because of this it is not only the best commonwealth, 'but the only one which can rightly claim the name of a commonwealth' (*Ut*, 239). Outside Utopia, Hythloday continues, 'men talk freely of the public welfare – but look to their private interests only' (ibid.), a lesson that is made even more striking in the 1551 English translation: 'For in other places they speak still of the common wealth; but every man procureth his own private wealth.'[32] In contrast, 'in Utopia, where nothing is private, they seriously concern themselves with public affairs' (ibid.). Notably, the word Hythloday uses for 'public affairs' is *negotium*, the descriptor of the active life he had rejected in Book 1. The tale thus comes full circle. Utopians 'seriously' concern themselves with public affairs, unlike Europeans, who cloak their self-interest in concern for the public welfare.

In Europe the cultural norms generated by institutions encourage vices that destroy the commonwealth, eradicating the natural bonds that unite it. The most important of these, as we might have expected, is pride. It is the 'one single monster, the chief progenitor of all plagues' that has prevented the adoption of the customs of Utopians (*Ut*, 245). The problem with pride is that it requires and necessitates inequality, because 'Pride measures prosperity not by her own advantages but by others' disadvantages' but rather by standing over others: 'Pride would not consent to be made even a goddess if no poor wretches were left for her to domineer over and scoff at' (*Ut*, 243). Utopians have eradicated pride, but in Europe, Hythloday concludes, 'Pride is too deeply fixed in men to be easily plucked out' (*Ut*, 245). Of course, this is precisely the language that Morus had used in his debate with Hythloday; one cannot always 'pluck out' these deep-seated vices, but rather do one's best with them.[33] One has to work with people as they are.

Hythloday himself proposes some compromises through which the 'burden' of poverty and misfortune imposed by private property can be 'lightened to some extent', though not 'removed entirely' (*Ut*, 105). For instance, 'a statute might be made that no person should have a monetary income beyond that permitted by law', 'special legislation might be passed to prevent the monarch from being overmighty and the people overweening', or 'public offices should not be solicited with gifts, nor be put up for sale'; but he rejects such compromises because they would only alleviate and make 'less acute' the ills of the commonwealth instead of curing them (ibid.). Such measures, of course, might be perfectly acceptable to the more pragmatic Morus and are reflective of the sort of compromises that Morton had suggested to Hythloday's speech in Book 1.

At the end of Book 2 the reader returns to the mind of Morus the narrator, who reflects on Hythloday's tale. Morus notes that the utopian way of life 'utterly overthrows all the nobility, magnificence, splendor, and majesty which are, in the estimation of the common people [*publica...opinio*], the true glories and ornaments of the commonwealth' (*Ut*, 247). He ends the book by reflecting that there are many elements of the utopian commonwealth that he would 'wish' rather than 'hope' to see realized (ibid.).

The Lessons of *Utopia*

It is an enigmatic ending, and the reader is left wondering what More's views really are on the matter. Does he think that philosophers should engage in politics, even in a world corrupted by private interests? Does he think that private property should be done away with and all goods held in common? If one were only to read *Utopia*, it might be better to leave these queries open. More's text invites more questions than it answers, and this is probably the way he intended it.[34] However, if we want to place *Utopia* in the context of More's thought more widely, it is worth interrogating these themes a bit further, using as corroborative evidence the comments he makes elsewhere. Although there is always the possibility that More changed his mind between works, the consistency and recurrence of his vocabulary allow us at least to suggest that the views he put forward in his less enigmatic texts can help us understand the puzzles of *Utopia*.[35]

In More's 1510 *Life of Pico della Mirandola* – which was a translation of the 1496 biography written by Pico's nephew – the eponymous character sets out views on the theme of the active and the contemplative life that are very similar to Hythloday's. He is concerned with his liberty and considers 'worldly business' to be servitude. The three letters More appends to his biography all deal with this subject, especially the last one. In it, Pico della Mirandola (1463–94) answers his friend Andrea Corneo's suggestion that he enter 'the civil and active life' (*LPM*, 85). Corneo (paraphrased by Pico) had advised him 'not so to embrace Martha that ye should utterly forsake Mary' (*LPM*, 86), thereby drawing on the distinction between the biblical sisters who served Jesus in two different ways: Martha, who attended to the business of welcoming him, and Mary, who sat at his feet and listened to his words. This tale was often used to justify the contemplative life; for, when Martha chides Mary for not helping her, Jesus declares that it is Mary who has chosen the better path. Corneo, however, suggests a middling way – that Pico should not completely leave behind contemplative affairs but still engage with worldly ones: 'I desire you not so to embrace Martha [business] that ye should utterly forsake Mary [contemplation]' (ibid.). More goes even further, however, and adds his own gloss on the reference, expanding the original letter that he is translating. He adds: 'I am content that ye study, but I would have you outwardly occupied also' and 'Love them & use them both, as well study as worldly occupation' (ibid.).[36] More thus suggests a fully combined and balanced approach, whereas his source text had just advocated the addition of limited time for contemplation.

This balance is more easily advised than achieved, however, as the paratexual letter in *Utopia* from More to Gillis attests. More's active life leaves very little room for study, which is why his *Utopia* has come to the publishers so late. He tells Gillis that his 'other tasks left me practically no leisure at all'; he must devote 'almost the whole day in public to other men's affairs, and the remainder to his own' (*Ut*, 39). In a world of private ownership, More doesn't have the time for contemplation that Utopians do. So what is one to do? Is it indeed impossible to embrace both Martha and Mary in the real world, where ownership is not held in common?

The answer that More seems to arrive at is one first articulated by Augustine. For Augustine, well read as he was in both Plato and Cicero, the important element is an internal reorganization of priorities. What is common and shared must be prioritized over that which is one's own.[37] More expresses the same idea in 1533, in a passage of his *Apology* that mirrors the final line of *Utopia*. In the *Apology*, More tells his reader that it would be wonderful if the world were filled with people who were 'so good' that there were no faults and no heresy needing punishment. Unfortunately, 'this is more easy to wish, than likely to look for' (*ATM*, 166). Unlike in *Utopia*, in the *Apology* More goes on to explain what this means. He writes that, because of this reality, all one can do is 'labour to make himself better' and 'charitably bear with others' where he can (ibid.). In some ways this suggestion is counterintuitive, as it demands an attention to one's own mindset that is seemingly at odds with More's focus on the common. However, the shift towards what is held in common has to begin with the individual (assuming that one does not live in Utopia).[38]

For Augustine, the accumulation of goods, the attainment of fame or favour, and the build-up of political power are not to be sought for their own sake, as ends, but are acceptable as means to attaining some higher end. Things of this world, though fleeting and untrustworthy, can be used to good ends, and it is solely for this reason that they ought to be invested with value. As John Colet – More's friend, mentor and fellow student of Augustine – admonishes: 'Use well temporal things. Desire eternal things.'[39] More repeats the idea in his own works, claiming that we ought not to consider the 'outward goods of fortune' – such as 'riches, good name, honest estimation, honourable fame & authority' – as important for our present life, but rather 'by the good use thereof, to make them matter of our merit with God's help in the life after to come' (*DC*, 209). By thinking of the issue this way, we see the two questions from the two parts of *Utopia* – the active versus the contemplative life and common versus private property – come together.

These two sets of debates often converge in More's writing. In the *Letter to a Monk*, written three years after *Utopia*, More writes that 'God showed great foresight when he instituted all things in common' and 'Christ showed as much when he tried to recall mortals again to what is common from what is private' (*LPM*, 279). This is because 'corrupt mortal nature cannot cherish what is private without detriment to what is common' (ibid.). Once we 'call anything our own', our interests are diverted 'from the service of the common good' (*communium cultu rerum*; ibid.).[40] More's point is not to suggest that property *should* be held in common, but that a discussion of common property serves as a reminder to value common things (such as the common good) over individual ones, including our own. He gives the example of corrupt religious orders, whose members place their own religious practices far above others': they value 'whatever is exclusive to their order more than everything that is common to all religious orders' and 'prize all that pertains to the religious' more than 'lowly and humble concerns that are not only not private to them but are common to the whole Christian people' (*LPM*, 281). This lesson is reflected as well, he suggests, in the choice between active and contemplative lives. In choosing the contemplative life, 'God may find that what you have been doing is avoiding responsibility', by 'wrapping your talent up in a napkin, thus wasting it inside for fear of losing it out-of-doors' (*LPM*, 303). Both these habits fuel 'personal pride, the most dangerous habit there is' and place faith in private interest over and above 'the Christian religion', which is shared by all (ibid.). Whether one considers the good of the commonwealth or the good life, the focus should be on what is common.

These lessons are repeated, with some variations, in one of More's later works, the *Dialogue of Comfort*, written while he was in the Tower of London. Although in this text More adopts a slightly more suspicious view of the active life, a wholly contemplative life is still condemned as self-serving. Through the character of Anthony, he disparages those who are not willing to trust in God enough to face a world of temptation, 'whereby for faint heart they leave of good business, wherein they were well occupied, & under pretext (as it seemeth to them self) of humble heart and meekness, & serving God in contemplation & silence, they seek their own ease & earthly rest' (*DC*, 161). More adds that, if a man *truly* feels that he cannot do his duty publicly without falling into temptation, then he ought to retire from public life, but only after he has trusted in God enough to have made an attempt. One finds the same avoidance of extremes in the case of *negotium*, the opposite of contemplation, which he says can be 'the name of a devil that is ever full of business in tempting folk to much evil business' (*DC*, 167). If both contemplation and action are temptations to pursue ungodly paths, then the safest method is to trust in God and attempt to navigate between them both: 'for those temptations, while he that is tempted followeth them not, the fight against them serveth a man for matter of merit and reward in heaven' (*DC*, 170).

In *The Dialogue of Comfort*, More then turns immediately to the issue of ownership. Anthony suggests that economic inequality is in fact necessary to the commonwealth; there must be 'men of sub-stance...for else more beggars shall you have' (*DC*, 179). He gives an Aristotelian rejection of common property, arguing that it would lead to stagnation and indolence. If all the land were gathered and divided up evenly, Anthony tells his nephew, then everyone would be only a little better than a beggar. It would be, he says, as if one were to cut open a hen who laid golden eggs every day. You might get one or two for your trouble, but at the cost of the daily supply.

Notably, this analogy does not actually capture the idea of common property; Anthony does not address the suggestion of a communal coop of shared golden hens, so that no one would go without if theirs stopped laying. But the actual economic reality is not the point. Anthony gives an example similar to the Lucianic illustrations from More's early works: if one of two beggars is given a home and nice clothes on a temporary loan, the two are still equal, as that property does not really belong to the fortunate beggar. So, too, all people are equal despite economic inequalities – 'in this world, between the richest & the most poor, the difference is scant so much' (*DC*, 163) – because nothing truly belongs to us. What is important is how you view your place in the world, internalizing this fundamental Lucianic equality: 'if a man keep riches about him for a glory and royalty of the world...taking the poorer for the lack thereof, as one far worse than himself: such a mind is very vain foolish pride' (*DC*, 184). However, if, on the other hand, he doesn't love his riches but uses them for the benefit of the commonwealth, then he has done as much as, or even more than, one who gives his riches away. This is all about an orientation of the mind and soul away from what is private and towards what is common.

More carries this lesson into yet another of his last works, one also written in the Tower of London but left unfinished upon his death: *A Treatise upon the Passion*. He condemns those who internal-ize the false and artificial inequalities of this world: 'how much more foolish abusion [distortion][41] is there in that pride, by which we worldly folk look up on height, and solemnly set by our self, with deep disdain of other far better men, only for very vain worldly trifles that properly be not our own?' (*TP*, 8). He lists the things from which people derive this sense of pride over one another – several of them had also appeared in *Utopia* – and demonstrates how foolish it is to measure one's worth with that of others, when we consider that in fact it is not even one's own. 'Gold and silver', for instance, are 'no part of our self, but of the earth', and, although the 'wool of [a man's] gown' may be finer, 'as fine as it is, a poor sheep wore it on her back before it came upon his...And why should he be now better than she by that wool, that though it be his, is yet not so verily his as it was verily hers' (ibid.). In fact, he goes on to say, we cannot actually speak of 'other men's and our own' because 'I can see nothing (the thing well weighed) that any man may well call his own' (ibid.). Recalling the example of the pageant or the beggar's borrowed estates, More writes that, 'as men may call him a fool that beareth himself proud, because he jetteth[42] [struts] about in a borrowed gown, so may we be well called very fools all, if we bear us proud of any thing that we have here' (*TP*, 8–9). Nothing in this world actually belongs to us; it is all 'borrowed ware' from God, which must be returned at the end of our lives. Private ownership is a fiction. In this way Utopia is more 'real' than Europe.

These lessons in *Utopia* and in More's later works are clearly related, then, to those of his poetry and translations of Lucian. The short 'pageant' of life, the dangerous nature of pride, these are all foundational to More's comments, in *Utopia*, regarding a reorientation towards 'common things'. There is no clearer sign of this connection than in the 1518 edition of *Utopia*. There the map of the island bears an uncanny resemblance to a skull – a *memento mori* – designed to remind people of their impending death (Figure 2.4).[43] *Utopia*, like the skull, reminds us that nothing is truly our own, inviting us to lead lives dedicated to the commonwealth.

The remaining issue is how one in practice relates this remembrance to the difficulties of counsel-giving that Hythloday had mentioned in Book 1. The clearest direction is given in More's *Four Last Things*, written shortly after *Utopia*. In a crucial passage, More comes to discuss the active and the contemplative life in terms similar to those Hythloday had used, noting the objection that godly speech would either be ridiculed or endanger the speaker. Here More uses the idea of timely speech in order to promote a middling approach,

Figure 2.4 Map of Utopia by Ambrosius Holbein. Woodcut.
Source: From Thomas More's *Utopia*, Basel, 1518, p. 12.

as he had in the *Life of Pico*: 'And surely every thing hath [its] mean.
There is as scripture saith, time to speak & time to keep thy tongue'
(*FLT*, 137). He goes on to recommend that, whenever the conversation is 'naught and ungodly', it is better not to speak than to support
such an exchange. However, 'yet better were it than holding of thy
tongue, properly to speak, & with some good grace and pleasant
fashion, to break into some better matter' (ibid.). If one can change
the topic quickly, one ought to do so; such change is even better
than silence. The reason he gives returns us to the concept of one's
duty to serve the public, for in changing the conversation for the
better 'thou shalt not only profit thy self', which can be accomplished by keeping silent, 'but also amend the whole audience,
which is a thing far better and of much more merit' (ibid.). In other
words, remaining silent is, like the contemplative life, almost certainly motivated by pride or self-interest. It is true, More concedes,
that, if one cannot find a way of changing the subject and doesn't

have the authority to command silence, then it would be better to keep silent rather than 'blunt forth rudely, and irritate them to anger' (ibid). In most cases, however, one may be able to 'break into some better matter', which will serve the benefit of others (ibid.). It is all about judging the character of the moment.

This tactic sounds a lot like the 'indirect approach' that the character of Morus advocates in *Utopia*, certainly more than like Hythloday's 'thrusting ideas on people'. To drive this home, it is worth returning to the text and reflecting on the figure of Cardinal Morton, as described by Hythloday himself. Hythloday praises Morton both for 'his prudence' and for his 'virtue' (*Ut*, 59). In conversation Morton is both 'agreeable' and 'serious and dignified', and his qualities combine 'learning and practice' (ibid.). In other words, Morton combines the virtues of the active and the contemplative life; he can negotiate the realities of politics but remains virtuous. As we've seen, he takes Hythloday's highly philosophical – and indecorous – advice and presents it as something realistic and manageable. Although Morton doesn't appear in the text of Hythloday's second example, we can turn to More's *History of King Richard the Third* to see how Morton interacts with a council of flattering courtiers and with a tyrannical king. Even if a member of the tyrant Richard III's council, Morton successfully works behind the scenes to bring about Richard's overthrow and the arrival of Henry Tudor – the future Henry VII. He does so by playing his part, waiting for his moment and employing, for the good of the commonwealth, an indirect approach that plays upon the pride of others. In this way Morton heals a commonwealth torn apart by self-interest, bringing English realities more in line with utopian ideals, or rather English pageantries in line with *Utopia*'s realities.

Conclusion

With leisure time pressed upon him by his voyage on the continent in 1515, More had the opportunity to reflect on the classical and humanist debate over the active life versus the contemplative. For him, the question was intimately tied up with the theme he had explored in his earlier works: attention to the private over the common. The contemplative life was a life of pride and self-interest. The active life, on the other hand, demonstrated attention to what was held in common. Thus More, in *Utopia* and elsewhere, places the discussion of these two kinds of life next to a discussion of common versus private property as a way of arguing that the active life is the less proud and more community-oriented choice.

So did More 'mean' what he said in *Utopia*? Was he advocating for private property? For religious toleration? For the devaluing of gold? Did he really think that men and women should see each other naked before marriage? Or that divorce should be permitted? In most cases external evidence suggests that he would not have seriously mounted a plea for any of these causes, and in some ways this is precisely the point. Morus' objection to Hythloday is that his aims are too lofty and lack an understanding of the context in which they are to be applied. The stage play around them is problematic, but must not be ruined with too much truth. Raphael Hythloday is indeed a healer, like his namesake, the archangel Raphael, and, like him, is especially a healer of blindness; but Morus' point is that there is sometimes value to not seeing the truth of every single thing.[44]

In *Utopia* More is answering Erasmus, whose use of the stage play metaphor tended to favour Hythloday's arguments for a reclusive life and higher principles.[45] Whereas Erasmus, drawing on Aristotle, objected to rules that suited the *mores* of the people, More appears to plead for paying attention to customs and opinions and for tailoring to them one's words and actions. Erasmus agreed that deeply ingrained values could not be 'plucked out', but he focused on implanting virtues in the individual through education. More takes a different route, focusing on the beliefs of the community and on the role of the active individual within it when it comes to effecting considered change.[46]

Perhaps one of the most overlooked aspects of *Utopia* is More's analysis of public opinion, which not only keeps the commonwealth together, but – in contrast to More's contemporary situation – expresses 'real' values.[47] Rather than being used to support absurdities of the world (like the value of gemstones), in Utopia public opinion praises virtue, conceived of as a lack of pride and a dedication to the common good. More refers often to the *opinio* of the Utopians as essential to their way of life (*Ut*, 157, 159, 211). Public opinion becomes an expression of *vera nobilitas* – true nobility, not artificial and absurd hierarchies.

More goes far beyond other writers in his treatment of this idea. We've already seen how rhetoricians like Quintilian and Valla held that meaning was determined by common usage. This also meant that the orator needed to be concerned with what was variously referred to as *opinio communis* or *consensus civitatis*: the shared opinions of community members. Such an orator – and not the philosopher, Cicero maintained – was the one who would be concerned with 'practical philosophy' and had a duty to act for the public welfare.[48] This is the same division that Morus draws in Book 1 of *Utopia*: one between 'academic philosophy', which is concerned with high ideals and truth, and 'civil philosophy', which works within the bounds of public opinion. The deeply 'rooted' aspects of public opinion, for More, could not be changed, but people could be 'moved' to virtue on a given policy or idea. How to participate in the stage play while neither being fully overtaken by it nor disrupting it was a balancing act between these aspects of public opinion.

For More, Utopia may be the ideal, the true reality of our equality, but this does not mean that it ought to be implemented as it is in the world in which we live. Instead it is a reminder of our essential equality, which can help us make more virtuous decisions about how we might live our lives. If we accept what *Utopia* teaches us, we choose to live lives that avoid the sin of pride. We work within existing hierarchies, respecting their role in shaping our world but all the while acknowledging them as artificial. And we serve the commonwealth, holding the lessons of *Utopia* always in mind.

3

Richard III *and the Stage Play of Politics*

If *Utopia* teaches its readers lessons through reflection on a best possible world, *Richard the Third* is its dystopic counterpart. The comparison between these two texts ought not to be ignored; More was almost certainly writing both at the same time and thus probably had the same themes in mind. Clues in *Richard the Third* suggest that he began writing the text as early as 1513, two years before he began *Utopia*, and that he probably stopped writing around 1518, two years after *Utopia* was published. It is perhaps no surprise then that one sees many of the same issues confronted, albeit from a slightly different, slightly darker, perspective.

Like *Utopia*, *Richard the Third* is a commentary on the state of the commonwealth; but, whereas *Utopia* shows a commonwealth united, *Richard the Third* shows how a commonwealth can be torn apart. Despite this difference, *Richard the Third* draws upon the same understanding of the artificiality of this world that we find in *Utopia*, demonstrating the importance of public opinion to the stability of the commonwealth and the way in which self-interest and pride can destroy it. Unlike *Utopia*, however, and much more optimistically, the English *History of King Richard the Third* gives a clear example of an ideal figure who can make the situation in the commonwealth as 'little bad as possible'.

Texts and Contexts

There are two texts of *Richard the Third*, one in English – *The History of King Richard the Third* – and the other in Latin – *Historia Richardi*

Tertii – both of which purport to recount the events of the year 1483, beginning with the death of Edward IV in April.[1] The Latin version ends with the coronation of Richard III in July 1483, and the English continues up to the beginning of Buckingham's rebellion later that year. In both texts, More also details past events, such as Edward IV's marriage to Elizabeth Woodville in 1464. The key figures are nobles, primarily Edward IV's brother Richard, Duke of Gloucester, who would become protector to young King Edward V and, later, himself king, as Richard III. More reports that Richard was considered responsible for the death of his nephews, who stood between him and the crown, and who disappeared in the Tower of London. Richard is supported by a group of nobles, most notably Lord Hastings (c. 1431–83), whom he executes, and the Duke of Buckingham (1455–83), who by the end of the English text is being persuaded to turn against Richard. The former queen, Elizabeth Woodville (1437–92), also plays a role in attempting to protect her young sons, as does her family, which is quickly eliminated by Richard in his climb to power. Edward IV's former mistress and the current mistress of Lord Hastings, Jane Shore (c. 1445–c. 1527), also appears (though unnamed), and John Morton is present throughout the history, although he only comes to the forefront at the end of the English version. Finally there is the constant presence of the 'people', whose spectatorship exerts constant pressure on the political actors.

Richard the Third presents the reader with just as many puzzles as *Utopia*, if not more. First, there is the issue of the two different versions, neither of which was finished or published during More's lifetime.[2] The English *History* and the Latin *Historia* seem to have been written more or less simultaneously. This is an unusual composition technique; More must have moved back and forth between the two texts while writing. One is not the translation of the other. This becomes even clearer when comparing the two texts. While they have the same plot and characters, and they detail (more or less) the same events, there are dramatic differences between them, indicating what sort of audiences More intended for his works had they ever been published.[3] As Latin was the lingua franca of scholars across Europe, the Latin *Historia* must have been designed for More's humanist audience, presumably the same as that of *Utopia*. In it More takes the time to explain English traditions and customs, which he skips over in the English version. In some descriptions and explanations the Latin is more detailed and poetic, making clearer connections to the classical historians that More was drawing upon. There is a universalizing and classicizing tendency in the

Latin version. When referring, for instance, to the parliament, More calls it *senatus* (a 'senate'), recalling the role of the senate in the Roman republic; he even states that it has 'supreme and absolute' authority (*HRT*, 321).[4] More justifies this approach in his *Confutation of Tyndale's Answer* in 1533; he writes that, if one found in a 'Latin chronicle the term *senatus Londinensis*', it ought to be translated not as 'senate', but as 'mayor and aldermen' or, depending on the circumstances, as 'mayor, aldermen, and common council' (*CTA*, 287). The English version roots the history solidly in the English context and assumes much more local knowledge than the Latin, confirming that this text was for an English audience, perhaps one specifically within London. More importantly, the English version, though likewise unfinished, goes further than the Latin, giving the history a more optimistic ending, and thus is a little clearer about the lesson of the text.

Ars Historica

For the humanists, history ought to have concrete lessons, which connects it to their study of rhetoric and of moral and political philosophy. In addition to poetry and translation – at which More had already shown himself proficient by 1513 – this was one of the genres with which a young humanist ought to be thoroughly familiar.[5] In the Renaissance there were two potentially competing, though often combined, views of how to write history, which were related to the perceived purpose of such writing. One saw history as a 'mirror' of past events; the emphasis was placed on eyewitness accounts and sources. The other approach saw history as a literary exercise that was meant to persuade the reader; thus it often included long invented speeches. In other words, just like travel literature and the dialogue genre, history could be used to blur the line between fiction and reality, one of More's recurrent themes. More plays with both these historical methods in *Richard the Third* in order to explore more fully the ideas of artificiality and authenticity in politics.

Histories and chronicles were also an essential part of medieval literature. The More family certainly had at least one medieval chronicle; More's father had written down the date of his son's birth on the back of a copy of Geoffrey of Monmouth's (c. 1100–c. 1155) history. The humanist tradition should not be thought of as a break with this medieval tradition, but rather as a variation on its theme. Humanist histories contributed a greater focus on causation to the medieval foundations of the genre, a focus that went beyond the assumption of providence; and this is why humanist historians like More began to interrogate the psychology of figures at the heart of historical events.[6] They also evinced a renewal of interest in historical truth by weighing various authorities and witnesses, a technique that More both typifies and plays with in his *History*.

Both versions of More's *History* are interlaced with his commentary on the reliability of the stories and rumours he repeats, in an attempt, he claims, to stick to the truth. As he writes, 'whosoever divines upon conjectures may as well shoot too far as too short' (*RIII*, 9), so he questions the reliability of what he presents. More constantly qualifies his recording of events through phrases such as 'as men constantly say' (*RIII*, 8), 'some wise men also ween [think]' (ibid.) or 'this have I by credible information learned' (*RIII*, 9). This conscientious presentation of the reports of More's sources is juxtaposed with the façade and pretexts cultivated by his historical actors.

In his other works More also appears dedicated to a historical form of writing focused on the presentation of truth. His epigrams include several that criticize the humanist Germain de Brie (in Latin Germanus Brixius, 1490–1538) for a 1513 poem recounting the events of a battle between the French and English the year before. More probably read de Brie and wrote his critique while he was beginning his own history. He writes that, because de Brie's work 'is not at all true, it is not history' (*LP*, 221). The major issue is de Brie's bias towards the French against the English; More writes '[l]et historians begin to show either prejudice or favoritism, and who will there be to lend any credence at all to histories?' (ibid.).

That being said, More does allow for fabrication when it serves a higher purpose, a greater truth than that of historical fact. He criticizes de Brie not because his history contains some falsehood, but because it contains no truth whatsoever. De Brie had no witnesses to draw from, there were no survivors of the battle he recounts, and thus he felt free to invent details. As More jokes, 'when you [de Brie] represented heroic Hervé fighting with four weapons and a shield all at the same time...your reader ought to have been informed in advance that Hervé had five hands' (*LP*, 223). More does not say that a history cannot be written when there are no eyewitness accounts available, but that de Brie was the wrong historian to do it, as, 'for him to learn the whole truth, the right thing would have been for him to be aboard himself – amidships' (*LP*, 221). In addition to a joking suggestion that de Brie ought to have been among those slaughtered that day, More is also pointing to de Brie's inexperience regarding the matters he was attempting to relate. By the mid-1510s More may have thought he was practised enough in London politics to fill in the gaps of his witnesses, and thus he invents a number of long rhetorical speeches in the style of other humanist histories. These speeches may be inventions but, as they advance More's lessons about politics, he would still consider them to have contained truth, in the same way in which a novel can be said to hold truth, even though it is a work of fiction.

More's historical method follows closely the instructions of Lucian in his 'How to Write History'. Lucian tells his reader that histories should avoid eulogies and panegyrics, instead presenting events as truthfully as possible. This statement is consistent with a desire that histories be exemplary, for 'history has one task and one end – what is useful – and that comes from truth alone'.[7] If it can also 'give pleasure', then that is a welcome addition, but its true purpose is 'the publication of truth'.[8] This being said, it is a different understanding of truth from the strictly empirical one we tend to embrace today. Like More, Lucian does allow room for the addition of speeches, as long as 'his language suit[s] his person and his subject'; and, if a 'myth comes along', the historian should tell it 'but not believe it entirely' so that the reader can decide its veracity.[9] The 'truth' can be established with invented speeches, as long as they seem plausible and impart a lesson that is itself true. Finally, in setting out his history, the Lucianic historian will appeal both to the learned and to the common person, by using words 'such as ordinary folk may understand and the educated commend', an idea that perhaps inspired More's simultaneous composition for English readers and for the European scholarly elite.[10]

More also continues to draw on Lucian in the theatrical language he uses throughout his history to describe figures and events, reflecting, once again, the eternal truth of human equality and the artificiality of social inequality. For More, politics is artificially constructed, and hence demonstrating the 'truth' of political history is actually to demonstrate its artificiality. *Richard the Third*, then, is a truthful representation of falsity and uses falsity only to express truth. Its ultimate lesson is how to negotiate such falsities in the service of truth, in line with Colet's admonition that worldly things must be 'used'.

Sources

In composing *Richard the Third*, More's classical exemplars tended to be Roman, perhaps because these authors – such as Sallust (86–35 BCE) and Tacitus (56–117 CE) – focused on periods of turmoil and on corrupt political figures.[11] If Greeks such as Plato provided the material for the ideal state of a commonwealth, the Romans furnished the content of a corrupt one. The Roman historian Sallust, a contemporary of Julius Caesar, treats the theme of usurpation and corruption and gives sketches of historical figures, much in the same way in which More describes Richard III and Jane Shore. Importantly, Sallust, like More, emphasizes the way in which the pride of the nobility results in faction, leading to the destruction that he details in his history.[12] In Sallust, this is almost always rectified by way of a 'carefully staged speech' given by a virtuous orator, and one wonders if this is how *Richard the Third* would have ended, with Morton taking on that role.[13] For Sallust, this is the purpose of history, to remember those of 'mental virtue' rather than those who possess fleeting physical or material wealth.[14] Like Lucian, Sallust emphasized the importance of the historian's impartial telling of events and, like More, was explicit in his views of his sources.[15] More would have been familiar with Sallust – he was also a favourite of Augustine's – and may have been giving lectures on his work in Oxford in 1513, about the time he was writing *Richard the Third*.[16]

Tacitus also provides an important source for More. Tacitus' *Annals* had only been rediscovered in the decade in which More was writing, so More was one of the first Renaissance writers to use these Latin texts in composing a history. Tacitus too drew on Sallust, but imposed a more chronological form on history and went deeper in investigating the darker side of politics. Tacitus employed a much more dramatic, perhaps even tragic, form than Sallust, and it is one that More appears to consciously adopt. Tacitus and More both attempt to paint portraits of their main characters – Tiberius and Richard – and do it in similar ways, paying close attention to their motives and to what we now would think of as their psychology. Both their subjects, importantly, are gifted actors or dissimulators, who know how to play a role in order to achieve their ambitious ends. For instance, both Tiberius and Richard appear to refuse the political position they are working so hard to achieve, in an attempt to sway their respective audiences. More than other classical historians, Tacitus was concerned with the relationship between virtue and action and with the associated question of appearance and reality, which could then be manipulated or communicated:[17] in other words, precisely the same questions that More explores in his works.

More may also have been familiar with a handful of Renaissance histories that recounted the period of Richard III's rise to power. It is especially tempting to draw a comparison with that of Polydore Vergil (c. 1470–1555), who began his *Anglica historia* as early as 1505; it was completed in draft form in 1512–13 and published in 1534. There is every reason to believe that More was aware of Vergil's work and may have even read it around 1513. However, the similarities between these accounts are limited, which leads us to suspect that much of what More included in his history was drawn from his own witness accounts and unpublished sources.

It is almost certain that More got much of his information about the period from his time living in Cardinal John Morton's household, and perhaps from Morton himself. Serving dinner to the great lords who visited Morton less than a decade after the events he describes, More would have overheard every relevant rumour and detail he needed to furnish his history. It has even been suggested that Morton was the author of *Richard the Third*, a theory that has been soundly rejected, but Morton may have left papers that More used in his composition.

Not all of More's sources need be so noble; his history demonstrates an interest in the experience and sentiments of ordinary people. More records that one story in his *History* came from his own father; the events to which it pertains happened only a stone's throw from his childhood home in Cheapside. It is probable that his accounts of public opinion, which play such a large role in *Richard the Third*, derive from sources like his father and his contemporaries, whom More would have encountered regularly in the Inns of Court and guilds. Generally More does not name these witnesses. This omission may seem surprising, given how truth was valued in historical writing. Naming sources, especially an exalted eyewitness such as Morton or a respected man such as John More, would be a crucial way to gain credibility, but More does not do this. The reason may have been to shield them, but Morton had died by the time More was writing and mention of him as a source could not have damaged his reputation.

Reference to these anonymous witnesses was more likely part of More's attempt to reinforce the undefined nature of the atmosphere of opinion and hearsay that surrounds the action of the plot, forming a constant pressure on the minds of the actors. We have already seen how rhetoricians like Cicero and Quintilian saw 'common' or public opinion as essential to the persuasive work of the orator. This also translated into the related *ars historica*. For Quintilian, history, like rhetoric, was concerned with belief (*opinio*) versus knowledge (*scientia*), and medieval historians placed value on *fama vulgans*, public opinion or rumour, alongside *natura*, nature, in substantiating their history.[18] More goes even further in treating these ideas in *Richard the Third*, exploring, as in *Utopia*, how public opinion can make or break a commonwealth.

Public Opinion and the Stage Play of Politics

We have already seen More's use of the stage play metaphor a number of times. In Lucian's dialogues and in More's poetry life itself was a performance, revealing a perpetual foundation of natural equality that renders ridiculous the pride exhibited by so many. In *Utopia* the character of Morus asserts, like Cicero, that the active citizen ought to play his part in the stage play of politics without upsetting the performance, even though he might see through it. As we have seen, these two uses of the metaphor of the stage play are not actually all that different. More is telling his readers that, although they must acknowledge the inherent falsity of the world, thereby resisting any impulse to pride, they have to use the things of this world for divine ends, which requires them to take up their roles in performances they know to be false. In his *Richard the Third*, More makes his most famous statement of this metaphor, developing its lessons throughout the work with references to public opinion.[19] Whereas on the idealistic island of Utopia public opinion was harnessed for the good of all, in *Richard the Third* More demonstrates how it can be manipulated for tyrannical ends.

In the opening pages More gives a description of the dying Edward IV, placing emphasis on his reputation among the people. More writes that they obeyed Edward 'not in a constrained fear, but in a willing and loving obedience', primarily because he had 'left all gathering of money', which 'is the only thing that withdraws the hearts of Englishmen from the prince' (*RIII*, 5), and had even managed on his deathbed to bring the warring noble factions to peace. This account cannot be relied upon as 'truth', however; the panegyric nature of this description of Edward is at odds with the nature of one that is presented later on, when Edward is presented as being ruled by lecherous appetites. In addition, the suggestion that Edward managed to appease the fighting lords with his death-bed exhortation is shown to be false. This speech is ignored by the nobles, whose factions create the opportunity for Edward's brother Richard to take the throne. More's initial presentation of Edward is thus just one perspective on his reign out of many, the truth of events being difficult to determine.

The same attention to shifting reputations is clear in More's description of the other characters as well. One of the most moving scenes in the history is that of the penance of Jane Shore, a former mistress of Edward IV, in which the gaze of Londoners becomes a penetrating force; and her subsequent reputation is forever altered by the display. Caught up in the removal of the duke of Hastings, 'for the manner sake', Richard accuses Shore of witchcraft, but the 'colour does not work' (*RIII*, 54). Instead Richard lays against her a charge that 'all the world wist [knew] was true', yet 'every man laughed at to hear it then so suddenly so highly taken': that 'she was nought [naughty][20] of her body' (ibid.). Richard attempts to portray himself 'as a goodly continent prince clean & faultless of himself, sent out of heaven into this vicious world for the amend-ment of men's manners' in punishing Shore (ibid.). But this tactic backfires, for Shore is 'so fair & lovely' that 'her great shame won her much praise', especially 'among those that were more amorous of her body than curious of her soul', but also among those who were glad 'to see sin corrected' (*RIII*, 55). They perceived 'that the Protector [Richard] procured [her penance] more of a corrupt intent than any virtuous affection' (ibid.). This episode demonstrates an interesting interplay of reputations. Richard seeks to discredit and dishonour Shore in order to build up his own standing. When he can't make a pestilent rumour stick among the populace, he uses an already existing well-known fact, but one that is generally accepted. The people sees through this attempt; Shore's reputation is improved as a result, and Richard's standing drops.

As we can see from this example, especially in regard to the most politically successful of More's figures, this building and maintain-ing of reputations is self-conscious. Richard III in particular is described as a consummate actor no less than as a manipulator of opinion. More writes that he 'was close and secret, a deep dis-simuler [dissembler][21]...outwardly companable [companionable] where he inwardly hated, not letting [omitting] to kiss whom he thought to kill' (*RIII*, 323). This is even clearer in the Latin version, where More writes: 'He could adopt any role, then play it out to perfection...just as expediency urged him to sustain or abandon it' (*HRT*, 325). He is particularly aware of the opinion of the people and he and his supporters are always keen to maintain a good reputation. For instance, in discussing whether or not they ought to remove the sons of Edward IV from sanctuary, the duke of Buckingham reminds the councillors that, if they were to let the princes escape from their grasp, 'all the world would say' that they had failed as councillors (*RIII*, 29); and they decide, for 'the avoiding of all manner of rumor', first to send in the archbishop of Canterbury to try to convince the queen to release her sons from sanctuary rather than to remove them forcibly (*RIII*, 33).

In this debate over breaking sanctuary, it is Richard himself who most clearly sets out the importance of maintaining a good reputation: 'it redoundeth greatly to the dishonour both of the king's highness and of all us that been about his grace, to have it run in every man's mouth, not in this realm only, but also in other lands (as evil words walk far)' that they have not done their duty as councillors (*RIII*, 26). Such opinion is not only far-reaching, but long-lasting and pernicious: 'such evil opinion once fastened in men's hearts, hard it is to wrest out, and may grow to more grief than any man here can divine' (*HRT*, 361). Public opinion, Richard suggests, has power.

Richard is particularly adept in the art of paradiastole (from the Greek *paradiastolē*) or 'rhetorical redescription', a rhetorical technique whereby a vice is described through its associated virtue.[22] For instance, instead of calling someone miserly, you would call them thrifty. Commonly writers spoke of this technique as 'colouring' or 'cloaking' the vice, and the same strategy was often used in morality plays, in which the character of a vice would dress up as a virtue to try to trick the central characters. More was familiar with the figure of paradiastole, making reference to it in his *Supplication of Souls* in 1529. He accuses heretical writings of advancing 'falsehood under pretext of plainness, cruelty under the cloak of pity, sedition under the colour of counsel, proud arrogance under the name of supplication' (*SS*, 114–15). Importantly, he notes that it is especially the 'simple reader' who 'might by delight in the reading be deadly corrupted' (*SS*, 114).[23]

In *Richard the Third*, the duke of Buckingham, speaking for Richard, redescribes the queen's concerns about removing the princes from sanctuary, calling them 'womanish fear, nay womanish forwardness (*RIII*, 26).[24] The queen recognizes this strategy, noting that she can perceive 'whereunto his painted process draws'

(*RIII*, 38). The most obvious example concerns Richard's execution of Hastings. To combat the 'fame' of Hasting's death, which spread 'swiftly through the city' (*RIII*, 52), Richard attempts to 'set some color upon the matter' (ibid.) by sending out reports of Hastings's (fabricated) plot against Richard, and, 'for the further appeasing of the people's mind' (*RIII*, 53), he issues a proclamation denouncing the sins and vices of Hastings.

So how successful are these techniques? More suggests that generally there is a split among the people regarding how these performances are perceived.[25] The 'vulgar' or common people, it seems, are easily convinced. The 'wise' are not. One of Richard's first attempts to deceive the populace, as a whole, is to convince it that the queen's family members, whom he had executed, were devising a plot to overthrow Edward V. To do so, he piles up barrels of armour in carriages, suggesting that they were going to use it in their rebellion. More writes that 'it made the matter to wise men more unlikely', because they realized that rebellious men would have been wearing their armour, not storing it in barrels, 'yet much part of the common people were therewith very well satisfied' and thought the punishment well deserved (*RIII*, 24). As More remarks elsewhere: 'So unfailingly unreliable is the common herd [*vulgus*], always ready at a moment's notice to take the wrong side' (*DT*, 527).

By the time Richard is planning his coronation, however, the entire population, wise and vulgar, begins to take note. More writes that there was 'some manner of muttering among the people' (*RIII*, 44), even though they didn't know what had caused their suspicions. Even 'the common people...that wave with the wind' and the 'wise men also & some lords' began to 'mark the matter and muse thereon' (*RIII*, 44–5). More attributes this awareness to a 'secret instinct of nature' that makes people aware of 'such great things' (*RIII*, 44) as the sea swelling before a storm, although he acknowledges that it may also have been the murmurings of just a few, which quickly spread to others.[26]

From this point on in the history, the population is often tipped off to the falsities of the claims being made to them, frequently through the poor timing of Richard and his propagandists. People were easily able to see the falsity of Richard's attempt to discredit Hastings after his execution, because the proclamation followed so closely on the heels of Hastings's crime and execution that it must have been prepared in advance. As More reports, 'every child might well perceive, that it was prepared before' and an anonymous schoolmaster remarks: 'Here is a gay goodly cast, foul cast away for haste' (*RIII*, 54). In other words, the good (in the sense of successful) trick was thrown away because of its ill timing. Poor timing also hinders Richard's attempt to get the support of the entire populace to take the English crown. In order to ascend to the throne, Richard has first to disinherit his nephews, the sons and heirs of Edward IV. In order to convince the people that the princes are bastards, Richard employs the services of preachers who can 'colour' the matter, hoping that they might 'frame the city to their appetite' and 'incline the people to the ghostly purpose' (*RIII*, 58–9). But Richard misses his cue to appear triumphantly before the people. Thus, instead of crying out for Richard, the listeners 'stood as they had been turned into stones, for wonder of this shameful sermon', and the preacher, upon discovering how much the people despised him for it, 'withered & consumed away' (*RIII*, 68).

When Richard cannot successfully manipulate public opinion in order to gain the people's consent, he fabricates it. Directly after these failed sermons – 'allowing an interval of only one day', More notes in the Latin version (*HRT*, 455) – the duke of Buckingham approaches the people to try to get its approval for Richard's coronation. Buckingham gives a long speech to the citizens assembled there, assuring them that the matter is not only 'profitable to all the realm', but also advantageous 'to you the citizens of this noble city' (*RIII*, 69). He is, however, met with silence. So he repeats the speech 'so well and ornately, & nonetheless so evidently and plain, with voice gesture and countenance so comely and so convenient, that every man much marvelled that heard him, and thought that they never had in their lives heard so evil a tale so well told' (*RIII*, 75), but he is answered only with muttering. Finally, supporters of Richard, placed at the back of the hall, begin to shout 'King Richard!' and are joined by apprentices and other young men. The rest remain silent, but this fabricated consent is enough for the nobles to claim that they have the support of the city.

The next day Richard and Buckingham stage a final performance. Buckingham asks Richard to receive the crown, and Richard refuses. Buckingham must convince Richard to take the throne, despite the fact that everyone involved knows the lengths Richard had gone in order to get it. It is a classic example of the rhetorical figure of accismus (from the Greek *akkismos*), 'apparent refusal', in which one feigns refusal of something actually desired.[27] It is after this event that More presents his clearest articulation of the metaphor of the stage play of politics. The people leave the scene, 'talking diversely of the matter, every man as his fantasy gave him' (*RIII*, 80). Some people suggest that 'men must sometimes for the sake of manner not acknowledge what they know', just as

> in a stage play all the people know right well, that he who plays the soldan [sultan] is perchance a souter [shoemaker]. Yet if one should can so little good [be so foolish as] to show out of season what acquaintance he hath with him, and call him by his own name while he standeth in his majesty, one of his tormentors might hap to break his head, and worthy, for marring of the play. And so they said that these matters be Kings' games, as it were, stage plays, and for the more part played upon scaffolds. In which poor men be but the lookers-on. And they that wise be, will meddle no further. For they that sometime step up and play with them, when they cannot play their parts, they disorder the play & do themself no good. (*RIII*, 81)

Here as in *Utopia*, it is difficult to know at first where authorial intention lies. The view that More presents has resonance with the Lucianic tradition: life, especially the artificial conventions of politics, is a stage play, and hence it is performed upon 'scaffolds'.[28] The character of Morus in *Utopia* had also said that one ought not to disrupt a play in progress. However, in *Utopia* and elsewhere, More's lesson is that especially educated men ought not to be merely spectators but rather should play their part within the drama, to the best of their ability; what they cannot make good in the commonwealth they should make as 'little bad' as they can.

Enter John Morton. Throughout the *History*, Morton plays his part in the unfolding drama. He first appears in the secret council meeting at which Hastings is arrested. We know this because he participates in a peculiar exchange with Richard before the council meeting begins. Upon arriving, Richard turns to Morton and asks for some strawberries that are growing in his garden. Morton is all too happy to oblige and sends for some. This innocuous but strange moment is actually very telling and contains multiple layers of meaning. First and most obviously, it demonstrates Morton's role in events. He is, without doubt, playing his role in Richard's drama, saying his lines and going along with the play at hand. Only later do we discover that all the while he was actually plotting against Richard, intending to have him replaced him with Henry Tudor, the future Henry VII. The scene also demonstrates Richard's tyrannical desire to have all things for himself – a desire very different from his later assertion that 'the title and profit and ownership' of the realm belongs to the people (*HRT*, 481).[29] Richard hears of the strawberries in Morton's garden and immediately desires them for himself. Most importantly, this episode gives away, in an oblique fashion, the deception latent in the minds of both parties: the reference to strawberries makes a veiled allusion to a passage in Virgil that belies the frequent use of this fruit as a symbol of virtue and goodness:

> You, picking flowers and strawberries that grow
> So near the ground, fly hence, boys, get you gone!
> There's a cold adder lurking in the grass.[30]

Richard is certainly an adder, covered as he is by all that pretence of virtue; but Morton – the real embodiment of goodness – is at the same time a danger to Richard, and his own betrayal is highlighted by the tacit reminder in the Virgilian allusion.

More describes Morton at length in *Richard the Third*, more than he does in *Utopia*. Morton is a man 'of great natural wit, very well learned', but also one of 'great experience' who has 'a deep insight in politic, worldly drifts' (*RIII*, 90–1). Morton had navigated similarly perilous waters before. He had served under Henry VI, the Lancastrian king and an enemy of both Edward IV and Richard III, and had fled with Henry's family when Edward IV came to the throne. After Henry's death he served the Yorkists Edward and then Richard, but meanwhile 'found the mean' to turn Buckingham to his plans in order to gather forces to support the new Lancastrian claimant, Henry VII (*RIII*, 91). He is exactly the mix of learning and experience, ideals and pragmatism that More seems to advocate in *Utopia* and throughout *Richard the Third*. He is also a good illustration of More's portrait of the tyrannicide – the tyrant killer – in his response to Lucian from the *Translation* of 1505. More wrote there that the tyrannicide is 'a resourceful man, one not only strong-handed but (much more) strong-hearted; able in stratagem rather than force; one who knows how to lay plots, hide his traps, make the most of opportunities' (*TL*, 109).[31]

This focus on 'opportunities' is important. In the stage play passage above, More warns against those who reveal 'out of season' their understanding of the artificiality of politics; and in *The Four Last Things* he writes of speaking at the correct moment or as occasion demands.[32] Morton, unlike Richard, knows his opportunities, as he is taking 'always the occasion of [Buckingham's] coming' and using Buckingham's pride in order to 'prick him forward...and so keeping him close within his bonds that he rather seemed to follow than to lead him' (*RIII*, 92–3). This is an 'indirect approach', as

Utopia's Morus would put it, and one that Morton had applied to Richard as well; for '[Morton's] wisdom deceived [Richard's] pride – to [Morton's] own deliverance and [Richard's] destruction' (*RIII*, 90). In a parallel to the use of accismus in the election scene, Morton, who is placed in Buckingham's custody after being arrested by Richard, makes Buckingham convince him to give his advice. Morton uses a fable, reportedly from Aesop, in order to justify his feigned reluctance to comply – while also reinforcing the theme of constructed truth in politics. In his tale, the lion had proclaimed that any horned animals found in his realm would be killed. An animal with a lump of flesh on his head flees upon hearing this decree. When asked why – after all, he does not have a horn – the animal answers: 'But what [if the lion] call it a horn, where am I then?' (*RIII*, 93). This tale communicates to Buckingham Morton's fear that the thought in Morton's head, though not treasonous, might get labelled 'treason' and lead to his punishment. It also supports the general theme of the text, that in politics reality is constructed – and largely by the powerful. Of course, Morton himself has constructed his own reality as well, because the thought in his head is indeed treasonous. Thus Morton, a man with little power but with both a great ability to play his part in the fiction and a willingness to use this ability for the benefit of the commonwealth, emerges as the one most able to effect positive change and to unite the commonwealth.

Unity and Disunity in the Commonwealth

In his *Epigrams* More translates a poem from Greek that captures perfectly the lesson Morton expresses through his fable: 'The impression [*opinion*] one creates has great influence, great weight, in the affairs of men. You have no desire to do any harm; but, if you seem to have, you are done for' (*LP*, 117). But why is reputation so important to the powerful figures in *Richard the Third*? After all, the duke of Buckingham makes clear that Richard doesn't actually need to be elected by the populace; its consent is fabricated. Richard manages to take the crown despite his lack of widespread popular support. So why do all the figures in More's history place great store by popular opinion?

For More, the consent – *consensus* – of the whole people confers sovereignty. We've already found this message in the Latin poems, and it will appear again in his analysis of church governance (Chapter 4 here). The people's consent comes up often in *Richard the Third* as essential to the good governance of England. Richard pays lip service to this idea in his acceptance of the crown, declaring that 'no earthly man can govern [England] against [the people's] wills' (*RIII*, 79), and, in the Latin version, that 'your solid consensus [*consensus*] supports me' (*HRT*, 481). This idea had also been central to Buckingham's speech. Buckingham tells the populace that the nobles were 'resolved in a mighty consensus [*consensus*] to approach the Protector' (*HRT*, 467) and – after the shouts from the crowd – approves of the 'nomination which you have tendered to him with such perfect consensus [*consensus*]' (*HRT*, 473). The juxtaposition of these claims to consensus against the division evident throughout the history creates a striking contrast. By placing such importance on the role of the people and of its consent, More suggests that, although England is a hereditary monarchy, the population at large does have a part to play in its politics. In part this rests on a Ciceronian belief that it is the people's view of a public orator's proposal that determines the actions of the polity. If the people as a whole is moved to support a proposal, that proposal ought to go through. If it is not, the proposal ought to be rejected. In contrast with this Ciceronian view, Richard completely ignores the fact that the people is clearly *not* moved by Buckingham's speech.[33] This combines with a tradition of custom and consent in English political thinking expressed by the fifteenth-century writer John Fortescue, who in turn was borrowing from Augustine the idea of a commonwealth united through love and common interest.[34] We do not get to see fully, in *Richard the Third*, the results of Richard's choice to proceed without popular consent, but we know what they are: Henry Tudor's invasion and accession to the throne. So there is a reason why a self-interested political figure would want to remain in the people's good graces. This may be why all the characters in *Richard the Third* are keen to have the crowds on their side. As Edward IV states: 'Ill-gotten goodwill [*gratia*] is soon lost, whereas that which is earned the right way remains stable and durable' (*HRT*, 333).

But there is a stronger reason why reputation is important for the commonwealth. For More, who draws primarily upon Augustine, it is the love of the people that keeps a commonwealth united. Speaking of Edward IV, More writes that 'love of his people and their entire affection toward him' held the commonwealth together and would have continued to do so, if private interest hadn't got in the way (*RIII*, 5). In the Latin version the word used for this mutual love is *gratia*, which can also be translated as 'popularity'. Thus there is a direct connection between the popularity of a figure and the unity of the commonwealth. *Gratia*, this love for and from the people, or the popularity with it, must be maintained for the good of the commonwealth.

This description of Edward as inspiring love among the people is juxtaposed with a description of Richard, then duke of Gloucester, by whom 'all the bands [are] broken that binden man and man together' (*RIII*, 6). Richard is corrupted, unnatural both in body and in soul. Rather than uniting the nobles, as Edward had aspired to do, Richard plays upon the factions that already exist between them. Edward had exhorted his nobles to peace and unity in order to protect his son's reign and makes clear that it is not just his sons' well-being that is at stake, but that of the whole realm:

> while either party laboureth to be chief, flattery shall have more place than plain and faithful advice, of which must needs ensue the evil bringing up of the Prince, whose mind in tender youth infect, shall readily fall to mischief and riot, & draw down with this noble realm to ruin. (*RIII*, 11)

Notably, in the Latin version, the key word is, once again, *consensus*: 'for without a consensus, it [their advice] cannot turn out well' (*HRT*, 333). Debate among the nobles will lead to 'internal sedition' within the realm (*HRT*, 337). The nobles should be united through love and the acknowledgement that they are all 'Christian men' (*RIII*, 12) held in 'common humanity' (*HRT*, 333).

This unity, Edward says, can be threatened by ambition and 'desire of vainglory and sovereignty' (*RIII*, 12), or by 'pride and the lust for supremacy' (*HRT*, 335). This is, of course, what happens; the nobles in *Richard the Third* become just like those Hythloday describes in *Utopia*, so preoccupied with their own private interests and ambitions that they destroy the commonwealth. When Edward ends his speech, the nobles exchanged 'as good words as they could' and 'joined their hands together, when (as it after appeared by their deeds) their hearts, were far asunder' (*RIII*, 13). This is another performance, and private interest tears apart the bonds of love that should come from a recognition of commonality.

It is this division, More reports, that gives Richard the opportunity he needs in order to rise to power: '[Richard] now thought that their division should be (as it was indeed) a fotherlye [favourable] beginning to the pursuit of his intent, and a sure ground for the foundation of all his building' (*RIII*, 10). What gives Richard his opening is not just division, but the private interest that causes this division. As More writes, Richard 'set the foundation of all his unhappy building' 'upon that ground' of the queen's desire to advance her family's interest (*RIII*, 14). This desire for personal gain is most clearly brought out in the case of Buckingham. Perverting Morus' advice in *Utopia* that whatever one cannot make good in the commonwealth should be turned into as little bad as possible, Buckingham decides that, 'since the common mischief could not be amended, he would turn it as much as he might to his own commodity' (*RIII*, 43).

This disunity spreads to the people as well. More reports that, when the queen entered sanctuary with the princes, the people spoke 'diversely' about it (*RIII*, 22). The Latin version gives more detail:

> the different bands rushed about here and there, exchanging defiances according to the factional zeal or the fear which had brought them together. And as each was inclined by a positive or negative bias, so some speakers attempted to minimize the gravity of the deed while another group sought to exaggerate it. (*HRT*, 355)

The populace thus engages in precisely the sort of rhetorical redescription that Edward had warned would provoke further discord: 'For a hostile witness often makes something innocently done appear sinister or a prejudiced hearer makes a minor offense into a major one' (*HRT*, 333).

In the English version More tells his reader how, especially after the murder of his nephews, Richard himself becomes torn apart. First this happens inwardly, through his own personal turmoil: 'he never had quiet in his mind – he never thought himself sure' (*RIII*, 87). Ultimately Richard is physically torn apart through his defeat in battle, 'slain in the field, hacked and hewed of his enemies hands… torn and tugged like a cur dog' (ibid.). Even Richard cannot escape the destructive effects of self-interest.

The commonwealth, however, begins to heal, largely through Morton's efforts. More reports that, not long after Richard's murder of his nephews, there 'began the conspiracy, or rather good confederation' (which emphasizes the unity of the movement) 'between the Duke of Buckingham and many other gentlemen against [Richard]' (ibid.). This rebellion, as we've already seen, comes about through the duke's pride and self-interest, which Morton is able to turn to the good of the commonwealth. Like Richard, Morton uses the nobles' self-serving pride as an opportunity; but, unlike Richard,

he turns it to the good of the commonwealth, making a bad situation as 'little bad' as he can. He cannot cure people of their pride,
but he can use it to the benefit of all. Morton restores the unity of
England through the marriage of Henry VII (a Lancastrian) to Elizabeth of York, the daughter of Edward IV. This marriage brought
'infinite benefit to the realm, by the conjunction of these two bloods
in one, whose several titles had long enquieted [disquieted] the
land' (*RIII*, 82). As More wrote in his coronation poem to Henry
VIII, the union of York and Lancaster in this marriage removed
all 'internal strife' and generated a son, Henry, who in himself
'represent[s] both sides of the quarrel which usually arises' (*LP*,
109). Through unity, the peace of the commonwealth is restored, at
least for a time.

Riot

Many reasons have been proposed as to why More didn't finish
and publish his *Richard the Third*, ranging from political prudence
to lack of time. Both of these may have been factors. By the end
of the period in which More appears to have written the text,
his own situation had changed dramatically. In 1513, when he probably began the work, he was a London lawyer and a relatively
unknown humanist scholar. By 1518, More was one of Europe's
leading humanists and a rising court presence with a close relationship to the king. Especially this second shift, from city to court,
was a dramatic change for More, who in February 1516 had declared
to Erasmus that, although he had been offered a royal pension,
'I have not as yet accepted it, and I do not think I ever shall' (*SL*,
70). He was reluctant, he writes, to leave his position in the city,
'which I do prefer even to a higher one', and feared that, if he
retained it while taking a pension from the king, the recurrent tensions between court and city would cause Londoners to lose faith
in him (ibid.).

More's apparent change of heart has elicited just as much specu-
lation as his decision not to publish *Richard the Third*; some even
maintain that he was deceiving Erasmus in claiming to be reluctant
to join the court: another instance of accismus, perhaps? We
will never know for certain either why he stopped writing *Richard
the Third* or why he chose to abandon London for the court but,
in considering both, we cannot ignore the dramatic events of May
Day 1517.

The years 1516–17 were difficult ones for London; it was a severe winter and a contagious and virulent disease known as the sweating sickness struck the city in April 1516. The miseries of the city were vented on London's foreign merchants, who were accused of taking trade away from English tradesmen. By the end of April 1517 the growing spats and disputes were coming to a head, and it was rumoured that 'there was a plot to cut to pieces all the strangers in London' on May Day.[35] The night before, More and the other city officials were called to an emergency meeting at the Guildhall, and More was asked to draw on his most powerful connections to help tackle the crisis. He was sent to meet with Wolsey and other members of the council, and a curfew was imposed.

This measure came too late, however, and by 11 p.m. violence had broken out across the city, especially near More's own home in Cheapside. More intercepted the rioters at St Martin's Le Grand, a foreign neighbourhood just north of St Paul's, probably about midnight. It appears from the records that, whatever he said, More momentarily managed to calm the rioters; but it was only a short reprieve. As the rioters quietened, bricks and hot water were thrown down from the windows, stirring them up once again. No report indicates that More was hit, but an official standing near him was; in his anger he cried out 'Down with them!' and the riot was ignited once again.

Edward Hall's later *Chronicle* claims that the rioters numbered about 1,000, though a contemporary ambassador's letter says that it was closer to 2,000.[36] Given that most of the rioters were concentrated in the crowded area around Cheapside, their number would have seemed impressive. The Venetian ambassador reports that they sacked the house of the king's French secretary, who escaped with his life only by climbing up the belfry of the adjoining church.[37] Cannon shots were fired from the Tower of London, and one report suggests that 15,000 troops surrounded the city and 10,000 troops entered, once the gates had been won back from the rioters.[38] Even the more modest account notes that a week later there were still 5,000 troops in the city to maintain order, at a time when London's population was only about 50,000.[39]

With hindsight, the danger was not very great; generally the foreign merchants were well armed, so the rioters could do little damage. No one was reported to have been killed during the riots, although a contemporary report claims that this was only because Wolsey had been 'forewarned' of danger, perhaps by More himself.[40] Wolsey and several other lords rode into the city towards dawn.

There they found that the gates had been locked and several of the prisons emptied, as the rioters 'had overpowered the forces of the Lord Mayor and other city officials', including More.[41] The lords forced their way through and arrested about seventy of the ringleaders. By dawn the riot was over.

More cannot have been unaware of the connections between the events of May 1517 and elements in his account in *Richard the Third*, though it is impossible to know which came first. In *Richard the Third* those who take up the shouts of 'King Richard!' at the Guildhall are the apprentices – those who are 'delighted with any kind of change' (*HRT*, 473); in the same way, reports of the May Day Riot, including More's own in his *Apology* (*ATM*, 156), suggest that the main participants in the riot were the young apprentices of the city. Accounts of the aftermath of the riot also sound a great deal like the pageantry and artificiality of *Richard the Third*, as the stage play of politics was used to good effect and was indeed performed upon scaffolds. Francesco Chieregati (1479–1539), the papal nuncio, reports that sixty of the rioters were hung in 'gibbets all over the town' while others were given the traitor's death by hanging, drawing and quartering.[42] Another 400 were destined to the same fate, but Queen Catherine of Aragon (1485–1536), 'with tears in her eyes and on her bended knees, obtained their pardon'.[43] This, Chieregati says, was an act 'performed with great ceremony'.[44] In other words, even if this appeal to Henry's mercy was real, it still had the air of a political performance about it.

The greatest performance, however, would come shortly after, on 22 May, when Henry publicly announced this pardon. Chieregati writes that Henry had Westminster Hall hung with 'tapestry of cloth of gold' and a 'canopy of brocade'.[45] There he assembled all the nobles as well as a large company of Londoners, 15,000 in all.[46] Hall reports that this assembly included the officials of the city – certainly Thomas More among them – who were there 'in their best livery (according as the Cardinal had them appointed)'.[47] Wolsey then proceeded to make a long speech 'to the people, reproving them for their rebellion' and for the danger they had posed to king and realm, and the king followed with his own speech, though Chieregati does not record its contents.[48] The prisoners were then 'paraded' in, 'with ropes round their necks, as if about to be executed', and they immediately 'threw themselves on their knees, shouting "Mercy!"'.[49] At that point, Wolsey and the nobles joined in, falling to their knees and begging the king to pardon the prisoners (knowing full well that he had already done so). The king, moved by this display, 'after addressing the people again, pardoned the rioters and had them released, so much to the popular satisfaction, that everyone wept for joy'.[50]

These events seem to have had an effect on More. He had written at length about the common humanity that ought to bind all people, particularly within a commonwealth, and most especially in a city such as London. In the early hours of 1 May 1517 he had witnessed first hand how this unity was violently torn apart at the instigation of a few preachers and petulant apprentices, and he had stood powerless against it. And it was the pageantry of politics that had ended the conflict to everyone's satisfaction. In sum, participation in the artificial stage play of politics, at the level of the court, could produce results that involvement in city governance could not.

This realization seems to have had an effect on More's own role at the court. By the autumn of 1517 he was on a second diplomatic mission to the continent, this time to Calais. There is some suggestion that More was already a member of the Privy Council by this point, but more probably the mission was one last task in finalizing this appointment. When he was finally made a Privy Councillor in March 1518, his payments were 'back-dated' to September 1517, when he was in Calais.[51]

While on the continent, More checked on the progress of a new edition of *Utopia*, this time published in Paris, and received a pair of paintings of Erasmus and Gillis as a commemoration of his time in Antwerp and of the work it had produced. Although only two years had passed, More's life had changed substantially since 1515. Now one of the most renowned humanists in Europe, he would soon resign his positions in the city in order to pursue a career at the court of Henry VIII. By the early 1520s he even moved his family out of London to Chelsea, a fashionable village just outside of the city, close to Westminster and ideal for those who were in royal service, like More.[52]

Thus, although perhaps battered by the events of May 1517, by autumn of that year More had every reason to be optimistic about his future. Unbeknownst to him, however, on 1 November 1517 the monk Martin Luther published his *95 Theses* in Wittenberg, Germany. The act itself was relatively unremarkable, but its impact was colossal. Having just written the history of a commonwealth torn apart, More would now turn his attention to the disunity that rent the whole of Christendom.

Conclusion

Given More's forays into translation, poetry and satire, it is perhaps
no surprise that his *History of King Richard the Third* also presents
the reader with a unique synthesis of sources and a reflection on his
recurrent central themes. By bringing together different methods of
writing history, More plays with the concepts of fiction and reality,
just as he had in *Utopia*. And, just as in *Utopia*, public opinion is at
the centre of this discussion of artificiality and truth. *Richard the
Third*, however, goes much further into interrogating the role of
reputation in the formation of public opinion and the ways in which
individual self-interest can damage a commonwealth. It also goes
further in the creation of an archetype of the educated and active
citizen. John Morton fulfils the role sketched out in *Utopia*; he works
within the pageantry of politics while retaining the knowledge of
essential truths and resisting the temptations of pride. He plays
instead upon the pride of others, knowing full well that it cannot
be uprooted and turning it to the benefit of the commonwealth. It
is by Morton that the commonwealth is healed, through the union
of the warring roses.

The discord and division portrayed in *Richard the Third* probably
reflects accurately the context in which More grew up, even if
More fabricates some elements of his history. He makes clear that
the disunity that threatens the commonwealth is based on the ambition and pride of the nobility, whose members refuse to heed
entreaties that they focus on their common humanity and Christianity and place these values over and above their private interests. At
its worst, such disunity spreads to the people as well, threatening
its place as the source of the consensus and consent foundational
to the commonwealth. Richard III disregards or manipulates this
important element of consent and, although we do not see this in
the unfinished text, the idea may well be that his fall has come about
in large measure because he did not truly gain the necessary consent
of a united people.

More's context changed dramatically after 1517; however, this
focus on the need for consensus and union, expressed through what
is held in common, remained central to his thought. He continued
to be dedicated to these central principles and firm in his rejection
of what he saw as proud self-interest, be it in scholastics, in nobles,
or in 'heretics'.

4

The Common Corps of Christendom

Even before the massive schism and upheaval that would become known as the Reformation, More had shown that he believed strongly in the importance of unity. For him, the greatest danger to this ideal was pride and the self-interest it fostered. It is perhaps no surprise, then, that More came to view the Lutheran movement through this lens, attributing to the 'heretics' the sort of proud acrimony that he had condemned in puffed-up scholastics and nobles.

But the challenges of the Reformation context also required More to engage with topics he had not formerly treated. More gave his attention to the issue of authority more fully than he had done before. So far as he was concerned, the major question arising out of these theological controversies and of their attendant political disputes was the location of a single and irrefutable source of authority. This matter required him to reflect more consciously and explicitly on the themes of human nature and political legitimacy. As a result, More's extensive (and in consequence often unread) texts written after 1520 yield some of the clearest and most mature statements of his thought. More's emphasis on 'the common' and his fear of pluralism led him to articulate a theory of church governance that drew on republican and conciliar writings and gave the consensus of the people a prominent role in the generation of authority.

Background

More would not concern himself with the growing religious upheaval on the continent until six years after Luther published his

95 Theses. In fact, from 1517 to 1523 he would write very little at all, because he found himself inordinately busy and had little time for scholarship.[1]

In the autumn of 1517 More was on his second diplomatic mission for Henry VIII, and by March 1518 he was officially in royal service as a councillor. His title was 'Master of Requests' and his function was to receive many of the petitions that came daily to the crown. It was a job for which his background as lawyer and judge prepared him well. Unofficially, More's role entailed much more, and he became the intermediary between Cardinal Wolsey and the king. The corpulent cardinal couldn't always be at the young king's side; but More could, and his letters suggest that he was. More became a close companion to the king, and later biographies suggest that his role extended beyond the one that Wolsey had in mind, as Henry apparently spoke to More about intellectual as well as political matters. It would probably be too much to call them friends – humanist *amicitia* was a relationship between equals – but there probably was at least a bond of mutual respect between them.

By 1521 More controlled much of the access to the king – the council couldn't even send letters to Henry without their going through More – and he had the king's signet seal, which allowed him to authorize royal expenditure. He was able to secure appointments for friends and family and may have had a hand in pushing forward certain policies. He was also accruing significant wealth along with his elevated status. In the same year he was knighted and appointed undertreasurer, a position that secured him the second highest salary in the exchequer.

More's close proximity to the king meant that he would have known when the king came across a copy of Luther's work for the first time (probably in 1518) and began to compose a response to it (which was not published until 1521). Henry's pamphlet was titled *Assertio septem Sacramentorum adversus Martinum Lutherum* (*The Assertion of the Seven Sacraments against Martin Luther*) and earned him the title of *Fidei defensor* ('Defender of the Faith') from the pope. More had a hand in the production of the text, although probably just an editorial one. In a letter to Thomas Cromwell (1485–1540) written later, while he was in the Tower of London, More claimed that his only role in the *Assertio* was to advise the king against attributing supreme power to the pope. It is unclear whether this claim was some kind of politic back-pedalling or a gesture indicative of More's views on the authority of the papacy.

There is little evidence that More was in any way inclined to participate in the debate over Lutheranism until Henry called on him to do so. Henry needed More's reputation and rhetorical skill, because Luther had answered Henry's pamphlet with a vehement rejoinder, *Martinus Lutherus contra Henricum Regem Angliae* (*Martin Luther against Henry King of England*). In it he called the king a 'swine', a 'lying buffoon', said that he was 'strumpet-like' and, worst for Henry, 'effeminate' and spoke of him as vomiting pus and shit. In short, it was not the sort of pamphlet a king of England would be used to receiving, and Henry could not stoop to responding in kind. So he asked More to step in. The result was the *Responsio ad Lutherum* (*Response to Luther*) written in 1523, which we will consider in the subsequent section.

After the *Responsio,* with the single exception of the *Letter to Bugenhagen* (an extensive text written in 1526 but printed posthumously), More did not make another volley into these debates for the following six years. When he did, it was, once again, by official request: his friend Cuthbert Tunstall (1474–1559), bishop of London, asked him to defend the church against 'heretical writings'. This time More was specifically invited to make his contributions in English, in an attempt to counter the influence of vernacular Lutheran texts on a literate English audience. Tunstall wrote to More that he

> will never find a better way of spending any leisure hours you can snatch away from your official duties than in publishing in English for the common man some books that would help him see through the cunning malice of heretics and so keep him alerted and better fortified against these traitorous subverters of the church.[2]

For this task, More was given a unique licence to read the heretical books making their way into England. His first English treatise on the matter, *A Dialogue Concerning Heresies*, was published in June 1529 and spoke directly to Tunstall's request. A second one, *Supplication of Souls*, followed in September; it was written against Simon Fish's *Supplication for the Beggars*, which had circulated earlier in that same year.

There was a second break in the publication of these texts, which occurred between the end of 1529 and early 1532, during which time More served as Lord Chancellor, the highest political post in England under the king and one not usually given to a layman.[3] When he resigned in 1532, promising not to concern himself with affairs in

England, he turned his attention back to the debates on the continent, though he knew full well their connection to events at home. Henry's desire to overrule the pope on the question of the annulment of his marriage to Catherine of Aragon had fundamentally changed the English political climate, especially with regard to the role of the papacy. More had been given the post of Lord Chancellor after Cardinal Wolsey's failure to procure this annulment. Although in some ways his appointment makes sense – More had taken care of many of the affairs of state while Wolsey was preoccupied with the 'King's Great Matter' – in other ways it is odd, because More was even less likely than Wolsey to satisfy the king on this matter. As early as 1527 More had given the king his opinion on the desired annulment, which was almost certainly not in line with the king's wishes. In 1529 Henry may have thought that he could still win More over to his cause, or in any case he was happy to let More run the country while others sorted out the annulment, paving the way for his marriage to Anne Boleyn (c. 1501–36).

The solution, allegedly proposed by Thomas Cromwell, Henry's new minister, was a break with the authority of Rome that would allow Henry, as head of his own church, to decide on the validity of his marriage to Catherine. This proposal, as we shall see, posed a greater problem for More than simply that of Henry's abandonment of his first wife. A day after the convocation at which the ecclesiastic assembly officially handed its spiritual powers to the king, More approached Henry and resigned his post. After working closely together for fourteen years, More and Henry would never see each other again.

Without the affairs of state to occupy his time, More turned his attention fully to the various attacks on the Catholic Church. The first part of his *Confutation of Tyndale's Answer* had been published in March 1532; the second followed in spring 1533. His *Apology of Sir Thomas More* – a misleading title, as its true purpose was to answer Christopher St German's (1460–1540) *The Division between Spirituality and Temporality*[4] – was published in 1533, as was the *Debellation of Salem and Bizance*, written against St German's response to the *Apology*. The last text published in More's lifetime was *The Answer to a Poisoned Book*, written in response to an anonymous work called *The Supper of the Lord*, which in turn had answered More's *Letter to Frith* (published in 1533). These texts, as we can see, were polemical in the truest sense, each one specifically responding to a definite opponent or text (or both) and often prompting a rejoinder. More was participating in a Europe-wide battle of ideas that he had embarked upon, at least initially, on behalf of the king. Unfortunately the situation in England was rapidly changing. What had begun as a defence of the king was now an attack against him. To reinforce, as More was doing, a 'Universal' – that is, the Catholic – Church, with its governing and spiritual centre in Rome, was to deny Henry's supremacy as head of his own church in England, which in turn threatened the validity of his marriage to Queen Anne and the legitimacy of their daughter, Princess Elizabeth.

On 12 April 1534, while walking from St Paul's to his old home in Cheapside, More was handed a summons to appear before a panel and swear an oath in recognition of the Act of Succession, which had passed in March. This act proclaimed Anne Boleyn as queen and her children as Henry's heirs. The preamble stated that Henry was head of the Church in England. More refused to take the oath. Five days later he was imprisoned in the Tower of London, where he would largely remain until his execution in July 1535. He continued to write in the Tower, producing there his *Dialogue of Comfort*, his *Treatise on the Passion*, his *Treatise to Receive the Blessed Body* and his *De tristitia Christi* (*On the Sadness of Christ*) – works that would become essential to the trajectory of English Catholicism in the next century.

Style

There is a tendency to draw a firm dividing line between More's 'humanist' phase, which ended roughly in 1520, and his 'polemic' phase, which began with the *Responsio ad Lutherum* and ended with the final works before his death. In some senses this line of separation is correct; More's context changed dramatically in this time and his attention turned to different matters and debates. In other ways, however, we should be careful not to draw too firm a distinction between the works of these two periods. More did not become a different person in 1522, completely dissociated from his humanist background. Throughout this period religious matters were intimately intertwined with humanist ideas. To More and others like him, they would have appeared as two sides of the same scholarly coin.

More's humanism is especially clear in the form that his polemical writings take. In a number of these texts, especially those that come at the beginning and end of this period, he continues to play with the barrier between fact and fiction, employing the dialogue form and using his intimate knowledge of rhetoric to great effect. In line with More's previous works, these themes and techniques urge the reader to reflect on the construction of reality, especially through language.

In *A Dialogue Concerning Heresies,* More once again becomes a character in his own dialogue, although, unlike in *Utopia,* in this text it is clear that he is its authority, which perhaps indicates More's increasing desire to avoid the ambiguity of his earlier dialogues. More's interlocutor, the Messenger, is a student who has recently been taught at one of the universities rife with heretical ideas. He comes to More to test out these ideas and to learn tactics for refuting them. He is thus truly the messenger of Lutheran doctrine, one who is not to be shot down but instructed in ways of defending oneself against such pernicious principles. This background story renders the work more interesting to read, with engaging characters, but also transforms it into a teaching text.[5] Unlike many of More's other polemics, which address one specific opponent, *A Dialogue Concerning Heresies* engages with a variety of works and ideas, directly fulfilling Tunstall's request for an English response to the heterodox texts that had been published in the previous decade. Thus it is more wide-ranging than some of More's other works from this period, staging debates on a variety of theological questions, including the status of saints and relics, the value of pilgrimages and the oral tradition of the church.

More's other major dialogue from this period is *A Dialogue of Comfort Against Tribulation,* which would be his last. In this text More goes significantly further afield, placing his scene in Hungary, which faces a Turkish invasion. His interlocutors are Anthony and Vincent, an uncle and his nephew, the senior Anthony taking on the role of Socratic authority, though Vincent brings his own curiosity and contributions to the discussion. Of course, by placing the dialogue in such a distant foreign context, More, as in *Utopia,* was actually seeking to reinforce the reflection on England. Elsewhere More often made comparisons between the infidel Turks and the heretic evangelicals, presenting the former as less ungodly than the latter on the grounds that they did not have the same exposure to Christian teaching. For More, Hungary on the eve of a Turkish invasion becomes the perfect parallel to an England facing the threat of heretic ascendancy in 1534.

Even though it is not a dialogue, the *Responsio,* too, is couched in a fictional context. In the first edition More writes as Ferdinandus Baravellus (Ferdinand Baravello), a student at a Spanish university who has been convinced and 'tricked into' writing the *Responsio* against Martin Luther, who is nothing but a 'wrangler' and not deserving of such treatment (*RL*, 7). In the second edition the persona of Baravellus is dropped and Guilielmus Rosseus (William Ross) takes its place. The whole book, although still in Latin, is thus given a more English context. A number of prefatory letters are added, like in *Utopia*, as well as some poems at the end, which support this fiction. Throughout, More himself remains unidentified.

As many of the texts that he was countering were published anonymously, More plays along, giving dramatic names to his opponents. This technique has the effect of recalling the dialogue form, or at the very least adding a layer of fiction.[6] In *A Supplication of Souls*, Simon Fish becomes 'the beggars' proctor', another word for 'advocate', as well as someone sent to collect charity on another's behalf: 'they be also our proctors and beg in our name, and in our name receive your money' (*SS*, 119). In *Answer to a Poisoned Book* More calls his anonymous opponent 'Master Masker', in response to his name for More: 'Master Mock'. Although More would probably have known that Christopher St German was the author of *A Treatise Concerning the Division of Spirituality and Temporality* and of *Salem and Bizance*, he professes not to in the *Apology* and in the *Debellation*. Largely, this apparent ignorance was to avoid the charge of opposing royal policy – by 1532 St German was writing on behalf of the Crown – but it is also consistent with the theatricality of More's other polemics. St German becomes 'the Pacifier', an ironic title, as More was accusing him of stirring up controversy and discord between clerics and laypeople.

The use of dialogue tropes not only has the effect of making the texts more entertaining and thus readable, but also plays with the construction of reality. As far as More was concerned, the evangelicals were trying to present a distorted vision of the world through their writings and translations, to which he draws attention by way of the names he gives them. By calling Fish the 'beggars' proctor', More makes allusion to the persuasive rhetoric that such an advocate may use, imputing to him recourse to paradiastole, remarking that he was 'alway[s] covering his poison under some taste of sugar' (*SS*, 118) as he was 'rolling in his rhetoric from figure to figure' (*SS*, 127). By calling the author of *The Supper of the Lord* 'Master Masker', More calls attention to the ways in which this writer used language to mask his real intentions, just as he masked the real presence of Christ in the Eucharist.[7]

Despite such accusations, More does not shy away from employing his own rhetorical figures throughout his polemics. In the *Confutation* he uses alliteration to make his arguments stick – 'fast fettered in his holy heart' (*CTA*, 575) – and opens the text with a whole page of rhetorical questions – a trope known as pysma (from the Greek *pusma*): 'And what can be [a] worse kind of infidelity, than to make books of heresies, and call them the right faith? And what more abominable infidelity, than to abuse the scripture of God to the colour of their false belief?' (*CTA*, 5). Driving home the seditious nature of heretics, More employs diasyrmus (from the Greek *diasurmos*) – a type of refutation through a ridiculous comparison:

> surely to make men heretics and then bid them be meek…standeth as well with reason, as to make a man drunk, and bid him be sober, make him stark mad & bid him be well advised, make him a stark thief, and bid him see he steal not. (*CTA*, 30)

And he tends to conclude in a climactic way, in line with the figure of accumulatio:

> Finally, aside from his most wicked lies, and his most stupid contradictions, and his thousand follies, which we have exposed from here and there, we also proved that corrupt method of disputing by begging the initial premise which he thought he had so very wittily cast in the teeth of others. (*RL*, 321)

He was especially known for his irony, which is why he is identified as 'Master Mock' in *The Supper of the Lord*. Almost two decades after More's death, Thomas Wilson notes in his *Art of Rhetoric* that More's writing was the greatest English example of 'this kind of delight', irony, or a 'pleasant dissembling', which makes his work difficult to interpret.[8]

Even with these attempts to lighten the prose, there is no question that the polemical works, especially the *Responsio* and the *Confutation*, are long and detailed texts, very different from the pithy wit of *Utopia*. In these works More adopts a traditional form of defence of the church, used by church fathers such as Augustine and Jerome and adopted by the scholastics, which involves long verbatim quotations from his opponents' work, accompanied by a detailed refutation.[9] This method makes for a cumbersome and lengthy text; the *Confutation* runs at around a million words.

The structure of texts like the *Confutation*, however, also invites questions about methods of reading. The *Confutation* was almost certainly not meant to be read from cover to cover but rather consulted as a reference text, the reader – probably an educated English layman – dipping in and out as necessary.[10] More tells his readers that they 'shall not need to read over any chapter but one' (*CTA*, 9–10). Each section begins with a long fragment from Tyndale's text on a particular topic, followed by More's commentary, which rarely runs for more than a few pages; this makes it quick reference reading. The *Responsio* has many marginal notes, which allow the reader to get a sense of almost every paragraph at a glance. It even contains an 'index of those things which are contained in this work', with the relevant page number. In other words, a reader, having encountered the work of Luther or Tyndale, could look up the relevant passage in More's response, getting the other side of the debate. As More writes in the preface to the second edition of the *Responsio*, '[Luther's] work does not require an answer if one considers both sides of the question [*utramque partem*]. But how many persons do you think will be so diligent?' (*RL*, 19). So he provides this other side of the question for his readers, in an attempt to stage an argument against the heretics.

Heresy

Heresy was not new in the 1520s. The Catholic Church had been burning heretics since the fourth century. England passed its own law condemning heretics to the stake in 1401, in an act called De Heretico Comburendo ('On the Burning of Heretics'). Thirteen years later, the state's role in detecting and punishing heresy was expanded; the state became the chief institution, over and above the church, required to take the lead in the persecution of heresy.[11] In particular, the English church was concerned with the rise of Lollardy, a heretic sect led by John Wyclif (c. 1331–84) that had many parallels to the later Protestant movements. These persecutions continued into the reigns of Henry VII – under whom twelve Lollard heretics were burned – and Henry VIII. In May 1511, six years before Luther's *95 Theses*, ten people were burned in Kent for denying that the bread of the Eucharist was the body of Christ, and in 1520–2 another eight were burned in Coventry.[12] Thus, although there was a sharp increase in the persecution of heresy over the sixteenth century, the difference was primarily in scale; concerns about the spread of heresy had been a part of the English worldview for well over a century.[13]

One can mark the escalation of these concerns in England from early 1521. Lutheran writings had been circulating there since at least 1520, and they found support especially in underground Lollard circles. Wolsey, then Lord Chancellor as well as a cardinal, was reluctant to do anything about it, especially as there had been no official condemnation of Luther's works. This all changed in the spring of 1521, when the Vatican excommunicated Luther, ordered his books to be burned and outlawed their publication and circulation.[14] On 12 May 1521 Wolsey, *Assertio septem sacramentorum* in hand, held a grand book burning of Luther's texts in St Paul's churchyard, to announce these new measures publicly.

At first this display and the ban on books seem to have worked. However, by the middle of the decade it was clear that evangelicalism, absorbed as it was into the existing networks of Lollardy, was not easily uprooted. The major issue was not the writings of the German Martin Luther, as Wolsey may have expected, but the scriptural translations of an Englishman, William Tyndale. By the summer of 1525 Tyndale had completed an English translation of the New Testament. This translation not only made the New Testament accessible to the literate Englishman but, as More would point out, it significantly undercut the support for church authority based on scripture, for instance by translating *ekklēsia* (usually understood as 'church') to 'congregation' and *presbuteros* (usually 'priest') to 'senior'. Another burning was held at St Paul's, and this time it was copies of Tyndale's Bible that were thrown in the flames. It did nothing, however, to stop the tide of heretical books, to which other English authors – such as Simon Fish (d. 1531) – made their own contributions.

The prosecution of publishers and preachers began in the late 1520s. One of the first to be arrested was Thomas Bilney, who had been preaching Luther's doctrine around London. Although he recanted and was released in 1529 by Wolsey, he would continue to preach and was eventually burned in Norwich in 1531, shortly before the first of the London executions later that year. More himself led a raid on heretical books among merchants in the Steelyard in January 1526 and searched William Tyndale's old home in 1528. Given that tensions were rising, it is no surprise that Tunstall had written to More, requesting help towards the discreditation of the persuasive heretical texts. Tunstall's tactic did not work, however. The first public burning of an evangelical in England took place in February 1530 in Kent. Another five followed – three in

London – before More's resignation from the chancellorship in 1532, and at least another fifty before the end of Henry's reign.

There were two central and interrelated issues that defined the battle lines of this complex debate.[15] The first was the definition of the church. For Catholics, the church was the visible church that had existed throughout the centuries and had its centre in Rome. The evangelicals, contrastingly, expanded upon the beliefs of the *devotio moderna* (Modern Devotion) movement and upon Erasmus' reformism to insist on an invisible church, one lacking ceremony and hierarchy. This was related to their view of scripture, which they saw as taking priority over the decrees or dictates of the institutional church. For evangelicals, the *written* word of God was the key to God's truth. The primary source for it was scripture.[16] In the eyes of Catholic writers like More, this belief neglected, first, the unwritten word of God, which was written in the hearts of people, and, second, the fact that the scripture had in fact been determined by the church.[17] In short, according to evangelicals, salvation lay in a simple study of scripture, not in the ostentatiously visible church.[18]

In many ways the beliefs of evangelicals and those of humanists such as More do not seem so distinct, a fact of which both parties were well aware.[19] Many evangelicals were humanists in that they had received an education in the classics, were dedicated to the principle of returning *ad fontes* ('to the sources'), recognized people's essential equality and questioned absurd social practices, hierarchies and ceremonies. When Erasmus refused to join their movement, the evangelicals were shocked, and he was nevertheless adopted as a Protestant hero in the decades after his death.

In particular, both More and Luther drew their inspiration largely from the works of Augustine and regarded the community as central to the church.[20] They both recognized a division between the 'spiritual' and the 'secular' sphere – the former eternal and characterized by equality, the latter finite and defined by hierarchical order.[21] They were both horrified by riot and chaos and recognized the need for politics to mitigate violent disorder.[22] More, like Erasmus, at times struggled to defend the distinction between his views and those of evangelicals. He wanted to continue emphasizing the importance of what is inner, eternal and divine, but he also needed to defend a visible, material and often corrupt church.

The dividing line was over the evangelical argument for individual conscience, as opposed to the 'consensus' of the community. As we've seen, for More and generally for humanists, classical or 'pagan' learning was essential to the study of scripture.[23] It went alongside the study of the church fathers, and this was accepted church doctrine. Without such guidance one could interpret the word of God incorrectly, which would lead to heresy and damnation. For evangelicals, nothing was relevant outside the written word of God in scripture, and it was up to the individual to interpret it. According to Luther, all Christians are priests and there needn't be an intermediary between people and God's word.[24] In his view, God communicates directly with the individual via scripture. In More's view, he communicates with the body of the church – the community of Christians – through the Holy Spirit. To break off from this community is to reject God himself. For this reason, the notions of 'custom' and of a 'consensus' of the community once again take centre stage.[25]

For More, heresy was 'a sect and a side way…from the common faith and belief of the whole church' (*DCH*, 37–8). This definition was a common one; it emphasized the dangerous disunity that, More felt, heresy inherently contained. Heresy was a type of treason, 'the treason to God' (*SB*, 68–70), and should be punished with the same severity; it is 'accompted [accounted] as great a crime as is the treason committed against any worldly man' (*ATM*, 136). Recall that, for More, unity in the commonwealth was the key to its preservation, as we saw in *Richard the Third*. Heretical sects endangered that unity, implicitly introducing the threat of sedition. Evangelicals

> break the union of the church, and make sundry sects, and kill their Christian brethren…they break the peace and unity both of the church and the faith, by making of sects and sowing sedition and dissention, to stir up rebellion and insurrection against their neighbours and their governors, and thereby cause the robbery, pillage, spoil, and murder of their good Catholic Christian brethren. (*CTA*, 485)

Although More's remarks may seem extreme to a twenty-first-century reader, the suggestion that those who did not conform to the Catholic Church were violent and dangerous traitors was relatively commonplace and expressed both legal precedence and public sentiment.

According to More, the threat to the state posed by heretics required that heresy be punished severely, and punished by the state (*DCH*, 483). As More writes in his *Confutation of Tyndale's Answer*, 'every good man hath good cause both to be angry and to burn up too, such pestilent seditious persons as not only by jesting, railing and biling[26] all those that are in dignity, provoke to rebellion the people that should obey them' (*CTA*, 911). The danger posed by heresy is so great, More declares in his *Debellation of Salem and Bizance*, that it should be prosecuted quickly, for a 'slow sober order...may not all, & always, be kept, neither in heresy nor treason, nor some other great crimes neither, without great hurt and damage to the common weal' (*SB*, 70). A slow approach would allow heretics to 'poison other good simple souls in the mean season' (*SB*, 71).

The violent punishment of heresy by secular authorities, More contended, was a response to the violence perpetrated by heretics, and one that equalled it: 'yet had they never in deed fallen so sore to force and violence against heretics if the violent cruelty first used by the heretics themselves against good Catholic folk had not driven good princes thereto'. (*DCH*, 406). Princes were 'driven of necessity' by the 'importune malice of heretics raising rebellions' to set 'sorer and sorer punishment thereunto' (*CTA*, 956). In other words, the heretics had started it: 'the Catholics Church did never persecute heretics by any temporal pain or any secular power until the heretics began such violence themself' (*CTA*, 954). More had in mind violent conflicts on the continent, such as the German Peasants' War (1524–5) and the Münster Rebellion (1532–5).

The first evangelical martyrs of the English Reformation were burned while More was Lord Chancellor.[27] Later accounts suggest that More took a personal hand in the torture of such prisoners. These rumours must have existed at the time, because in his *Apology* of 1533 More addresses them head on, writing that lies were spread about that 'in my house while I was chancellor, I used to examine them with torments, causing them to be bounden to a tree in my garden, & there piteously beaten' (*ATM*, 117). This account matches precisely the report later given in John Foxe's *Acts and Monuments* (first published in 1563). He denies ever having done such things, but proudly declares that he has certainly punished heretics, just as he would punish any thief or murderer, who would be likely to cause more pain if he were allowed to go free (*ATM*, 117). He admits of two instances in which he was directly involved in the punishment of a heretic in his own home; neither episode would have been perceived as unduly cruel according to sixteenth-century views of corporal punishment. The first was the punishment of a boy in his household who was repeating heresies to other children. More 'caused a servant of mine to stripe [whip]' the boy, More reports, just as he would punish any child (*ATM*, 118). The second episode involved a man in his community recently released from Bedlam, a hospital for the mentally ill, who would lift women's skirts and throw them over their heads during the mass. More 'caused him as he came wandering by my door, to be taken by the constables and bounden to a tree in the street before the whole town, and there they striped him with rods' (*ATM*, 118). If More's denial is true, this latter tale may be the basis for the suggestion that More whipped heretics like James Bainham against a tree near his home.

Authority

As a 'sect' or 'division', any kind of heresy was by its very nature a threat to the unity of the commonwealth, which More so valued. But Lutheranism was especially pernicious in his view, as it held the idea of *sola scriptura* – authority by scripture alone – to be one of its essential pillars. Lutheranism fundamentally challenged the concept of authority, both in terms of establishing truth and in relation to political order. This had unsettling consequences for the stability of the commonwealth, for evangelicals seemed to be proposing an antinomian universe, in which a Christian man needed no laws but could be ruled by scripture alone: 'But they say therewith that the laws & precepts of their sovereigns do nothing bind the subjected in their consciences' (*CTA*, 30). This view, More contended, would 'make all people lawless...as to let all run at riot without any bond or bridle' (*CTA*, 585). This sort of anarchy terrified him.

Although More, like most humanists, agreed that fewer laws were better – recall that Utopians needed few laws because they were educated properly – he did not support the idea that people could live without any laws. People were *more* free, he thought, under law than without it, because without laws they would be subject to the arbitrary rule of magistrates: 'if you take away the laws and leave everything free to the magistrates' – that is, to their discretion or under their arbitrary rule – 'either they will command nothing and they will forbid nothing, and then magistrates will be useless; or', more worryingly, 'they will rule by the leading of their own nature and imperiously prosecute anything they please, and then the people will be in no way freer, but, by reason of a condition of servitude, worse' (*RL*, 277).[28] In addition, the populace is also likely to stir up sedition and rebellion. The teachings of the evangelicals, More contends, 'bring the people into the secret contempt and spiritual disobedience, & inward hatred of the law, whereof must after follow the outward breach [of the law], and thereupon outward punishment & peril of rebellion, whereby the princes should be driven to sore effusion of their subjects' blood' (*CTA*, 31).

The nature of the evangelical heresy put its adherents on an inevitable slippery slope towards rebellion, as evidenced by the conflicts in Germany.

For the most part More writes in favour of political obedience, although he, like his evangelical opponents, wavers on the subject.[29] Luther opposed resistance until 1530, allowed some possibilities for resistance in the early 1530s, and eventually came to support it in the late 1530s.[30] Tyndale followed Luther's somewhat meandering path on the matter of obedience. According to him, subjects must disobey a ruler's commands if the latter contravene the laws of these subjects' faith; but he also maintained that tyrants exist in order to punish sins, and in consequence subjects ought not to resist them.[31] More, as responder to both Luther and Tyndale, does not take a clear and consistent line either. He objects to the idea that subjects must obey their rulers only as far as the law of God allows, which opens up the possibility that a person would disobey, or even rebel against, a prince who ruled contrary to God's laws. Certainly the 'commodity' of the people is not enough reason to rebel against a ruler. More writes in his *Confutation of Tyndale's Answer*:

> God although he will that the governors and rulers of the world should be good and profitable to the people, yet will he not that the people shall measure the duty of their obedience by the only rule and measure of their own profit and commodity, but that they shall obey their princes and other rulers and governors, because that they be their governors and rulers, and because that God hath so commanded. (*CTA*, 56)

More does, however, defend the view that obedience is limited by God's law. He writes that Jesus commanded obedience to secular authority but did not mean 'that they should obey any commandment that by God were forbidden, nor to set God's law aside for men's traditions' (*CTA*, 353). Secular authority, he seems to suggest, operates in the silence of scripture. Jesus was 'forbidding them to refuse to fulfill the commandment of their rulers, whereof there were no mention made in scripture, where the commanded tended to virtue, good manners, or God's honour' (ibid.). Although More objects to Tyndale's idea that 'a Christian man is bounden to obey tyranny, if it be not against his faith nor the law of God' (Tyndale, as quoted at *CTA*, 32), he does so on the basis of Tyndale's interpretation of the 'law of God', taken together with the view that everyone has the authority to provide his or her own interpretation in the same way.

One begins to distinguish more clearly between these two positions by considering the question of who decides whether or not secular authority is operating within the bounds of God's laws. One of More's greatest concerns about the rise of heresy was its destruction of a final arbiter in settling such questions. He was terrified by the idea of a relative truth. As he writes in his first polemic, *Responsio ad Lutherum*, 'you will find nothing else [in Luther's work] but these two propositions: that nothing is true and certain apart from evident scriptures; [and] that all other traditions are the work of men and are left to the free choice of the individual' (*RL*, 93). As he later goes on to demonstrate, even the 'truth' of scripture is left to individual discretion, because all other sources of authority are rejected; hence Lutherans have no single 'truth' at all. He gives the example of an outsider, a Turk, who wishes to join Luther's church. More suggests that such an individual would not know where to go to learn the faith, because there is no structure by which he would determine who has the authority to teach him. And if he takes the scripture 'in hand himself', he is likely to fall into errors, as the scripture can be difficult to interpret without guidance – a lesson More took from Augustine.[32] As More writes, 'though the scripture be true in itself: yet…it is not so plain but that many difficulties arise thereupon' (*CTA*, 270). The Lutheran attack on church authority, he asserts, leaves no single source of truth, so that 'everything would thus be uncertain…there would be as many varieties in faith as there would be heads among the people' (*RL*, 619).

The problem, as we might now come to expect, is one of pride. For More as for Augustine, pride is the mother of all heresy, because it implies belief in one's ability to know better than the institutions and authorities of the established church. Luther's heresy is especially problematic in that it encourages pride in others, telling them that they too have the power to interpret scripture according to their own judgement, which is different from that of the church. As More says, now 'every obstinate heretic, every prattling fool, every smatterer in scripture, shall be judge over all the general councils, and over all the whole corps of Christendom, to tell them all that himself understandeth the scripture better than they all' (*CTA*, 343). In short, heresy, for More, leads to anarchy, in which both intellectual and political authority are dismantled:

> with the papacy abolished together with the decrees of councils and monastic vows and all universities and absolutely all doctors, the people would neither be ruled by laws nor obey rulers nor listen to

doctors, but would be so free and unbridled, with the freedom of the gospel of course, that no one would be forced, nor commanded, nor counselled nor taught anything. (*RL*, 159)

At the heart of this problem is the heretics' transfer of authority from the people, as a corporate whole, to single individuals. Luther removes 'the authority of judging doctrines…from the people and delivers it to anyone whatever' (*RL*, 613). More often repeats this distinction between 'the people' – *populus* – and 'anyone whatever' – *quislibet* – and gives examples such as that of the conspirator Catiline, who would have been saved from death on condition that, 'if, when condemned by the senators, he appealed to the people, when condemned by the people he appealed to anyone whatever'; for then 'the just condemnation of everyone would not have had force so long as anyone at all like him would be found among the people' (*RL*, 613). More accuses Luther of using the same tactic:

> since he senses that the people also, indeed above all, condemn his doctrines…he finally reduces the matter to the point where he leaves the power of judging to anyone whatever. For he hopes that nothing can be said so absurd that he will not find at least one person somewhere agreeing. (*RL*, 615)

By transferring authority from the corporate whole to individuals, one necessarily runs up against the issue of a plurality of views and the loss of a single authoritative truth.

Human Nature

This rule of individual judgment stands in stark contrast with what More takes to be the proper establishment of truth. For Luther, the only natural law or lesson that was 'written in the hearts' of people is that there is a God; everything else is given in scripture.[33] More maintains that, in addition to the *written* word of God, in which the evangelicals place their faith, there is the *unwritten* word of God, which God inscribed in the hearts of all people. This is the 'true gospel of Christ' that was written 'before the books of the evangelists' (*RL*, 101). In fact it is by this unwritten word that the written word can be determined, interpreted and understood. More refers to this unwritten word as a 'secret inward instinct' by which we can determine the 'traditions taught by God' as well as the scripture (*CTA*, 381). As he puts it, God decided that it was more 'convenient for the law of life, rather to be written in the lively minds of men, than in the dead skin of beasts' – a reference to calfskin, the primary material used in the production of vellum (parchment), on which the codex (the modern book with pages) was written (*DCH*, 143–4). We may recall that Utopians had never heard of Christianity and yet were 'most holy'; and they were drawn to Christ's teaching when they encountered it. In the context of Christian Europe, this inward knowledge of God's word allows the church to maintain unity, for

> God by his word unwritten did teach his church to know his words written, and made the church agree therein by his spirit, which maketh men of one mind and one custom in the church, and which spirit keepeth both the words written and the words unwritten in perpetual knowledge and observance in his church. (*CTA*, 381)

This view requires a certain account of human nature. More is not as systematic or elaborate in setting out his understanding of human nature as other writers and philosophers; it was not his goal or intention to expound on this subject. It is clear, however, that he does entertain certain beliefs about how people think and feel, upon which he bases his understanding of a 'truth' held by all.

For More, God works in the individual both inwardly and outwardly. The 'inward motion' is the 'seed of God' – human reason – which is given to every person from birth, even before baptism. Just as the senses bring the human being to an understanding of reason, so, too, the senses combined with reason bring the human being to an understanding of those things that are 'above reason': faith in the divine. Because of this, one can say that a child, even before baptism, has 'habitual belief', just as he or she has 'habitual reason' before education. Neither is reflective or trained, but both are there.[34] Outwardly, God provides 'occasions' through which a person can come closer to him: 'God inwardly worketh with the will of man walking with God, in well using and applying convenient occasions toward that outwardly given by God' (*CTA*, 889). Reason leads to the 'assent and obedience of faith'. For More, faith and reason go hand in hand, reason being a 'handmaid' to faith. Just as reason separates humans from 'brute beasts', so faith separates Christians from the heathen (*DCH*, 118).

This relationship between inward and outward causes provided the foundation for More's account of the freedom of the will, which he contrasted to the limited Lutheran view on the subject. Luther objected to Erasmus' suggestion that a person could turn towards or away from God voluntarily, at will. People were entirely dependent on God's will for their salvation, and their own choices had no part to play.[35] The will can only be exercised on things that are below humanity, not above it. In More's view, a person has freedom of choice in his or her actions but is capable of good acts only through God's grace. This grace, however, is given freely to all, 'like the light of the sun', and thus the choice of good or bad behaviour is left solely to the individual: 'Evil men neglect [grace] when it is offered, good men embrace it, and both do what they do according to their own free will' (*LB*, 51). In this way More, echoing the teaching of the church, is able to reconcile salvation through God's grace with the justification of punishment: 'Thus a man who is saved is saved by grace, and yet free will is not inoperative' (*LB*, 51). More retains free will against a deterministic view of the universe, safeguarding both legitimate punishment and God's omnipotence.

The Common Corps of Christendom

It is God's unwritten word in every person that allows for the creation of the single Universal Church, built on consensus:

> the Holy Spirit of God interiorly inspires His church with truth...He alone makes those who dwell in a house to be one of mind, that he teaches so that they understand the same thing, judge the same, teach the same, prove the same, confess the same, follow the same. (*RL*, 623)

This consensus is what marks the true church out from all others. God wrote the same word in all individuals' hearts, so where there is dissension there must be a misinterpretation of that word, but 'where the Spirit of God is, there is agreement' (*RL*, 632). This consensus stretches not only across the globe but across time as well, making the pride of the heretics even more striking; they oppose the consensus of every Christian over the past 1,500 years.

For More, this consensus is largely tacit, represented by the uninterrupted continuance of custom in the church. As he writes in the *Responsio*, 'the custom of the Christian peoples in matters of the sacraments and of faith has the force of a more powerful law than has any custom of any people whatever in civil matters', because it is inspired by the Holy Spirit (*RL*, 415). This is the 'common consent of the church' (*DCH*, 169) and, once this is decided, 'it cannot be but that thing must needs be true' (*DCH*, 224).

This consensus is unanimous when it comes to 'things to be believed' within the church, because, as the church is defined by consensus, anyone who believes differently is automatically outside the church (*RL*, 623; *CTA* 922). This kind of consensus is distinct from the explicit majoritarian consent required when it comes to 'things to be done', both in the church and in politics. More writes that, 'if no one has the power to establish a single syllable for the Christian man without his consent,' as Luther seems to propose,

> then neither the king nor the whole people can establish any law which is valid against anyone who opposed it at the time it was proposed....according to this reasoning, should everyone unani-mously agree, yet the law can have force only until a new citizen is born or someone is enrolled as a citizen. (*RL*, 279)

Within the commonwealth universal consent is not required, but within the church all believers tacitly participate in a long-accepted universal consensus that establishes doctrine.

Interestingly, one can observe a shift in More's arguments about unanimity and consensus from his earliest polemics to his later ones. In the *Responsio* he contends that the Catholic Church is clearly the true church on the grounds that 'it is by far the greatest part of the Christian world' (*RL*, 609). In other words, it has the majority opinion in the Christian world, and hence it must be correct. As time goes on and the evangelical movement grows, More begins to move away from this argument, holding instead that the 'Catholic Church is [Christ's] perpetual apostle, how many nations so ever fall therefrom, and how little and small so ever it be left' (*CTA*, 252). By the 1530s More wants to emphasize that it is not the size of the church but the consensus within it that marks it out as the true church.

The church is defined by the consensus within it. It is

> the common known catholic people, clergy, lay folk, and all, which what so ever their living be...do stand together and agree in the confession of one true catholic faith, with all old holy doctors and saints, and good Christian people beside that are already passed this fifteen hundred year before (*CTA*, 480–1)

– and again 'the common known multitude of Christian men' (by this he also means women 'good and bad together': see *DCH*, 205).

More claims that the church cannot mistake the articles of faith necessary for salvation, because Jesus promised that he would leave behind a guide, the Holy Spirit, to serve mankind after his ascension. There must, then, be an institution that is designed to receive this guidance, and this institution can be none other than the church.

Mankind's guide is certainly not mere scripture, More asserts, because determining the truth of scripture requires an outside authority. It is the church that, 'by secret instinct of God' (*DCH* 181), chose the four gospels from all the possible alternatives and gave the correct interpretation of scripture. The church is thus the surer authority, because it needs no external support. This authority, as we've seen, is established through the long and extensive consensus over the years across Christendom. More does run into a slight problem here, as at least a part of his defence of the church as an authority is in fact scriptural. In making this argument he continually returns to those biblical passages in which Jesus promises to remain with his church 'unto the end of the world' (*DCH*, 147) and never to let it err: John 16: 13 and Matthew 28: 20. Although More has recourse also to other arguments – namely about the historical unity and constancy of the church – he does use the church's interpretation of these two scriptural passages to support the claim that the church has the authority to interpret scripture.[36]

More's insistence that there has to be a final authority on spiritual questions makes him able to overlook this circularity in his argument; and he determines that there is no better contender for such a final authority than the church. The church 'may be used as a sure judge, for to discern between the right faith and the discerning of the true doctrine & the false' (*CTA*, 399). The truth that the church gives needs no further verification; there is no higher authority to check it against: 'believe you the church, not because it is truth that the church telleth you, but ye believe the truth of the thing because the church telleth it' (*DCH*, 251).[37]

We may contrast the tale of the Turk who wishes to join Luther's church with that of a man whom More calls 'E', who encounters Christianity for the first time. Whereas the Turk was uncertain as to where to go for guidance and was eventually forced to rely on his own uninformed judgement, E would 'travel through so many Christian nations and would perceive everywhere the same faith, the same teachings regarding what is necessary for salvation' (*RL*, 191). He would also be able to consult 'the writings of ancient holy men' and perceive 'that all the holy doctors from the time of Christ's passion even to the present time have consistently agreed on these same points' (*RL*, 191). Because of this evidence, 'E would have no doubt that, if there is any true church of Christ on earth, it is this congregation' (*RL*, 191). Unlike the Turk, E can count on the manifest consensus of the Catholic Church to guide him to truth.

This foundation of precedent, consensus and tradition tends to make More take a conservative line on legal reform. This is especially clear in his debate with St German, who proposes changes in heresy law. More writes that St German seeks to change 'laws already well made', which he 'would have made worse' (*SB*, 15). In short, if a law isn't broken, we shouldn't try to fix it:

> if a man would come forth & labour us to break every old law long used in this realm, which he could not prove but that it were good enough, but yet would needs have it changed, because that if it were not to make, himself could, he saith, make it better. (*SB*, 138)

The problem for More is not reform in general, but that these laws are well established by parliament and by the general council and that St German, like the heretics, is proud in his assumption that he knows better than the great authorities:

> his request is no better, but in effect even this, that against every wise man's reason well approved hitherto, every man should in this matter now, either trust unto his, or else that the leastwise every man to his own, and instead of a better old law, make a new much worse. (*SB*, 119)

More's articulation of the neophobia typical of his age comes with a more distinctive argument about the dangers of pride and the importance of what can be held in common.

This being said, More contends that there can still be room within the church for debate and disagreement, which can be the foundation for change. Although on all matters 'necessary for salvation' the church holds singular authority on the basis of consensus, there can still be discussion about less important meanings of scripture, which can be debated by a 'sober theologian truly worthy of God' (*RL*, 127). In addition, More asserts that God does not always show his truth all at once, but 'leisurely, suffering his flock to commune and dispute thereupon', and allows them 'with good mind & scripture and natural wisdom, with invocation of his spiritual help, to search and seek for the truth' (*CTA*, 248). People are permitted to vary 'in their opinions' until God decides to 'reward their virtuous diligence' by leading them 'secretly into the consent and concord and belief of the truth' (ibid.).

This gives some scope for reform and change, for God may only give partial indications of his truth at any given time, through progressive revelation: 'in diverse times there may be more things farther and farther revealed, and other than were disclosed at the first' (*CTA*, 923). Anything that the church has decreed on the basis of God's inspiration may be changed the same way: 'as [the church] made it by the spirit of god, so it may break it by the same spirit', which is the same as to say that, 'as God made it, so himself may break it, if it so shall please him' (*CTA*, 322). Such drastic changes, however, only apply to 'things to be done & not in truths to be believed' (*CTA*, 923). Circumstances may change, and thus there might be different ways of doing things on the basis of those circumstances, but 'in matter of belief and faith, which be truths revealed & declared by God unto man', there can 'never any thing be by God revealed after, that can be contrary to any thing revealed by himself before' (ibid.). Once something has been established as an article of faith, it is not to be disputed.

In More's later writings, particularly the Tower works, he provides further detail on the 'profession' of faith requisite for becoming part of the body of the church. The key is communion, through which a Christian becomes incorporated into the church by sharing in the body of Christ.[38] Communion requires true belief, not just the action of receiving the Eucharist; recipients have to recognize the true nature of the act. In so doing, they receive 'the participation of the mystical body of Christ, that is to wit the church and congregation of saints' (*APB*, 76). The Eucharist becomes both a means of entering this corporate body and a symbol of it: the 'church and congregation is gathered together as many members into one body Christ' in the same way in which 'the bread ... is one loaf made of many grains of wheat, and the wine ... is one cup of wine made of many grapes' (ibid.). It is for this reason, More writes, that the Eucharist is also called 'communion', because it not only signifies the union of saints, but also 'effectually make[s] it' (*TP*, 154). Christ, through his death,

> in giving his own very body into the very body of every Christian man, he doth in a certain manner incorporate all Christian folk and his own body together in one corporation mystical ... And so are we, as I say, by the receiving each of us that loaf that is himself mystically, all incorporate together & all are made of one loaf. (*TP* 175)

Representation and the General Council

In order for the 'secret instinct' given to each individual to be translated into church doctrine, the governance of the church must be organized in such a way as to allow people to express this inner voice of God. In other words, because God's truth is known through common consensus, the people must hold power in the church. More proposes two ways in which truth can be expressed in the church. The first is through a 'perfect persuasion and belief so received through Christendom' (*DCH*, 164), the sort of tacit consent that we have already examined. This is usually generated over time, through custom, and is a consensus communicated through writing: 'out of the books of those who have lived before us we find out that knowledge [of their faith], and thus we discover...the public faith of the whole church through many ages' (*RL*, 251). Second, truth can be discovered 'by common determination at a general council' (*DCH*, 164). Where there is no consensus expressed through writers – primarily the church fathers – it is up to the general council to decide on the question.

More names the general council as the ultimate governing authority in the church, and he remains attached to this largely conciliar position throughout his polemical writing. When he does speak of the pope's supremacy, he claims to be reluctant to do so and relies on others' arguments rather than making his own. Often he simply avoids the question altogether, as in the *Confutation*, where he notes: 'This catholic known church is that mystical body [of Christ]...Of which body whether the successor of Saint Peter [the pope] be his vicar general and head under him, as all Christian nations have now long taken him, is no part of this question' (*CTA*, 398–9). He writes that he purposely avoids the question so that he may establish the church as the body of Christ without entering into the difficult issue of whether 'the pope must needs be head and chief governor' (*CTA*, 577). He takes this line not only in the late 1520s and early 1530s, when political prudence demanded silence on the topic of the pope, but as early as the *Responsio*, when the pope's supremacy was still vehemently defended in England: 'I had not intended, reader, to say anything at all in this passage on the power of the pope, nor was I so much drawn to this...as forcibly dragged here against my will' (*RL*, 139).[39] He acknowledges the problems with the papal office, calling Luther a necessary 'scourge of God, to the great good of that See [of Rome]', who will be thrown into the fire once it has whipped it back into shape (*RL*, 143).

There is some difficulty in determining whether this apparent ambiguity over the issue of the pope reflects More's genuine desire to refrain from the fractious debate or is evidence of his conciliarism. Certainly other opponents of Luther, such as John Fisher and Henry VIII himself, had no problem berating Luther for his disrespect for the pope. More, instead, explicitly sets up the general council as the clear governing authority of the church, in a way that seems to go beyond what political prudence may demand.[40] For More, the council is representative of the entire body of the church; the 'synods and councils...do represent the whole church...likewise as parliament representeth the whole realm' (*CTA*, 146). Thus, although one might say (to borrow More's example) that England passed a law condemning heretics, what is really meant is that *parliament* passed this law. The same manner of speaking, More asserts, can be used with the councils of the church. To take a second analogy, More suggests that the same idea of representation is clear in the case of ambassadors, to whom 'princes give...full authority in such things as they send them for to do, as much as they might them self, if they were there present in their own persons' (*CTA*, 940). In this same way, the general council has the full authority of the body of Christian people.

In thinking of the church and council this way, More was drawing from a rich tradition of medieval corporatism. For many medieval writers, the church was a *corpus mysticum*, a 'mystical body', in which individuals were transformed into a single unit. This was often paralleled by the *corpus reipublicae mysticum*, the 'mystical body of the commonweal', in which individuals were transformed into a 'people'. Primarily More was drawing on the medieval conciliarists, who held that the infallible and supreme authority of God did not reside in the pope but rather in the church's general council, as it represented the body of the church, the *corpus mysticum*.[41]

Medieval conciliar thought also furnished More with a specific concept of 'representation', according to which a small body can be thought to stand in for the whole, just as the parliament does for the realm of England, as More himself says. This is representation as authorization, and it requires precisely the sort of corporatization implied by the *corpus mysticum*.[42] This position can be contrasted with the view that the unity of the church is achieved through its representation in a single individual, the pope.[43] Thinkers in this tradition held that it was only through representation that the church was united into a single whole. For More and his predecessors, for instance Marsilius of Padua and Bartolus of Sassoferrato, the church's formation as a single united corporate body was prior to its representation and was in fact a requisite for it.[44]

More shows by means of a thought experiment how this representation as authorization in the general council could have taken place. In the *Confutation* he asks his reader to imagine that, sometime during the reign of Pope Gregory the Great (c. 540–604, reigned 590–604), the whole Christian body was called together for a meeting, perhaps on Salisbury Plain. This assembly, he says, could only be gathered with great difficulty; people had to leave their work behind, take their entire family with them and travel great distances. In consequence, while they were there, they decided

> to take an order and make a law among them there, that for any need that should at any time after happen, there should never more all the whole people be called again together. And that such an assembly so gathered together, should represent the whole people, and should have the same authority full and whole, in all laws after to be made, and all doubts of scripture or questions of the catholic faith to be declared [as if all were present]. (*CTA*, 937)

The purpose of this 'imagination' is to show that, if such an assembly had been (or ever were) gathered, its members would have made such a decision, investing their authority into a representative general council; and thus, More asserts, one can proceed as if it had happened. This may at first seem odd, but reflects the same logic as saying that you can legitimately borrow an item from an absent friend, because you know that she would have happily given it to you had she been there. As More writes: 'For be the thing never so false and impossible too, yet may it be put and admitted, to consider thereby what would follow or not follow thereupon, if it were both possible and true' (*CTA*, 938). In this way More creates a hypothetical moment of authorization to legitimize the general council as truly representative of the whole common corps of Christendom.

Trial

More gives his clearest and most resounding statement of these views on the church and its governance in the refutation of the charges of treason laid against him in the last years of his life. These charges began early in 1534, when he was accused of writing against the *Articles* written by the King's Council in support of Henry's marriage to Anne Boleyn. His printer and nephew William Rastell

(1508–65) was interrogated by Cromwell but was able to show that More's most recent work was published before the *Articles* and hence could not have directly opposed it. More wrote personally to Cromwell to defend himself, promising him that he would never write anything against Henry; and indeed, although More continued to write, he published nothing else in his lifetime.

That was not his last letter to Cromwell, however. Over the coming months More was repeatedly forced to defend himself. A few weeks after the Rastell incident, More's name was included on a Bill of Attainder – a parliamentary act convicting the named of treason – on account of involvement with the Maid of Kent, a nun who had spoken against Henry and his new marriage. The case was weak and More's name was eventually struck from the bill, but it worried More enough to make him write repeatedly to Cromwell, and even to Henry, proclaiming his innocence. In a long letter to Cromwell, More gives an abridged history of his involvement with the 'King's Great Matter', declaring that Henry had assured More that he should never do anything against his own conscience, 'and that I should first look unto God and after God unto him' (*SL*, 209). For this reason, More told Cromwell, he was able to continue in his service to the king without involving himself in the matter of the annulment. Now that Anne was anointed queen, More says that he would happily uphold the legitimacy of the marriage and of Anne and Henry's heirs.

More also turns to the question of the papacy, telling Cromwell that he 'nothing meddle[d] in the matter' (*SL*, 212). He writes that he initially 'was myself sometime not of the mind that the primacy of that see [of Rome]' came about through the institution of God, until 'I read in that matter those things that the King's Highness had written' in the *Assertio* (ibid.). He claims that he urged Henry to leave this bit out of his book, in case a conflict would later arise between Henry and the pope, but Henry refused. Subsequently, he tells Cromwell, he has seen the primacy of the pope supported by so many and 'by such general councils so confirmed' that he feels he has to believe that it has been instituted by God or, at the very least, that it is essential to the well-being of the church: 'that primacy is at the leastwise instituted by the corps of Christendom and for a great urgent cause in avoiding of schisms, and corroborate by continual succession more than the space of a thousand year' (*SL*, 212–13). In other words, because the common corps of Christendom, through the general council as well as by tacit consent, had decreed the continued necessity of the pope's primacy, to deny it would be to take the position of a prideful heretic, like those More had written against. It is not relevant, he writes, whether it was God or the church that instituted this primacy; either is strong enough to authorize it.

More continues to put more stock in the council and in consent than in the pope's primacy, as he writes to Cromwell, 'never thought I the Pope above the general council' nor 'advanced greatly the Pope's authority' (*SL*, 214). Whereas he is unsure about the institution of the pope's primacy, he says with surety that, 'as for the general councils assembled lawfully…the authority thereof ought to be taken for undoubtable' (*SL*, 213). The councils are what provides authority and stability to the church, for without them, 'were there in nothing no certainty, but through Christendom upon every man's affectionate reason, all thing might be brought from day to day continual ruffle [disorder] and confusion' (ibid.). In fact he encourages Henry (through Cromwell) not to allow any denigration of the council; after all, 'in the next general council it may well happen that this Pope may be deposed and another substituted in his room [place]' (*SL*, 213–14).

All of this is consciously in line both with More's published beliefs and with the Henrician regime. More is attempting in this letter to defend himself from accusations of supporting the pope over Henry, and so there is an obvious danger in taking it at face value. Yet More is not being disingenuous; he had indeed never written that the pope was above the general council – not even in the early 1520s, when he was not just safe to write such things but also actively encouraged to do so. Nevertheless, More's biting wit remains as sharp as ever in his remarking that he had in fact discouraged the king from advocating the pope's supremacy. And there remains a dangerous edge to the letter: More argues that, 'sith [since] all Christendom is one corps, I cannot perceive how any member thereof may without the common assent of the body depart from the common head' (*SL*, 213). Although More is speaking about the futility of a discussion of the primacy of the pope, and not about Henry's regime, he was surely aware of how dangerous a sentiment like that was, as it implied that Henry could not legitimately break with the Universal Church. A few weeks later, parliament passed the Act of Succession and its associated oath, and by the middle of April More was told that he must swear to it. He agreed to the body – the legitimacy of succession via Queen Anne – but refused to swear to the preamble, which stated that Henry was head of the church in England.

Following his arrest, More wrote to his daughter in a lengthy letter that, although he acknowledged his duty to obey the king, this 'was one of the cases in which I was bounden that I should not obey my prince', as 'in my conscience the truth seemed on the other side' (*SL*, 221). Here he appears to be repeating the argument from the 'silence of scripture', which he had set out in the *Confutation*; for he notes that, in cases where 'the [church] doctors stand in great doubt', 'the King's commandment' resolves all uncertainty (ibid.). But in this case there is no such doubt, and hence the church is the higher authority, both in terms of knowledge and in terms of obligation. More tells the commissioners that, rather than being in the minority by refusing the oath, he is in fact in the majority, standing alongside the rest of the body of the church. 'If there were no mo[re] but myself on my side and the whole Parliament upon the other,' he says, 'I would be sore afraid to lean to mine own mind only against so many' (ibid.). But this is not the case, for on his side is 'as great a council' as that of the parliament, 'and greater too', because it represents the whole church (*SL*, 222). And so he should not change his conscience 'to the council of one realm, against the general council of Christendom' (ibid.).

On his reasons for objecting to the oath, however, More refused to speak. The commissioners, he reports, denied him guarantees of safety if he spoke his mind, and so he refused to give his reasons. The time to 'break into some new matter' was past, as he had written in his *Four Last Things* (*FLT*, 137), and hence, by his own reckoning, silence was the only remaining option. He writes in the prayer book that accompanied him to the Tower of London that a 'meek man…during tribulation…should neither speak proudly nor resort to wicked words'.[45] There was another reason to remain silent, and that was the 1534 Treason Act, which declared it high treason to 'maliciously publish and pronounce, by express writing or words, that the King our sovereign lord should be heretic, schismatic, tyrant, infidel or usurper'.[46]

Cromwell pressed More on this silence, objecting that, when More was Lord Chancellor, he had compelled heretics to answer whether or not they believed the pope to be the head of the church; so why shouldn't Cromwell force a response from More on the question of Henry's supremacy? More responded by once again questioning the authority of a single part of Christendom against the whole of it, united. When he was Lord Chancellor, the status of the pope was 'recognized for an undoubted thing' throughout 'the corps of Christendom', whereas Henry's status of head of the church was 'agreed in this realm' but 'the contrary taken for truth in other realms' (*SL*, 251). More, as he himself claims, had been the enforcer of a universal truth. Cromwell is not. Just as Henry's treason law, which condemns to death all those who deny his supremacy, is contradicted by a law from the common corps of Christendom, which is the higher power, so 'a man is not by a law of one realm so bound in his conscience, where there is a law of the whole corps of Christendom to the contrary' (*SL*, 252).

On 1 July 1535 More was tried and, once condemned, at last broke his silence.[47] Although four counts were laid against him at his trial, his silence and the legal maxim *qui tacet consentire videtur*, 'he who keeps silence seems to consent', protected him against the first three.[48] The fourth, however, stuck. This was the charge that, on 12 June, More had maliciously denied the king's supremacy in conversation with Richard Rich (1496/7–1567), the Solicitor General. Rich reported that the two of them, lawyers both, had participated in the 'putting of cases' – a theoretical discussion of legal cases common among lawyers.[49] According to the indictment, Rich had asked whether it would be treason to deny that he, Rich, were king, if parliament had decreed it. More agreed that it would be and that he, More, would be bound by it, because it was something he could 'give his consent to'.[50] But More put to Rich a 'higher case', asking him whether parliament could decree that God was not God. Rich denied this possibility, responding with a 'middle case': If parliament could decree that Rich be king, why does More deny that it can make Henry the head of the church? More responded, as he had to Cromwell earlier, that the difference was in the matter of jurisdiction. A citizen 'cannot give his consent' to Henry's supremacy in parliament because 'many foreign places do not affirm' this supremacy. In other words, as he had indicated to Cromwell, the problem was that England was only a small part of Christendom: the power of deciding over the headship of the church lay with the general council as a representative of the whole body of Christendom.

Rich made a record of this conversation with More and reported it to Cromwell, seemingly unaware that it could be of any use in the proceedings against More.[51] Cromwell, however, realized its worth, and it was on this evidence that More was declared guilty of treason and condemned to death. In the account of the trial given by More's son-in-law William Roper (1498–1578), Rich went beyond the report he had given Cromwell, declaring that More ended their conversation by stating outright that, just as parliament could not decide that God was not God, 'no more could the Parliament make

the King Supreme Head of the Church'.[52] Unfortunately we cannot
be sure what More might actually have said, or what was presented
at his trial.

According to Roper, once the verdict was given, More insisted
on his right to speak and gave a scathing criticism of the validity of
the Act, seeing as it was 'directly repugnant to the laws of god and
his holy church, the supreme government of which, or of any part
whereof, may no temporal prince presume by any law to take upon
him'.[53] This supreme governance, More declared, rightfully belonged
'to the See of Rome', which had directly inherited it from St Peter.[54]
This particular argument about the inheritance of St Peter (the pope)
is missing from the shorter, contemporary Paris Newsletter account
of the trial, in which More does not mention the pope at all, and we
might wonder if it was an addition made by Roper, who was writing
under the Catholic Mary I.[55] According to Roper, More then

> declared that this Realm, being but one member and small part of
> the church, might not make a particular law disagreeable with the
> general law of Christ's universal Catholic Church, No more than the
> city of London, being but one poor member in respect of the whole
> realm, might make a law against an act of parliament to bind the
> whole Realm.[56]

He quoted Magna Carta and Henry's coronation oath, and when he
was once again accused of standing against so many who supported the Act, More replied as he had before, that he stood with
'well learned Bishops and virtuous men' throughout Christendom,
as well as with all holy men and saints who had died.[57]

More was executed on 6 July 1535. According to contemporary
accounts, his final words were that 'he died [the king's] faithful
servant, and God's first', which reflected both the assurance that
Henry had allegedly given More on his entering Henry's service
and More's own views.[58] What was universal and common – Christendom – held a higher priority over any particular, even the realm
of England itself.

Conclusion

Much of More's thought on the place of the general council is in
line with that of his contemporaries; however, More's acknowledgement of the council's ability to depose the pope gives him a conciliarist edge. Although conciliarism was at its height in the fifteenth

century, there were certainly still conciliarist writers in the sixteenth, and More would have been aware of conciliarist literature,
most certainly through the work of Jean Gerson (1363–1429) and
perhaps also Pierre D'Ailly (1351–1420), as well as through his contemporaries Jacques Almain (d. 1515) and John Mair (or Major)
(1467–1550).[59] There had been a general council called in 1512,
which brought up once again, for these sixteenth-century conciliarists, the question of the relative power of council and pope, despite
its apparent resolution at the Council of Florence in the first half of
the fifteenth century. Almain in particular, like More, drew parallels
between the relationship of king and parliament and that of pope
and council when he advanced his claims about the relative power
of the latter over the former.

Interestingly, for Almain and Mair, the secular situation was
clear: the people – through their representative parliament – could
depose the king, and therefore the council could do the same with
the pope.[60] More never goes so far, though his own comparisons
between council and parliament might suggest a similar view, especially when we recall his earlier comments about the need for
consent in authorizing rule. Although in his later works More had
to be careful to defend secular authorities and hierarchies, there
remains in them a latent republicanism, and it is possible that he
saw the king as an analogue to the pope: legitimate through the
consent of the people and through centuries of tradition, but ultimately under the authority of the people's representative institution
– and we might recall here the power that More affords the parliament in his *History of King Richard the Third*.

More's faith in the church, conceived of as the body of the people
and represented in the Council, bestows governing authority on
the church by reason of its unerring expertise, expressed through
consensus – a lesson shared with the conciliarists and with More's
fellow humanists. For Erasmus, consensus can be a way of determining theological questions; and, like More and other contemporary Catholics, Erasmus saw this consensus as existing through
the centuries.[61] According to both More and Erasmus, the church is
held together through consensus; where this does not exist, there
is no church.[62] However, whereas Erasmus seems to uphold the
common idea that consent institutes rulers, he does not go as far
as More in claiming that the withdrawal of consent should also
remove sovereignty.[63] Although pope and council, just like king and
parliament, make up one sovereign whole, More seems to suggest
that the former derives its power from the approval of the latter as

well as from custom, both of which represent the opinion of the community.

One of the reasons why More wrote so vehemently against the evangelicals is that their views stood in complete opposition to those that he had already been cultivating. Luther's religion was designed to be personal and private, detached from the community that More valued. Furthermore, Luther directly contradicted More's argument from common sense by asserting that 'what is even more ridiculous' about Catholics' arguments that councils are the word of God is that they base such arguments on the justification that 'this is what kings and princes and people generally believe'.[64]

More has to shift perspectives on many of his previous arguments in order to mount a response to evangelicals. Before the 1520s, he had argued against those who took hierarchy and political order too seriously; after reading Luther's works, he had to argue against those who, he felt, did not take them seriously enough. He also developed a more authoritative voice in this period, no longer masking his beliefs behind translation, poetry and dialogue. Finally, this context requires More to delineate more clearly the limits of his egalitarianism. His version of equality does not tear down social hierarchies – this would disrupt the play – nor does it give some the right to oppose the authority of others. This latter approach, for More, was in fact fundamentally *un*equal, as it allowed people to consider themselves more knowledgeable than those who had come before them.

All that being said, More's focus on the common and the public at the expense of the individual and the private remains at the foundation of his thought. He maintains that too much emphasis on the latter is associated with pride and poses a danger to corporate entities. These popular bodies are what guides us to truth, and hence to fragment them through individual self-interest is to court anarchy, disorder, death, and hell itself. It was around these central themes that More produced volumes of text, and it was for these principles that he died, on 6 July 1535.

5

Influence

It did not take long for More's life and death to become the stuff of legend. However, between Catholic attempts to establish More as a martyr and Protestant propaganda that painted him as a foolish and zealous Protestant-hunter, More the thinker was all but lost. As ideological battles became increasingly divided along Protestant–republican and Catholic–absolutist lines, More's blend of Catholicism and humanism made him a somewhat awkward figure. Catholic writers downplayed his humanism, which was increasingly seen as a source of Protestantism, and Protestant republicans vilified him, even as they appropriated elements of his thought and writing.[1] As a result, the legacy of More's thought is difficult to trace and, given these distortions, any explicit influence tends to have very little to do with the intentions he had in writing.

Reputation

The Marxist writer Karl Kautsky (1854–1938) wrote in 1888: 'To most of the biographies of More a certain fragrance of incense clings.'[2] Indeed, the members of More's large and loyal family were the primary engine of his reputation in the period immediately following his execution, and their goal was to portray him as a saint and holy martyr.[3] Fleeing into exile on the continent under the increasingly Protestant Edwardian regime, the Mores returned under the Catholic Mary I (1516–58, reigned 1553–8), and the cult of Thomas More was established. With Mary's support, More's son-in-law William Roper published a collection of More's works in

English, a critical text for the dissemination of his thought. This text was circulated widely and ended up in the libraries of the majority of educated English households.[4] Extant copies reveal ownership by William Wake (1657–1737), an eighteenth-century archbishop of Canterbury, as well as by several prominent descendants of More himself, who used the opening pages of the book to detail their proud ancestry. Under Mary's reign Roper also produced the first biography of Thomas More, upon which every subsequent one has drawn.

Roper's is a sympathetic, even panegyric account of More. He opens by declaring his father-in-law a 'man of singular virtue and of a clear unspotted conscience...more pure and white than the whitest snow'.[5] Like More himself in his *History of Richard the Third*, Roper inserts into his account long speeches that he cannot have heard, in support of a larger general truth: the demonstration of More's virtue. Much of the practical day-to-day details – where More was living, the positions he held – can be corroborated through other sources, but the more elaborate elements that speak to More's importance and virtue are often fabricated.[6]

Roper was writing to vindicate not just More, but the Catholic Marian regime.[7] Many of More's humanist writings (such as *Utopia*) are omitted or downplayed in favour of portraying More's Catholic virtue. This was largely in order to distance More from Erasmus, who by the middle of the sixteenth century was seen by many as a Protestant hero.[8]

Roper's notes were used to furnish the detail of Nicholas Harpsfield's (1519–75) biography of More, which was also written during Mary's reign and for the same purpose. This biography was followed by a series of even more explicit hagiographies. Thomas Stapleton's (1535–98) *Life of More* was written in 1588, as the third and final part of a collection entitled *Tres Thomae* (*The Three Thomases*) that aimed to detail the lives of three saintly Thomases: Thomas the Apostle, disciple of Christ; Thomas Becket; and Thomas More. Another biography followed in 1599; it was titled the *Life of Sir Thomas More* and written by an author known only as 'Ro. Ba.', possibly Thomas More's great-grandson Robert Bassett (1574–1641). Ro. Ba. used much of the material previously set out by Roper and Harpsfield. His contribution was to add a series of anecdotes designed to show More's wit, most of which are dubious in terms of historical accuracy. The same may be said of the *Life* published in 1630 and written by another great-grandson of Thomas More, Cresacre More (1572–1649). On the whole, these accounts present a picture of More as a saintly scholar, though the emphasis is on his holiness, not on his humanism.

These hagiographical accounts were countered by two Protestant presentations of More that gained popularity in the second half of the sixteenth century. The first was the figure of More the fool, the 'Master Mock' of earlier Protestant propaganda.[9] Edward Hall's (1497–1547) *Chronicle* of 1548 concludes, 'I cannot tell whether I should call him a foolish wiseman or a wise foolishman' because his 'great wit' was 'so mingled with taunting and mocking'.[10] Even on the scaffold, Hall reports, More made jokes, asking the executioner to mind his beard when he cut off his head: 'Thus with a mock he ended his life.'[11] This image prevailed in a number of chronicles popular in the sixteenth century, including Raphael Holinshed's (1529–80) famous history.

Second and relatedly, there was the portrayal of More as the zealous Catholic persecutor of Protestants, most powerfully presented in John Foxe's (1516/17–87) *Acts and Monuments* – or *The Book of Martyrs*, as it is commonly known. Whereas the More family's image of Thomas More was fostered under Mary I and on the continent, Foxe's view of More arose out of the anti-Catholicism of Elizabethan England. First published in 1563, Foxe's book was an instant success; it was expanded and reprinted throughout the Elizabethan period, and even ordered to be placed alongside the Bible in English parishes. With the help of detailed and often graphic woodcuts, Foxe narrates the deaths of Protestant martyrs, placing them in the context of a long history of persecution of true believers. Foxe retains from Hall the mocking presentation of More, adding a measure of religious zealotry to his portrait. More comes across as a man of great learning and skill, but sadly mistaken in matters of religion and obstinate to the point of idiocy. There is a sense that Foxe is disappointed, even betrayed by More's choice to become one the leaders of the English persecution of Protestants and cruelly to seek the death of the godly men whom Foxe presents. Foxe famously repeats the story of More torturing men in his own home – the rumour that More had addressed in his *Apology*. Foxe includes two accounts of such torture in his edition of 1563, and only one is repeated in the subsequent editions. It seems likely that Foxe realized that the two had been conflated and removed one. Despite the circulation of the More family biographies, unquestionably Foxe's account would have been better known in the sixteenth and seventeenth centuries, especially in England, changing the way in which More's texts were read and interpreted.

Literature

Many Protestants made a link between More's religious beliefs and his writing and accused him of using too much rhetorical ornamentation, just as Catholics used incense and gold to adorn their mass. This judgement included *Utopia*; for some, 'utopia' became a byword for purgatory, since it was just as fictional.[12] Nevertheless, More did have some admirers who were more interested in his work than in his religious allegiances. In the period following his death, especially *Utopia* and his *Epigrams* were referenced repeatedly, both by Protestant and by Catholic writers. More's poems, in the words of the courtier and author Sir John Harington (1560–1612), flew 'all over Europe for their wit & conceit'.[13] Selections were used in schools and universities as models of Latin verse. For instance, they formed part of the curriculum for second-year students at Eton, some of whom later went on to translate and publish More's poems.[14]

More was also noted in the early modern period as a protector of the English language and innovator in this field, for instance by Thomas Hoby (1530–66), the 1561 translator of Baldassare Castiglione's (1478–1529) *Book of the Courtier*. The Oxford English Dictionary lists More's works as containing over 400 first occurrences. More's commission to address the evangelicals in the vernacular meant that he had to generate English words for debates that had previously taken place largely in Latin, which is why he is listed as the earliest source for terms like 'pacifier', 'political' and 'pretext', not to mention, of course, 'utopia'. As More himself had written in his first polemical English text, *The Dialogue Concerning Heresies*: 'For as for that our tongue is called barbarous, is but a fantasy' (*DCH*, 337).

The sixteenth century also saw the re-emergence of a fascination with rhetoric, and early modern rhetoricians admired More as an exemplar of classical rhetorical tropes. Richard Sherry, for instance, gives *Utopia* as his example of the figure called 'topothesia' (from the Greek *topothesia*, 'topography') –'the feigning of place, when place is described as peradventure [perhaps] such none is'[15] – and Thomas Wilson (1524–81) in his *Art of Rhetoric* praises More as the paradigm of rhetorical irony. Roger Ascham (1515–68), tutor to Elizabeth I, noted the *decorum* of *Richard the Third*, which, as a result of this feature, 'content[ed] all men'.[16]

Ascham was correct about the popularity of *Richard the Third*, as this text was absorbed into the growing number of chronicles and histories written in the sixteenth and seventeenth centuries. Both Edward Hall and Raphael Holinshed used More's *History* as a source for their own accounts of Richard's reign, which were then taken up in subsequent histories. Although its content was at first used without acknowledgement, More's authorship was later recognized and praised. For instance, in his *History of Great Britain* of 1602, John Clapham considers historians who had 'devised set Speeches, and Oration, to interlace with their true Histories', as More had done, noting: 'Among all which of this kind, that excellent Story of Richard the third, written by sir Thomas Moore…may worthily challenge the first place.'[17]

One of the greatest admirers of More, and especially of his *Richard the Third*, was William Shakespeare (1564–1616). There is no doubt that More's history was a significant influence on Shakespeare's own *Richard III*, which was probably written around 1592–3.[18] Shakespeare retained many of the details present in More's version, such as the exchange between Richard and Morton over strawberries.[19] Shakespeare also assimilates many of the lessons of More's text and even expands them, especially Richard's abnormality and deceptive ability, and the resultant division of the kingdom. Beyond *Richard III*, there are indications that Shakespeare had a great admiration for More, both as a man and as a writer. In *Henry VIII*, which is probably the result of a collaboration between Shakespeare and the playwright John Fletcher (1579–1625), More barely appears, but is described as 'a learned man'. The speaker, Wolsey, hopes that he may

> continue
> Long in his highness' favour, and do justice
> For truth's sake and his conscience; that his bones,
> When he has run his course and sleeps in blessings,
> May have a tomb of orphans' tears wept on 'em'.[20]

Given that More appears in the play only briefly, Shakespeare is counting on his audience's knowledge of him and his fate to give this foreshadowing resonance. More's relative absence from a play about Henry's divorce from Catherine is conspicuous, and Wolsey's speech is a rather out-of-place moment of tribute.[21]

The fact that More lacks a real part in the action of *Henry VIII* speaks to how controversial a figure he was in the late Elizabethan and early Jacobean periods. Shakespeare probably learned this lesson during his involvement in writing *Sir Thomas More* around 1592.[22] The play underwent severe censorship from the Master of the Revels, Edmund Tilney (1536–1610). Tilney advised that the playwrights ought to 'leave out the insurrection' – the 1517 May Day Riots – entirely, which eliminated a large portion of the text and some of the best writing.[23] Tilney also demanded that they remove the section in which More refuses to take the oath, obviously a crucial part of the plot, even though the playwrights had done their best to downplay the political significance of this act by giving no indication of why More was refusing to swear.[24]

The manuscript of this play shows the involvement of five different playwrights, including Anthony Munday (1560[?]–1633), who wrote the original text, Thomas Heywood (c. 1570–1641), who also used More's *Richard the Third* in his *Edward IV* of 1599, and Shakespeare. Shakespeare's contributions are few but crucial, one being More's speech to the 1517 rioters. Although entirely invented, the speech has at least the virtue of adhering to the historical method to which More himself was dedicated and it remains true to his character, or at least to what Shakespeare might have known about him. In the play More asks the rioters to imagine what would happen if they were to win and drive the immigrants away. By taking the law into their own hands, they would show 'how order should be quelled',[25] ensuring that other ruffians, 'with selfsame hand, self reasons, and self right', would also attempt to impose their will through force. This message speaks to More's concern about the anarchy that results from empowering a plurality of views.[26] Instead of making such an 'innovation', a concept More himself abhorred, the people ought to obey the king, to whom 'God hath his office lent'.[27] The rioters' 'mountainish inhumanity' stands in contrast to the commonality that Londoners ought to acknowledge having with the European 'strangers' in their midst.[28]

The play also captures other elements of More's thought, probably gleaned through the playwrights' familiarity with *Richard the Third* and *Utopia*. For instance, London is presented as a city of active and involved citizens, a 'civic body' united by love.[29] As More states upon returning to the London councillors after his courtly promotion, they are

brethren all – for once I was your brother,
And so am still in heart. It is not state
That can our love from London separate.[30]

Sir Thomas More was written and performed in London, and both reflects on and demonstrates More's special connection with the city.

Through the medium of the theatre, the playwrights were also able to explore More's ideas about the artificial nature of reality, which he often expressed through theatrical metaphors. For instance, the character of More asks his fool to dress like him when Erasmus first arrives, in order to test whether the philosopher can see past such costumes to the truth of things:

> I'll see if great Erasmus can distinguish
> Merit and outward ceremony'.[31]

This recalls both More's and Erasmus' dedication to seeing through things to the truth of the matter.[32] The scene also invites reflection on the low status of the actor, recalling More's many metaphors of costumes and stage plays as *memento mori*: the person who would have played More had no more right to wear such trappings than the servant.[33] More's fool states that he should 'grow proud' from wearing his master's shift.[34] This idea is reflected through the plot of the play; just when More's fortune is at its height, he must face death. This reminder is accompanied by another reference to clothing, namely an analogy around the point that clothes can cover the morbid realities of one's physicality only for so long.[35]

Just as in More's writing, this idea of the stage play is also extended into a discussion of the active life. As the character of More himself says, there is not much difference between a 'state pleader' and a 'stage player'.[36] After his promotion and directly before the scene in which he resigns, More participates in a play at his home in Chelsea, because one of the actors is late. Accepting the role of 'Good Counsel', More comments: 'We'll not have our play marred for lack of a little good counsel.'[37] This line is echoed shortly after, when the player finally arrives and More notes: 'Thus fools oft-times do help to mar the play.'[38] When it is suggested that More made an excellent player, the actor playing 'Wit' retorts that they ought not to 'meddle with any such matters'. Such language and metaphor recalls More' own treatment of the same issues in *Utopia* and *Richard the Third*.

Sir Thomas More is an important document, illustrating as it does the complexities of More's reputation and legacy in the period: More is presented as both foolish wise man and wise foolish man, and the play demonstrates diverse ways of imagining More in the latter half of the sixteenth century.[39] Although there may have been some demand for a play about More, even the most subtle allusions to the main aspects of his life and thought were not just contentious, but dangerous. References to him were censored and hidden in an attempt to avoid such implications. The play also demonstrates, however, how well known his legacy and reputation were, at least within London. Munday, the lead playwright, was a fierce anti-Catholic who had spied on Jesuits on behalf of the crown, giving evidence and witnessing their torture and executions.[40] Yet even he was drawn to the story and thought of Thomas More.

Early Modern Political Thought

As in the theatrical world, when it comes to the development of early modern political thought More is everywhere and nowhere. References to him and his work abound, and yet they seem to have no or little connection to More's own thought. Unsurprisingly, the most referenced text is, unquestionably, *Utopia*. An immediate success, by the mid-seventeenth century *Utopia* had been republished numerous times and into six different European vernaculars (German, Italian, French, Dutch, Spanish and English).[41] Largely because *Utopia* is so ubiquitous, it is difficult to establish clear and incontrovertible evidence of its influence.[42] In particular, the issue of property is brought to the fore by those writers who reference More or the concept of 'utopia', and their use of More's ideas is often more representative of the issues relevant to their contexts than of More's own concerns. As we've seen, while for More property was a useful way of thinking through the issue of how private interests divided common concerns, he himself was not interested in abolishing it. Due to his controversial associations, More's place in the history of political thought is largely one of misinterpretation, appropriation and obfuscation; but it is also one of significant influence and importance.

The first major political thinker to engage at great length with the work of More was the French jurist and political philosopher Jean Bodin (1530–96). More is referenced repeatedly in Bodin's mostly widely read work, *Six Livres de la République* (*Six Books of the Commonwealth*), published in 1576. Although Bodin notes, in what was rapidly becoming an early modern literary commonplace, that it is not his 'intent or purpose to figure out the only imaginary form and Idea of a Commonweal...as have *Plato*, and Sir *Thomas More*',[43] he does use elements of *Utopia* as foundation for his own ideas for political reform. For instance, when proposing that magistrates should have limited terms, Bodin notes that he is supported by not only 'the authority of the greatest Law makers, Philosophers, and Lawyers' along with that of all the 'ancient Commonweals', but 'also the authority of Sir *Thomas More*, chancellor of England, who in the Commonweal by him devised, maketh all the magistrates and officers therein annual…to avoid the inconveniences which I have before spoke of'.[44] Bodin was also impressed by the injunction in *Utopia* that 'nothing should be disputed or reasoned upon' by legislators 'the same day it was propounded' but should 'be still reserved unto the next assembly', so that 'he which had rashly and unadvisedly delivered his opinion, should not afterward enforce himself to maintain the same' – an idea that he associates with More alone.[45] Elsewhere, although he doesn't explicitly associate it with More, Bodin adopts a corporation theory of society, as More had done.[46]

Bodin, however, also opposes elements of the utopian commonwealth. In particular, he associates More with the idea of a mixed constitution, according to which a commonwealth is most likely to thrive if it combines democratic, aristocratic and monarchical elements. Bodin aligns More with Machiavelli in this belief, which Bodin himself considers to be 'neither grounded upon truth nor reason'.[47] Of course, More never explicitly backs this idea. The system in Utopia can be considered a mixed one, though More doesn't discuss it in these terms. Also, Bodin sees More as an advocate for the abolition of private property in securing the maintenance of the commonwealth, against those who staunchly defended property as essential to it. Bodin himself takes a middle position by suggesting that at least some measure of equality should be instituted and that this could be achieved by reforming inheritance laws, which may result in a more equal distribution of wealth.[48] Such a compromise perhaps comes closer to More's own vision, although it lacks the concerted attempt to break down private interest that defined More's thought.

Other political thinkers followed Bodin's lead, using *Utopia* as a foil against which to set their own ideas.[49] Alberico Gentili (1552–1608), one of the 'fathers' of international law, condemns what we may think of as the pragmatic military practices of Utopians, namely their willingness to engage in deceit in order to win a battle. As he writes, 'I greatly wonder at Thomas More, that great intellect of England, for approving such shameful deeds on the ground that thus the destruction and death of the innocent are avoided'.[50] He does, however, agree with the Utopians on one point: there should be religious toleration of all but atheism. 'Thomas More, a man of good judgement, tells us that every religion should be tolerated; except one which is contrary to nature.'[51] Once again, this is not a view that More would have endorsed. Although Utopians were right to institute religious toleration because they had not yet found the true faith, this was not the case in Europe. There any religion or sect that had the potential to undermine the unity of the Christian body and of the commonwealths it contained was to be uprooted, violently if necessary.

Although on the continent More might have been interpreted as an advocate for religious toleration, it was not likely that this mistake would be made in the British Isles. By the turn of the seventeenth century, More's reputation as a political thinker, always caught up in the intricacies of the relationship between church and state, had become part of the growing tension between absolutist and republican theories, which reached their height during the British Civil Wars in the middle of that century.

It is perhaps no surprise that More emerges as a prominent figure in the debates over the 1609 Oath of Allegiance, which required all citizens to swear loyalty to James I (1566–1625) and renounce all allegiance to the pope. James himself, in his *Apology for the Oath of the Allegiance* (as in More's title, 'apology' means here defence), attempts to discredit More by presenting him as a champion of those Catholics who may be inclined to refuse the oath. James suggests that More's death was only 'partly' related to an ideological stand against Henry's sovereignty. The prior cause of More's imprisonment and death was his denial of the king's marriage, which, James pointed out, was 'a very fleshly cause of Martyrdom, as I do conceive'.[52] This perspective on More's death was taken up by one of More's descendants, the priest and poet John Donne (1572–1631), whose *Pseudo-Martyr* of 1610 is (at least superficially) approving of the oath and of James's power to enforce it. Yet Donne still writes of More's integrity, quoting from both *Utopia* and More's translation of Lucian; and he notes, in his posthumously published *Biathanatos* (a work in defence of suicide), that More was a 'man of the most tender and delicate conscience, that the world saw since Saint Augustine'.[53] Elsewhere Donne associates *Utopia* with the republicanism that he had turned his back upon, once he was conquered by absolutism.[54]

As James and Donne demonstrate, More had great potential in the seventeenth century as a republican figure. He had been a friend of Erasmus, who was much admired by republicans; had written a widely read republican work (Bodin refers to *Utopia* as More's

'*Republic*'); and had stood against the tyrannical power of a king. And yet More makes few appearances in this guise. The reason is almost certainly religious.[55] Despite the reality of complex allegiances, it was generally perceived that Catholics were the upholders of divine right and monarchical absolutism, whereas Protestant sentiments were consistent with republicanism. More did not fit in. This tension between a republican and a religious perception of More is clear in the work of one of the period's greatest republican writers, John Milton (1608–74). In 1642 Milton praises More's use of the utopian form 'as a mighty continent', to teach 'this world better and exacter things'; but in his *Areopagitica* of 1644, which was a defence of free printing, Milton condemns *Utopia* as too restrictive.[56] More emerges not as a republican champion, as James had feared, but as a barely mentioned figure whose works, although acknowledged to be decent in form, leave much to be desired when it comes to content.

Even radical groups such as the Levellers and, later on, the Diggers made little mention of him, despite the fact that their works and thought favoured equality and the abolition of private property, and thus perhaps they owed most during this period to a reading of *Utopia*. These groups emerged in the tumult of the British Civil Wars (1642–51), in which the parliamentarian forces overthrew and executed King Charles I, establishing a republic under Oliver Cromwell (1599–1658). During the 1647 Putney Debates regarding the new constitution of the republic, Levellers such as Thomas Rainsborough (1610–48) argued that 'it is impossible to have liberty but all property must be taken away'; for, even if the monarchy were abolished, the average citizen would remain a 'perpetual slave' to the rich.[57] One of the Diggers' leaders, Gerrard Winstanley, wrote a utopian text entitled *Law of Freedom*, which was heavily indebted to *Utopia*; yet no mention was made of More or his work by either of these figures.

Of course, since More had been convicted of treason on account of refusing an oath to the king, the royalists – defenders of the king – couldn't claim him either, despite having read and been influenced by his work. Although not strictly speaking a royalist, Thomas Hobbes (1588–1679) was certainly not a parliamentarian or a republican and remains one of the most influential political theorists of the period. He mentions More only twice. Both are passing mentions of *Utopia*: attempts to distance himself from what he calls More's *jeux d'esprit*.[58] Both *Utopia* and More's *English Works* appear to have been in Hobbes's library, however, and there are signs that they exerted a greater influence than these two direct comments suggest.[59] Hobbes's concerns during the tumultuous 1640s and 1650s are very close to More's own. He, like More, was especially preoccupied with establishing a singular source of both epistemological and political authority. Whereas for More such authority was important in the face of the Reformation, for Hobbes it was essential in order to combat the growing instability of the Civil War period. For More, this authority was to be found in the body of the Christian people and expressed through the representation of the general council. For Hobbes, the corporate authority of the people was embodied by the sovereign, the 'leviathan'. Thus, although they invest power in radically different places, both Hobbes and More begin from similar problems and use similar tools to think through the question of authority.

By the end of the seventeenth century, some of the reluctance about using More in support of the power of parliament seems to have dissipated. In the 1680s Britain was in the middle of another political crisis. King Charles II (1630–85), restored in 1660, was aging and had no legitimate children. The heir to the throne was his brother James (1633–1701), a known Catholic, and his accession faced intense popular opposition. Debate raged over whether parliament had the power to appoint another monarch to the throne instead of James. In this context More once again came to be of use, this time as an advocate for the authority of parliament to decide the succession. John Somers (1651–1716), later Lord Chancellor, in his pamphlet *A Brief History of the Succession of the Crown of England*, argues that, if he is to convince his opponents of this power of parliament, there is no better authority for him to cite than Thomas More. More may have refused the oath written by parliament, but he did so because he doubted its ability to legislate on the king's supremacy, not because he denied parliament's ability to determine the succession. Somers writes that More 'says expressly...that the Parliament had unquestionable Authority in the ordering of the Succession, and the people were bound to obey them therein'.[60] Somers may have been aware of more than just the historical account of More's trial and defence, because he goes on to say that, for More, 'the People are bound in Conscience' to obey such laws and ought not to 'enquire whether they were made upon just Grounds', as this would undermine the authority of all laws: 'by the same Reason [the people] may pretend that all other Laws were made without just Cause, and refuse obedience to any of them', a sentiment that More expresses in his *Apology* (*ATM*, 96–7).[61] That being said, this is a trifling mention from a fairly minor author, and the larger debates occur with little or no reference to More or his works.

Utopias

More's influence on the genre of utopian writing is far more apparent and concrete. Like More himself, writers of the early modern period increasingly turned to the idea of a 'nowhere' in order to communicate arguments about their own political realities, and they almost always did so with at least passing mention of the text that inspired this growing genre.

One of the first European writers to engage at length with the utopian form was François Rabelais (1494–1553), a French writer and humanist known for his satirical style. Rabelais was certainly familiar with More's *Utopia* and adopted elements from it in his books *Pantagruel* and *Gargantua*, the first of which was published in 1532.[62] Rabelais uses his imagined characters and commonwealths in order to advance humanist aims in line with those of More and Erasmus. In particular, like More, Rabelais seems to seek a middle path through the question of the good life, combining the advantages of learning (in the character of Pantagruel) with those of experience (in Panurge).[63] It is Panurge who is able to cut through the meaninglessness of the puffed-up scholars whom the pair meet in their journeying. One such scholar is an Englishman named Thaumaste, who may have been a parody of More himself. As per Thaumaste's request, he and Panurge engage in a debate using only gestures, because Thaumaste wants to ensure that the debate remains focused on the acquisition of truth and is not sidetracked by the desire to win over the audience through rhetoric. Unsurprisingly, the debate is entirely meaningless, as it consists of exchanging a variety of gestures that have no significance to either participant, or indeed to the gathered audience. Thaumaste nevertheless admits defeat and leaves, announcing that he has learned valuable lessons that he publishes in a book in London, as the narrator reports. Rabelais' moral for the reader is ambiguous and certainly multifaceted, but it does seem that, in the attempt to uproot the desire to please the audience and thus to do without the rules of rhetoric and *decorum*, the scholarly debate between Panurge and Thaumaste loses all meaning. In other words meaning is constructed by, or in relation to, the masses that Thaumaste seeks to eliminate from scholarly discourse. It is a lesson that resounds with the humanist argument that sense is determined through use and consensus, which More had embraced, and with More's own desire to ensure that scholars never forget what is 'common', either in language or in purpose. In fact, although the text can be interpreted as imply-ing that Thaumaste foolishly attributes meaning to the gestures of Panurge, perhaps instead Thaumaste realizes this very lesson through the course of the debate, publishing his findings upon his return.

The dialogue *Sivqila: Too Good to Be True*, published in 1580 by the English writer Thomas Lupton (fl. 1572–84), is more explicit about the critique it levels against society. Lupton borrows from More's wordplay, establishing a dialogue between Sivqila – the Latin pronoun *aliquis* ('anyone') read backwards – and Omen – the Latin noun *nemo* ('no one') similarly read backwards – about the utopian country of Mauqsun – another Latin word read backwards: the adverb *nusquam* ('nowhere').[64] They compare Mauqsun to Ailgna (*Anglia*), England, employing the former as a mirror through which to behold the latter's faults. Lupton goes further than More in using his utopia as a vehicle for explicit social and legal reform.[65] The dialogue is also more one-sided. The character of Sivqila, a citizen of Ailgna, is not the active narrator of *Utopia* but rather functions more like the marginalia in *Utopia*, reacting to Omen's description of Mauqsun with comments like 'Oh that we had that law'.[66] These remarks are reinforced by marginal notes that draw attention to certain passages and lessons. Lupton's utopia, though still a dia-logue, is a strongly didactic one.

As it develops in the seventeenth century, the utopian genre begins to move away from the dialogue form and changes from a vehicle for critical reflection, as it was in *Utopia*, to one for laying out concrete social and legal reforms.[67] Tommaso Campenella's (1568–1639) *City of the Sun*, published in 1602, uses the dialogue solely as a framing device for the description of the ideal city.[68] The questions that the knight poses to the sailor, who has been to the city, once again take on the air of marginal comments, or even chapter headings. For instance, Campenella uses them to draw attention to a lesson that *City of the Sun* shares with *Utopia* and that may have been taken from More himself: 'when self-love is destroyed, only concern for the community remains'.[69]

One of the most famous utopias of the period is undoubtedly Francis Bacon's *New Atlantis* (written around 1624, published in 1627), which achieved a status comparable to that of Plato's *Republic* and More's *Utopia*. In this text Bacon demonstrates familiarity with

Utopia by referencing it while he simultaneously distances himself from it.[70] Bacon uses the literary convention of utopia in order to explore the positive benefits of 'natural philosophy' for society, especially highlighting the importance of institutionalizing science as a central part of the state.[71] Although the reforms suggested are not expressly social or political, Bacon is still trying to establish the important role that natural science plays in society, probably in the hope that this will elicit greater political support for it. His text continues the move away from utopia as a reflective critical form and towards a more didactic and prescriptive genre. In this case, utopia is used to lay out Bacon's scientific institution.[72]

Bacon's text also reflects on the idea that had inspired More's work: Erasmus' 'Pythagorean' adage 'friends hold all things in common'. This maxim was the foundation for the publication of Erasmus' *Adages*, in that it justified disseminating the knowledge they contained. Because the adage form allows for the easy communication of rich knowledge, by opening his collection in this way Erasmus frames it as a common store of wisdom, which he is sharing with his friends.[73] *Utopia* is likewise presented as a piece of common property that More shares among his humanist friends. It is itself a 'republic of letters', having no actual geographical presence, and the paratexts it contains indicate this shared ownership. Bacon similarly treats scientific knowledge in *New Atlantis* as something that ought to be shared among an elite community of scholars. Although a twenty-first-century reader is tempted to highlight the restrictions of scientific learning in Bacon's utopia, as scientific inquiry remains an elite activity Bacon's readers would almost certainly have been more struck by the *opening* of the enterprise of learning in *New Atlantis*.[74] Importantly, Bacon also argues for a common purpose of such learning. Relevant scientific results in his imagined city would be published widely, for the benefit of all. Thus, although knowledge itself is not *actually* common the way property was in *Utopia*, natural philosophers still pursue the common good rather than their own interests, embracing the reorientation of perspective advocated by More.

This idea was even more strongly articulated in the decades following Bacon's death. For instance, in the anonymous 1660 *New Atlantis Continued* the author writes that, in his version of Bacon's ideal state, 'we study the public good so much, that whereas we reward those that discover, so he is in some measure punished that conceals and hides a benefit which may pleasure his country'.[75] Such a person is considered to have done harm to his or her country by omission and is treated the same as one who actively works against the commonwealth. The cooperative and socially oriented nature of scientific study outlined in Bacon's *New Atlantis* inspired scientists of the next generation, many of whom backed the creation of the Royal Society, an institution similar to that of Bacon's vision.[76]

Although it inspired substantive change, Bacon's *New Atlantis* was classified by other writers as an imaginary or hypothetical community, alongside More's *Utopia*. By the mid-seventeenth century this growing body of 'utopian' works can really be said to form a genre. The scholar Robert Burton (1577–1640) was the first to discuss it in these terms in his *Anatomy of Melancholy*, in which he decides to set out his own 'poetical commonwealth' that should eliminate the problems of his world.[77] Burton seems to have been well versed in More's work; he makes at least twenty-five allusions to *Utopia*, eighteen of which are in the preface to the *Anatomy*.[78] When it comes to the biggest issue, property, Burton rejects the idea that common property leads to a successful commonwealth: 'I will have no...commons, but all inclosed...for that which is common, and every man's, is no man's; the richest Counties are still enclosed.'[79] The 'parity' or social equality in Utopia is (as Morus himself says), 'to be wished for, rather than effected'; such a levelling of hierarchy is 'absurd and ridiculous'.[80] Instead Burton will have not only property, but also inheritance; and he suggests a few minor reforms designed to provide for younger sons, so that they may live independently. Burton retains the need to place the public good over private interests in his commonwealth but sees private property as instrumental to this good.[81]

The same view of private property was also taken up in James Harrington's *The Commonwealth of Oceana* in 1656. Harrington uses the utopian form but strips it of its framework of travel and dialogue, using it purely as a way of setting out republican reforms in the context of Oliver Cromwell's Commonwealth. Nevertheless, the Morean inspiration is difficult to deny, and it is made even clearer by Harrington's acknowledgement of his respect for More.[82] Like More, Harrington believes that competing private interests tear a state apart and rejects the doctrine of those like Machiavelli, who believe that it is precisely this competition that holds a state together.[83] Harrington does not object to private property but seeks to equalize it, and he does so in the context of already existing property arrangements, so that those who already hold land will not be denied it.[84] Harrington's intention, like More's, is to remove the causes of greed and envy within the commonwealth, and his proposals begin to look a great deal like the rejected compromises that Hythloday puts forward towards the end of *Utopia*.[85]

Harrington's vision of equality of property influenced many political thinkers of the seventeenth and eighteenth centuries.[86] The view, taken for instance in Winstanley's utopian *Law of Freedom*, that private property ought to be abolished remained a minority one, seldom expressed. During the Enlightenment private property gained even more importance, because many thinkers, in stark contrast with More, placed great store by the efficacy of private interest – including greed and pride – in bringing about the common good.

The Enlightenment

More receives little mention from the best known thinkers of the Enlightenment period. Montesquieu's (1689–1755) *Persian Letters* bears some utopian influence, but Montesquieu prefers Plato's more realistic-sounding *Laws* to his *Republic* or to More's *Utopia*. Voltaire (1694–1778) and Jean-Jacques Rousseau (1712–78) make only passing mentions of *Utopia*, although the former's *Candide* and the latter's *Social Contract* both contain utopian elements. David Hume (1711–76) also makes a passing reference to *Utopia* in his essay 'On the Ideal Commonwealth', engaging in the common trope, begun by More himself, of differentiating his work from preceding utopias.

Hume treats More more extensively and more positively in his six-volume *History of England*. Hume depends heavily on More's *History of King Richard the Third* in his treatment of that period, placing as he does great credence on More's 'authority'.[87] In his own treatment of Henry VIII's reign, Hume refers to More as 'a man, who, besides the ornaments of an elegant literature, possessed the highest virtue, integrity and capacity'.[88] More becomes an exemplar of the 'usual progress of men's sentiments during that age' on account of his turn to religious zealotry.[89] He began with a 'very enlarged sentiment', which Hume says even in the eighteenth century would be 'deemed somewhat too free', but 'in the course of events', being 'so irritated by polemics', More became a violent persecutor of heresy.[90] Hume attributes More's resignation from the chancellorship to his concern that king and parliament would cause 'an alteration of religion' with 'which his principles would not permit him to concur'.[91] Although later on Hume says that 'nothing was wanting' from More's 'end' than 'a better cause, more free from weakness and suspicion', he does not think that this takes away from More's 'constancy and integrity', which remain 'objects of our admiration'.[92] More is the subject of two lengthy panegyrics, in which Hume praises the 'sanctity of his manners', the 'gentleness of his temper' and 'that frolic and gaiety, to which he was naturally inclined'.[93] Hume also notes that More was an accomplished scholar and praises his 'elegant genius and familiar acquaintance with the noble spirit of antiquity'.[94]

Although Hume respects More as a historical figure, he doesn't treat his thought at any length. For this we turn to a lesser known writer who was a critic and contemporary of Hume: the eighteenth-century Scottish philosopher Thomas Reid (1710–96). In a paper from 1794 entitled 'Some Thoughts on the Utopian System', written largely with the aim to oppose the violence of the French Revolution and Terror, Reid addresses the project of utopian thinking as a less violent alternative to revolutionary theory. 'Speculative' thinking, he suggests, can 'enlarge our Conceptions' and 'strengthen our Faculties'.[95] In particular, speculating about the best commonwealth allows us to seek the means to achieve the three ideal 'ends' of political societies: (1) 'to strengthen in the Minds of the Citizens the Principles of Virtue and true Religion'; (2) 'That the Temptations to wrong and criminal Conduct be as few as possible'; and (3) 'That publick Esteem, Honour and Rank be proportioned as exactly as possible to real Merit'.[96] These are all ends with which More himself would almost certainly have agreed.

Perhaps because these aims are largely consonant with More's own, whereas Hume had rejected More's *Utopia* in his essay on the ideal commonwealth, Reid embraces it. He finds there especially the means to the second end, lessoning the temptation to ill conduct, and declares that 'the Utopian System of Sir Thomas More seems to have the advantage of all others in this respect'.[97] In this Reid was certainly on the right track; as we saw in Chapter 2, More specifically wrote of the lack of 'opportunity' for vice in Utopia. Reid also identifies the central aim of *Utopia* as countering the divisive effects of private interest: 'In the System of private Property every Man has his private Interest, distinct, not only from the publick Interest, but from the Interest of every Individual with whom he has any connection or intercourse.'[98] Private property creates, in other words, an 'opposition of Interests' that leads to 'Disaffectation to the publick'.[99] In the utopian system, on the other hand, 'there are no publick Interests opposed to that of the Publick' and so no resultant conflicts between them.[100]

As essays such as those of Hume and Reid demonstrate, 'utopianism' flourished during the Enlightenment, though often without mention of More himself. It has even been suggested that the idea of a 'utopia' stands behind eighteenth-century philosophers' frequent use of the 'state of nature'.[101] Writers such as Rousseau referred to the idea of a state of nature, a state that existed before the creation of civil government, to theorize about human nature and natural rights and to compare their contemporary societies to this ideal standard. For some, including Rousseau, the concept furnished the necessary goals for making prescriptions about what an ideal society should look like, and this in turn created two ideal societies: one in the past and one in the future. Thus we see is a shift in utopian theorizing in this period: rather than being geographically remote, as the island of Utopia was, 'utopias' become distant in time, a feature that renders them powerful tools in the progressive liberal tradition of the Enlightenment era.

Socialism and Communism

This move towards conceptualizing utopia as a destination to be reached over time, or as a 'euchronia', and the original connection between utopianism and common property come together in the origin of socialism and communism around the mid-nineteenth century. The socialist movement sprung out of egalitarian, and especially republican, responses to the French Revolution,[102] as well as from the social changes brought about by the Industrial Revolution.[103] In this new context More re-emerges as a powerful philosophical thinker, alongside those who inspired him, such as Plato, and those who were inspired by him, such as Winstanley.

Early socialist thinkers like Henri de Saint-Simon (1760–1825), Charles Fourier (1772–1837) and Robert Owen (1771–1858) sought to establish socialist communities that applied the sort of reforms advocated in utopian writings of the seventeenth century. Although accused of utopianism and labelled as utopians by others rather than embracing the description themselves, these 'utopian socialists' altered the way in which utopianism was conceived of, further cementing its association with egalitarianism and shared property and establishing the meaning of 'utopia' as a concrete goal to be achieved.[104]

These socialist movements had strong connections with another key nineteenth-century philosophical tradition: utilitarianism.

Although there was substantial variation in the details of their thought, utilitarians, broadly speaking, valued the principle of the greatest happiness (or pleasure) for the greatest number and favoured reforms that brought about this goal. For most utilitarians, particularly Jeremy Bentham (1748–1832), the traditional founder of this school of thought, the principle of utility rested on a fairly straightforward calculation of happiness among those who lived at any one time. This understanding of ethics was adopted by Robert Owen in his 'utopian' writings and experiments, which were supported by Bentham himself, a stockholder in Owen's factory.

Bentham also helped to shape the curriculum of the young J. S. Mill (1806–73), who would go on to expand Bentham's understanding of utilitarian aims. For Mill, the greatest happiness principle differentiated between 'higher' and 'lower' order pleasures, just as More's Utopians had done. Higher pleasures might involve, for instance, the enduring joys of philosophy, whereas lower pleasures consisted of fleeting and often physical pleasures. According to Mill, the greatest happiness had to be calculated not according to all those living in one given moment, but by taking into account all people over time, which meant that 'progress' remained an important principle. To achieve the greatest happiness for the greatest number of people, society as a whole had to advance towards enlightenment – a temporal extension not unlike the one that More proposed in his understanding of the church.

Some writers noted the possible connections between More and utilitarianism. We've already seen how Gentili opposes what he takes to be More's (proto-)utilitarianism when it comes to warfare, an impression he derives from the Utopians' willingness to engage in craft and deceit in order to win a war. Mill himself does not call More a utilitarian, he only refers to him once, briefly, as a 'man of wit, wisdom and self-devotion'.[105] However, Mill's stepdaughter and collaborator, Helen Taylor (1831–1907), writes that in *Utopia* More 'lays down a completely Utilitarian system of ethics' as well as an 'eloquently and yet closely reasoned defence of Socialism'.[106] In her 1870 article 'Sir Thomas More on the Politics of To-Day' (for the *Fortnightly Review*), Taylor attempts to demonstrate that 'a Conservative English statesman' in fact supported movements deemed 'too new and bold for practical acceptance' by the conservatives of the nineteenth century, particularly on issues such as 'small properties, the enclosure of commons' and 'the education of girls'.[107] Taylor particularly uses More as a way to try to sway reluctant conservatives on the issue of property, interjecting into a long quotation from

Hythloday's speech on enclosures: 'I hope my readers will remember that this last irreverent remark proceeds from a pious conservative gentleman of the sixteenth, not from a philosophical radical of the nineteenth century.'[108] She gives a perceptive reading, hitting on the centrality of the common for More and suggesting that 'perhaps an "Utopian" philosopher might be defined as some one who makes uncommon applications of common sense'.[109]

There is some indication that Taylor saw herself in the same role as More's educated daughter Margaret Roper (1505–44), casting Mill as the modern Thomas More: 'Margaret Roper possessed talents which were often the subject of her father's delighted encomiums, and she was his favourite companion both in their home, and...during the imprisonment which preceded his noble death.'[110] At the time of writing, Taylor was Mill's constant companion and intellectual partner, and he died only three years later. As Taylor's work implies, there were close connections between utilitarianism and socialism – Mill himself had some socialist leanings[111] – and More could be placed conveniently at the intersection of these ideologies.

Socialists and communists most passionately claimed More as an intellectual ancestor. For most of the nineteenth century the terms 'socialism' and 'communism' were used interchangeably. One of the first to use the latter term was Étienne Cabet (1788–1856), a French writer and lawyer who in 1834 had fled to England, where he was primarily inspired by two Englishmen: Robert Owen and Thomas More. He later describes how he came across a copy of More's *Utopia* while working in the British Museum and 'was so struck by his fundamental idea that I closed the book without wanting to remember the details to meditate seriously on this idea of Community'.[112] Inspired by *Utopia* as well as by all the other utopian writings he could get his hands on, Cabet wrote a utopian work, *Voyage en Icarie*, which provided the basis for a number of settlements in the United States. In Icaria property is held in common and all citizens are equal. As in *Utopia*, Cabet's ideal community uses public opinion to ensure right action, although Cabet here goes further than More, removing courts of law entirely. Cabet's *Icaria* bears the most concrete, direct and self-conscious influence exercised by More on any work since the sixteenth century and consciously brings that influence into the growing communist tradition.

Although explicitly rejecting 'utopianism' as overly conceptual and abstract, Friedrich Engels (1820–95) and Karl Marx (1818–83), the authors of *The Communist Manifesto*, were inspired by the same kind of utopianism as their socialist forebears, and went further by turning it into a revolutionary goal rather than an unachievable ideal or a mirror for social critique.[113] Both had almost certainly read *Utopia*. Marx was especially partial to More's treatment of enclosure, and particularly to the image of sheep devouring men. In his 1859 *A Contribution to the Critique of Political Economy*, Marx, citing *Utopia*, notes that More 'deplored (denounced)' the 'violent economic upheaval' caused by the enclosure of land for sheep.[114] In *Capital* he references More's man-eating sheep and provides an extended quotation from *Utopia* on enclosure.[115]

In May 1882 Marx's daughter Laura Lafargue (1845–1911) gifted a copy of the 1869 English edition of *Utopia* to Engels. The copy has been heavily annotated with marks that resemble those Marx left in other books, though it remains unclear whether they were in his hand or that of Engels.[116] In particular the word 'hable' ('able') has been underlined at numerous points in the text, when it is describing limits on economic ability. The passage on sheep and enclosure has also been heavily lined, probably by Marx, and the top corner of the page appears to have been folded over for easy reference. There is reason to think it was Engels who underlined passages in the text relating to women's roles in Utopia; in 1884 he published *The Origin of the Family, Private Property and the State*, which treats the role of women in society.

Marx's and Engels's references to More in their works consciously place him as the first writer in the communist movement, sometimes even giving him some credit for it. For instance, Engels suggests that More was the first to set up the demand for 'justice', which was later corrupted by its appropriation into the machinery of capitalism,[117] and in the section 'Philosophy of True Socialism' in *The German Ideology*, Marx and Engels place More first in the list of English communists, where he is followed by the Levellers and Owen.[118]

This effort to establish More as an historical originator of communism went beyond their own work. In 1873 Engels wrote to Wilhelm Liebknecht about the possibility of an edition of More's *Utopia* that would open a 'social and political library', which would also include the works of Engels and Marx.[119] Interestingly, Engels notes that it may be difficult to 'unearth' a copy of *Utopia* in English, 'as all the old popular editions were bought up long since'.[120] Engels was writing from London, where there should have been plenty of editions of *Utopia*. However, it seems that he – and Marx – may have favoured the Ralph Robinson translation as being more 'popular' (meaning 'populist'), in contrast to the translation by the theologian Gilbert Burnet. It is possible that, finding few editions of Robinson's translation, Engels eventually sent his own copy to Liebknecht, leader of the German Social Democratic Party (SPD), which is how this copy of *Utopia* ended up with an SPD stamp.

Marx himself read at least the final two chapters of a work on the history of communist thought by Moritz Kaufmann (1839–1920): *Utopias; or, Schemes of Social Improvements: From Thomas More to Karl Marx* (1879).[121] Kaufmann was not himself a communist or socialist, he had published a critique of socialism in 1874, but sought in *Utopias* to dispel the 'unreasonable prejudice against socialistic literature', especially the idea that it contained 'nothing but idle dreams and fancies', showing instead its potential to recommend practical social reforms.[122] Kaufmann sets out a 'short History of Socialism', regarding it 'as a consecutive movement developed in the course of time, adapting itself to prevailing social conditions'.[123] For Kaufmann, utopian writers like More are mouthpieces for the opinions of the people, 'defining more clearly the vague socialistic tendencies of the times' and giving 'vent to their feelings in these poetical fictions'.[124] Rather than being simply poetical, however, these fictions had purpose: 'to satirise existing social inconsistencies' and to aim 'at social improvements and reforms'.[125] In particular, Kaufmann suggests that utopias seek to generate a world in which 'the unhappy consequences of egotism or private interest are prevented by legal enactments', and thus Kaufmann builds into his understanding of this genre at least part of More's intention in *Utopia*.[126]

Kaufmann describes More as Engels and Marx had done: as an early socialist who was concerned about the welfare of the 'labour class'.[127] He does concede, however, that More did not believe in the practicality of his reforms but set up *Utopia* as only a 'mirror of political and social evils of the times', rather than 'as a serious scheme for the entire transformation of society'.[128] He reads the dialogue of counsel as an example of Morus' 'indirect approach': *Utopia* is More's own indirect counsel to Henry VIII on social reforms.[129] Kaufmann sees More as a thinker 'far in advance of his own age', whose visions of 'the division of labour' were realized in 'our factory system', but whose pleas for short labour hours and recreation time for the working classes 'remain still among the *desiderata* of the present day'.[130] Although not strictly speaking a communist, because he did not argue for the application of his ideas, More remains for Kaufmann a pioneer of social reform to whom all subsequent reformers should look for inspiration.

Interestingly, Kaufmann seems to consider only the temporal dimension of utopias. As we saw above, there was a shift at the end of the seventeenth and eighteenth centuries from geographically to temporally distant utopias – a shift that made them a concrete goal to be achieved rather than simply a mirror suggesting reform. Kaufmann, however, thought that utopias either 'look backward to the past, a golden age', or '(since the spread of Christianity) they look forward to a brighter coming era for the realisation of their hopes'.[131] The same assessment of More's *Utopia* was made by the British writer William Morris (1834–96) in the 1893 preface to his utopian *News from Nowhere*. Morris writes that More gives 'a picture (his own indeed, not ours) of the real New Birth which many men before him had desired, and which now indeed we may well hope is drawing near to realization'.[132] *Utopia* itself becomes not a distant geographical place, but an achievable future.

Engels made an offer to read a draft of another work from this period that focused on the work of More: Karl Kautsky's *Thomas More and His Utopia*, published in German in 1888.[133] Although we don't have Engels' comments on this work, he seems to have approved of it, as he recommended it for translation into English in 1891.[134] Kautsky, a Marxist, went further than Kaufmann in placing More within the socialist tradition, explicitly calling him 'the first modern Socialist'.[135] Kautsky writes that the 'bases of [More's] socialism are modern', which is why More had to 'twist and turn' the 'resources of feudal times' in a 'truly fantastic manner to adapt them to his modern aims'.[136] Kautsky attempts to understand the nature of More's 'times', especially the 'beginnings of capitalism' and the role of the church and commerce, inserting More into a Marxist view of the stages of history at the moment of transition from feudal to capitalist society.[137] He then gives an account of 'More the communist', particularly in *Utopia*, which Kautsky argued was 'designed to exert an influence on the nation's destiny'.[138] Kautsky suggests that More 'assigned the championship of his standpoint to Raphael Hythloday', using him as a mouthpiece for his critiques and reforms.[139] The communism in *Utopia*, however, 'frightened nobody, for no communist party then existed' – and in fact, Kautsky maintains, it contained an acceptable bourgeois message about the role that the 'modern king' should play as 'the leader of the bourgeoisie'.[140]

Kautsky was one of the first respondents to More who attempted to go beyond the influence of *Utopia* alone. Kautsky draws on More's epigrams and polemical works as well as on *Utopia* in advancing his view of More's communism. In particular, he picks up on More's ambivalence when it comes to the issue of the pope, noting that '[More] wrote, in his *Confutation of Tyndale's Answer* (1532), that a general council is above the Pope'.[141] More, Kautsky maintains, saw the papacy as 'an international cohesive force, without which Christendom would dissolve'.[142] More understood the 'class struggle which underlay the Reformation', but did not understand that the papacy maintained order only through exploitation.[143] More turned to the pope rather than to the people as the limit on absolutism, which was his biggest mistake – one born out of the limited conditions of his age. More becomes, for Kautsky, a tragic figure who 'divines the problems of his age before the material conditions exist for their solution', a champion of 'the rights of the oppressed' who can never succeed.[144] This tragic genius, Kautsky maintains, can only be appreciated in the nineteenth century; 'only with the rise of scientific Socialism, has it become possible to do full justice to More the Socialist'.[145] Thus, 'although *Utopia* is more than four hundred years old, the ideals of More are not vanquished, but still lie before striving mankind'.[146]

Conclusion

Kautsky's appraisal takes us full circle to the scholarship on More in the twentieth century and to how More was used in a variety of debates up to the present day. If nothing else, this book has attempted to demonstrate that, in addition to being, as Erasmus called him, a 'man for all seasons', readily deployed in the service of a variety of purposes and ideologies, More was also a thinker for his own time. I'll end by saying a few words about what we might be able to conclude from such a reading of More.

There are at least three different ways in which one might approach the work of a past thinker, and they relate to the aims that a scholar may have. The first is to ask what that thinker was intending to do when she wrote. In what debates was she intending to participate, what was she aiming to argue? The bulk of this book has been an attempt to answer questions of this sort, as they provide the surest method of finding out a thinker's ideas. When we then go on to say that More thought something – for instance, that we must turn our attention to what is held in common in order to avoid the divisive effects of pride – we do so with the confidence that this was something he did indeed think, rather than an idea we have imposed upon him. From such a study we can see that More's works commented on a variety of subjects important to his time, such as language, the nature of authority, the role of public opinion and the unity of the commonwealth. More's ideas were not always consistent; they reflected the changing interests and events of his context. From this assertion we can draw conclusions about the period in which he lived: the kinds of debates that were happening and the ideas that were developed and deployed in those debates. From the more consistent aspects of his thought, such as the emphasis on what is held in common, we can start to understand what may have been most important to More himself, as he reflected on the context around him.

Second, a historian of ideas might ask what the influence of a thinker might have been, or what others thought of him or her. We have traced the legacy of More in the thought of writers from the sixteenth to the end of the nineteenth centuries and learned that More's ideas, the subject of our first question, became lost and misinterpreted in the centuries after he wrote, as he was shunned or appropriated according to the particular concerns of those who encountered them. Despite difficulties in following the trajectory of his thought, there is no question that More had a great influence on those who came after him, and so we can conclusively say that More's thought, as misunderstood as it may have been, deserves a place in a study of ideas.

Finally, we might ask what a thinker has to teach us today. I will end by outlining only a few suggestions about where such a line of investigation could take us in More's case. For my own part, I am less interested in an approach that starts with questions from our own context, such as 'Is More a communitarian?' or 'Is More's *Utopia* totalitarian?', though there might be reasons to ask such questions. Instead, if we look at More's ideas in their own context, we may be presented with new lines of inquiry that question our basic assumptions.

First, western society is built on a premise of individualism and self-interest, a legacy of the Enlightenment period and of thinkers such as Adam Smith and J. S. Mill. We've already seen how More's ideas inspired a response to such a perspective in the form of nineteenth-century socialism and communism. In the twentieth century the humanist republican ideas that underpinned More's work were also expressed in the form of 'communitarianism', presented as an alternative to the dichotomy between individualist liberal democracy and communism.[1] In the first decades of the twenty-first century the financial crisis has produced a stark division between those who maintain that self-interested capitalism continues to be the way forward and those who advocate policies that place the needs of the community first. Both the United States and the United Kingdom have seen the re-entry of socialism into mainstream politics, and a dichotomy has appeared between politicians who are deemed 'unifiers' and those who employ a 'politics of division'. In these respects, More's context and our own begin to look increasingly alike.

It is best, however, that we avoid drawing too many direct parallels. More's ideas, of course, preceded any reflection on 'individualism', which is why they are sometimes labelled 'totalitarian'. To use such an anachronistic twentieth-century term for sixteenth-century ideas obscures More's original intentions and, as a result, the ways in which his thought might provide alternative ways of thinking for us today. More's focus on what is held in common, and on the community, and his abhorrence for self-interested pride prompt reflection on the potentially damaging effects of self-interest. As More himself would maintain, it is not that private property needs to be abolished, but rather that we should shift our priorities internally, to what we hold in common, to an awareness of our essential equality and to the importance of the mutual affection that holds our community together. More would have undoubtedly provided an entertaining and scathing critique of the corruption of big banks, the rising disparity between rich and poor, and the self-interest that drives the capitalist system.

This relates to the second major theme that emerges from a reflection on More in our own time: the role of the public intellectual. As we saw, for More the questions of property and the matter of the best life were two sides of the same coin. Thus, just as we can use More's ideas to think about the tension between self-interest and the community's interest, we can reflect in the same manner on More's statements about the active role of scholars in the community. For More, hiding one's 'talents in a napkin' reflected a sense of pride and had a detrimental effect on the community. Instead intellectuals ought to serve the public, primarily by exercising a political role, for instance by proffering advice to political leaders.

Academics today are often torn between the requirements of scholarly publication and increasing calls to demonstrate the public utility of their work. More's opening letter to *Utopia* sounds all too familiar to the twenty-first century scholar:

> I am constantly engaged in legal business…I pay a visit of courtesy to one man and go on business to another. I devote almost the whole day in public to other men's affairs and the remainder to my own. I leave to myself, that is to learning, nothing at all.…Amid all these occupations that I have named, the day, the month, the year slip away. When, then, can we find time to write? (*Ut*, 39, 41)

Of course, for More, 'learning' ought not be self-interested. There is no inherent opposition between scholarship and public business, just a logistical one, for the two ought to go hand in hand. What is needed is bravery to articulate the truths that one has found in public, no matter the personal consequences; and, ideally, the position from which to do it.

More's most innovative contribution to our modern intellectual tradition is his reflection on the role of public opinion. As we've seen, the nexus of ideas around custom, consent, consensus and public opinion played an essential role in More's theory of language and meaning, of political order and legitimacy, and of religion. 'Common sense' provides the meaning of words; public opinion can either hold a society together, if it is oriented towards the common good, or tear it apart under the influence of self-interest; and custom demonstrates the guidance of the Holy Spirit over the church. Although, from a presentist standpoint, we might expect More to consequently take a firm line against censorship, his reflections on public opinion prompt the opposite view. For him, the 'vulgar' are easily misled, either through their own pride or through the pride of others, and so introducing them to complex and controversial ideas can lead to a dangerously misguided populace and a tainted public opinion.

There are three lessons we might want to take from More along these lines. First, public opinion can constrain and control, including in a positive way, by expressing, generating and perpetuating norms, as it does in Utopia. For this reason it is even more worrying that, second, it can also be manipulated, misrepresented and fabricated, as happens in More's *History of King Richard the Third*. Finally, More maintains that this consensus can be represented and can provide the necessary consent to rule, bestow legitimacy, transfer authority and communicate a higher authority. More goes further than his predecessors and contemporaries in generating this theory of what we now call public opinion – and also further than many thinkers in the five centuries since.

This is an especially pertinent contribution in the digital age. Just as the print revolution of the late fifteenth and early sixteenth centuries supported the proliferation of learning and ideas of the Renaissance, so too the introduction of the Internet has demonstrated the potential to create communities that cross borders, incite revolutions and democratize information. Again, we should not go too far in drawing connections between these two contexts; but we can turn to More to inspire a refocusing on this idea of public opinion in the digital age. When we consider the role of the Internet, this orientation comes together, as it did for More, with a concern for valuing what is held in common and for the new digital 'knowledge commons'.

There may be numerous other such contemporary issues that overlap with More's ideas, and a variety of other ways in which we might think through them, but the point here is not to dictate such lines of inquiry, nor to follow them through to their full conclusions. The intention of this book has been to provide an outline of More's thought, gathered from an analysis of his texts in their contexts. In so doing, we begin to encounter More not only as a historical figure but also as a profound – even classic – thinker.

Notes

Introduction The Thought of Thomas More

1. Miller 2005; see also Sylvester 1963.
2. It can be dangerous to attempt to see consistencies in the writings of a thinker. Because we tend to praise consistency and condemn variation, especially when the latter results in tension or contradiction, there is a temptation to pave over deviation. More is not always consistent, and there are indeed important moments of variation, contradiction and poor argumentation in his work. That being said, it may not be surprising that someone of More's temperament would strive for consistency in some basic principles, in line with both his religious and his intellectual allegiances.
3. See the *OED*, s.v. 'common, *adj.* and *adv.*' and Williams 1983, 70–2.
4. Kenny 1983, 1.
5. Fox 1982, 3.
6. Curtright 2012, 9.
7. Ibid., 120.
8. Richard Pace, as quoted in Surtz 1977, 184.
9. See McConica 2011, 22–4.
10. See Nauta 2007.
11. See Cummins 2002, 21–23, 112–18, 137.
12. See Hosington 2003.
13. Quintilian, *Institutio oratoria* 1.6.3; also quoted in Perreiah 2004, 30.
14. As Elsky 2013, 195 points out, such scholastic theologians commit the same crime as the propertied nobles in *Utopia*.
15. I have used 'evangelical' for the anachronistic 'Protestant' during the life of More, in line with the work of Diarmaid MacCulloch and Peter

Marshall; see MacCulloch 2002, 2 and Marshall 2002, 15. See also Mac-Culloch 2003, xx.
16. See Fox 1990, 151.
17. See Kempshall 2011, 372.
18. See Eden 1991; Baker 1999, 23.
19. See also Betteridge 2004, 4, 17, 27.
20. Kempshall 2011, 284–6, 288–9.

1 Early Life, Education and Poetry

1. Brown 2000, 181–2.
2. Biographical details here and in the subsequent chapters are taken from the *Oxford Dictionary of National Biography* entry by Seymour Baker-House and from Peter Ackroyd's biography; see Baker-House 2008 and Ackroyd 1999. For the controversy surrounding the date of More's birth, see Mitjans 2012.
3. McConica 2011, 23.
4. See Yoran 2010.
5. See Rappaport 2002 [1989].
6. Although most of More's sixteenth- and seventeenth-century biographers speak of him as living *in* the Charterhouse, Cresacre More's 1630 biography states that More lived 'near the Charterhouse': More 1828 [1630], 25. See also Guy 2000, 11.
7. For Augustine's insistence on the importance of pagan learning, and especially rhetoric, to the reading of scripture, see Kempshall 2011, 369–72.
8. See White 1982, 346.
9. Perhaps an English translation of Lorenzo Spirito's *Libro delle Sorti* or *Le livre de passe temps de la fortune des dez*, as suggested by Hubertus Schulte Herbrüggen; see Herbrüggen 2011 [1967], 15.
10. See Marsh 1998.
11. See *OED* online, s.v. 'match, *adj.* 1'.
12. See Greenblatt 1980, 27.
13. See Cooper 2010, 52.
14. Rummel 2004, xi, 50–1.
15. See McConica 1965, 17–19, 21–2, 29.
16. MacCulloch 2003, 102.
17. Rummel 2004, 40, 54–62.

2 Utopia and 'Common Things'

1. Baker-Smith 2011, 148.
2. Erasmus 1982, 15. See Eden 2001, 1–5 and Elsky 2013, 181–210.
3. Erasmus 1982, 15.

4. Eden 2001.
5. For more on the classical influences on *Utopia* detailed in what follows, see *CW* 4, cliii–clxxix.
6. Kristeller 1980, 10.
7. Plato, *Laws*, Book 5, 739c, in R. G. Bury's translation (Plato 1926).
8. Cicero, *De officiis* 2.73, in Walter Miller's translation (Cicero 1913); also quoted in Eden 2001, 101.
9. See Cave 1991.
10. See Hadfield 1998, 1–2.
11. Houston 2014, 10.
12. For more on the influence of Lucian on *Utopia*, see Baker-Smith 2011, 142–4.
13. *quicquid ad rempublicam bene instituendam pertinet, in hac velut in speculo liceat cernere* (*Ut*, 26).
14. See Parker 2002.
15. On this and the whole problem of the possible etymology of Hythloday's name, see Wilson 1992.
16. See Skinner 2002.
17. Erasmus 1992, 6.
18. Lanham 1991; see Hosington 2003.
19. My own translation (*philosophia ciuilior*).
20. My own translation (*cum decoro*).
21. *Totum est unus homo regnum, idque cohaeret amore.* / *Rex caput est, populus caetera membra facit.* / *Rex quot habet ciues (dolet ergo perdere quenquam)* / *Tot numerat parteis corporis ipse sui.* / *Exponit populus sese pro rege putatque* / *Quilibet hunc proprij corporis esse caput.*
22. Augustine 1998, 602.
23. See 'Enclosure', in Kinney and Swain 2001, 230.
24. The best geographical description of Utopia, with a comparison to that of England, is given by Goodey 1970.
25. It is unclear whether the notes are from Erasmus, Gillis or both. See Logan and Adams 2011, xxxi.
26. My own translation (*nihil est umquam priuati*). The *CW* edition renders this passage 'nothing is private *property* anywhere' (my emphasis), which reads more into the original Latin than is given.
27. Curtis 2006, 106. As we'll see in Chapter 4, More's account of church government is also conciliar.
28. Nauta 2009, 186.
29. Cicero, *De finibus*, 5.23.65; quoted in Lederman 2000, 255. For the relationship between Cicero and Augustine's views of the commonwealth, see Kempshall 2011, 97.
30. As Elsky 2013, 196 points out, More is making a pun on his own name in placing such emphasis on *mores*.
31. See Greenblatt 1980, 47–52 on the role of praise, blame, shame and public opinion in *Utopia*.
32. More 1551, R, 7r.

33. Baker 1999, 15 notes that Erasmus shares same view about 'plucking away' 'rooted' ills but that he takes a different approach in dealing with them.
34. See Burgess 2009, 17; Houston 2014, 20.
35. See the discussion in note 1 to the Introduction.
36. Curtright 2012, 31–2.
37. See Eden 2001, 128–34.
38. This inward turning is consistent with what other humanist writers advocated. For instance Petrarch, the founder of the humanist movement, rejected the search for the mystical island of Thule in favour of self-reflection. He wrote: 'If it is denied to me to search out these hiding places of nature and to know their secrets, I shall be satisfied with knowing myself' (as quoted in Cachey 2003, 89).
39. Quoted in Kinney 1986, xlvii.
40. 'anything at all which we can call our own attracts our attentions to itself and away from common interests' (*SL*, 130); see Wegemer 1993.
41. *OED* online, s.v. 'abusion, *n*. 2: Wrong or improper use; misapplication; perversion, distortion'.
42. Ibid., s.v. 'jet, *v*. 1: To assume a pompous or ostentatious gait; to strut, swagger, sashay'.
43. Bishop 2005.
44. Baker 1999, 20, 53–4, 73.
45. Fox 1986, 19, 20, 22, 32.
46. Ibid., 35.
47. See Greenblatt 1980, 47–52.
48. See Lederman 2000, 252.

3 *Richard III* and the Stage Play of Politics

1. I use the title *Richard the Third* to refer to both the English and the Latin texts when there is little difference between them or none, and I specify the edition when noting a difference. *Richard III* refers to Shakespeare's play.
2. See Hanham 2007.
3. See McCutcheon 2011, 52–3.
4. Rome's senate did, during parts of its history, have such power. Notably, it begins to decline under Emperor Tiberius, whom More compares to Richard III.
5. See Kristeller 1980, 6–7.
6. See Gransden 1997, 427.
7. Lucian 1959, 15.
8. Ibid.
9. Ibid., 71.
10. Ibid.
11. See *CW* 2, lxv–lxxx.

12. Wegemer 2007, 39–46.
13. Kempshall 2011, 41, 42.
14. Ibid., 42.
15. Ibid., 46.
16. Nelson 1977 [1943], 154–6.
17. Kempshall 2011, 519.
18. Ibid., 289–94, 354–5. Just as Boethius sees the authority for history as coming either from nature or from the times (Kempshall 2011, 285), More describes Richard's unnatural birth as proceeding from either *natura* or *fama* (*HRT*, 7).
19. For *Richard the Third* as a work of dramatic theatre, see Arthur Noel Kincaid 1977 [1972].
20. *OED*, s.v. 'nought, *adj.*, 3b: Wickedness, evil … (also) promiscuity, indecency'.
21. Ibid., s.v. 'dissimuler, *n.*'.
22. See Skinner 2007.
23. He also uses paradiastole in his explanation of how the characters of priests are redescribed as embodying vices: 'If they be familiar we call them light. If they be solitary we call them fantastic [odd]. If they be sad [serious] we call them solemn. If they be merry we call them mad. If they be companable we call them vicious', and so on (*DCH*, 296).
24. Logan 2007, 28.
25. See Beier 2012.
26. We'll see this 'secret instinct of nature' reappear as an important concept in Chapter 4.
27. For this and other rhetorical figures, see *The Forest of Rhetoric* at http://rhetoric.byu.edu.
28. Here More almost certainly intended the meaning of raised platform both for political proclamations and for theatrical performance, inviting his reader to make a comparison between the two. What is unclear is whether he also intended the meaning of a scaffold of execution, which the *OED* does not record as being in use until 1538.
29. See Eden 2001, 28.
30. Virgil, *Eclogues*, 3.92–3: *Qui legitis flores et humi nascentia fraga, / frigidus, o pueri, fugite hinc, latet anguis in herba.*
31. Curtright 2012, 69.
32. For more on the language of 'opportunity', 'occasion' and 'season', see Paul 2014.
33. Lederman 2000, 253.
34. Manley 1980, 104; Marius 1990, 33.
35. Francesco Chieregato to Vigo da Campo San Pietro, 19 May 1517, in Brown 1867, 385.
36. See Rappaport 2002 [1989], 15. Sebastian Giustinian to the Doge, 5 May 1517, in Brown (1867), 382.
37. Sebastian Giustinian to the Signory 5 May 1517, in Brown (1867), 382.

38. Francesco Chieregato to Vigo da Campo San Pietro, 19 May 1517, in Brown (1867), 385.
39. Sebastian Giustinian to the Signory, 5 May 1517, in Brown (1867), 382.
40. Ibid.
41. Ibid., 382–3.
42. Francesco Chieregato to Vigo da Campo San Pietro, in Brown (1867), 385.
43. Ibid.
44. Ibid.
45. Ibid.
46. Ibid.
47. Hall 1548, fol. lxiiir.
48. Francesco Chieregato to Vigo da Campo San Pietro, in Brown (1867), 385.
49. Ibid.
50. Ibid., 386.
51. See Guy 2000, 50–2 and Curtis 2011, 74–5.
52. Croot 2004.

4 The Common Corps of Christendom

1. The exceptions are mostly letters defending humanism, including the *Letter to Oxford* (1518), the *Letter to a Monk* (1519) and the *Letter to Brixius* (1520). In addition, More may have been writing the unfinished *Four Last Things* around 1522.
2. Quoted in Schuster 1973, 1139.
3. Curtis 2011, 83. More's publication of the first part of the *Confutation of Tyndale's Answer* preceded his resignation from the post of Lord Chancellor by two months, so there is no doubt that he continued to write during this period.
4. See More's comments in *SB*, 8.
5. See *CW* 6.II, 440.
6. See Baumann 2015, 99.
7. See *CW* 11, lxxviii–lxxxvi.
8. Wilson 1560, 79.
9. See *CW* 5.II, 804, 807.
10. Martz 1990, 31–2.
11. Wagner and Schmid 2012, 592.
12. McSheffrey and Tanner 2003, 2–3.
13. See Cavill 2014.
14. *CW* 8.III, 1149.
15. See Guy 1986.
16. Ibid., 200–1; see also Wannenwetsch 2003, 123; Wreidt 2003, 92, 95, 105–6.
17. Guy 1986, 202.

18. See Greenblatt 1980, 60–1.
19. Marius 1990, 32–5; Cameron 1991, 19–24.
20. Wannenwetsch 2003, 134; see MacCulloch 2003, 110–17 for the role of Augustine in the Reformation debates.
21. For the influence of Augustine on Luther and his view of two separate realms, see Whitford 2003, 181.
22. Ibid., 179.
23. See McConica 1965, 20.
24. Wreidt 2003, 101–2.
25. Marius 1990, 20.
26. 'bylinge' – a word it seems of More's own invention, as many were, but one that apparently did not catch on. Probably a verbal form of 'bile', the internal fluid thought to produce anger and obstinacy.
27. Rex 2011, 105.
28. *Leges ergo si tollas: et omnia permittas libera magistratibus: aut nihil neque praecipient: neque uetabunt: et iam inutiles erunt magistratus: aut naturae suae ductu regent: et pro imperio, quidlibet exsequentur, et iam nihilo populus erit liberior, sed seruituis conditione deterior* (RL, 276); see also DCH, 262. These passages betray the influence of neo-Roman – that is, republican – views of liberty on More's work. Although Cathy Curtis suggests that More is missing a neo-Roman account of *libertas* (Curtis 2006), we do see it here.
29. See Wreidt 2003, 87–8.
30. Cargill Thompson 1975, 181–8.
31. Cargill Thompson 1979, 24, 25, 26.
32. Chadwick 1986, 37.
33. Wannenwetsch 2003, 123.
34. A lesson that is sometimes applied to the Utopians; see Marius 1990, 27–30.
35. Wreidt 2003, 92, 110–11; see also Gatti 2015, 74.
36. Cummins 2002, 46–7.
37. This is a paraphrase of Augustine that had also been used by Henry VIII in his *Assertio*; see Marius 1978, 91.
38. See Baker 1996, 16 for the 'Utopian-like' element of communion.
39. See Marius 1978, 95.
40. Ibid., 95, 98–9.
41. See Oakley 1981; Burns 1991, 150–2; Oakley 2008, 124–36. Notably, as MacCulloch points out, there was no consensus among conciliarists about the source of the Council's authority (MacCulloch 2003, 40).
42. Runciman and Vieira 2008, 10.
43. See MacCulloch 2003, 26.
44. Runciman and Vieira 2008, 11.
45. Quoted in Trapp and Herbrüggen 1997, 118.
46. Quoted in Lemon 2006, 8.
47. For the documents of his trial, see Kelly, Karlin and Wegemer 2011.
48. See Guy 2000, 186–96.

49. Ibid., 192.
50. The indictment is quoted ibid., 189.
51. See Trapp and Herbrüggen 1997, 126; Guy 2000, 191–3.
52. Roper 1932, 92.
53. Ibid.
54. Ibid.
55. See 'Account in a Paris Newsletter' (August 4, 1535), in Wegemer and Smith 2004, 352–5.
56. Roper 1932, 93.
57. Ibid., 94.
58. Wegemer and Smith 2004, 355 ('Account in a Paris Newsletter'). Note that it is 'and God's first': 'and', not 'but', as is commonly thought. See Marc'hadour 2009, 31.
59. See CW 8, 1313.
60. See Burns 1994, 148–52.
61. Rummel 2004, xiv, 63–4.
62. Ibid., 96.
63. McConica 1965, 30.
64. Martin Luther 1991, 24.

5 Influence

1. Curtis 2006; Wooding 2000, 257.
2. Kautsky 1979 [1927], 81. The original German was published in 1988.
3. See Guy 2000, 11.
4. The British Library English Short Titles Catalogue lists fifty-three copies in the British Isles, fifteen copies in North America, and one copy elsewhere, which suggests a large original print-run.
5. Roper 1932, 3.
6. Conrad 1995.
7. See Duffy 2009, 179–85.
8. McConica 1963, 53.
9. See Wooden 1982.
10. Hall 1809 [1548], 817.
11. Ibid., 818.
12. Prescott 1994, xxiii–xxiv.
13. Quoted in Kilroy 2009, 31.
14. CW 3.II, 698.
15. Quoted in Prescott 1994, xiv.
16. Quoted ibid., xix; see also Sieman 2009, 53.
17. Clapham 1602, A, 3v.
18. Sieman 2009, 45.
19. See Hallett and Hallett 2011, 21; see also the discussion at p. 72 here.
20. Shakespeare and Fletcher's *King Henry VIII (All is True)*, Act 3, scene 2, lines 395–8, in Shakespeare and Fletcher 2002, 358.

21. There is some dispute as to whether this section of the play is Shakespeare's, or belongs to a younger writer: see Milward 1990, 26.
22. See Murphy 2005.
23. Quoted in Jowett 2011, 5.
24. Ibid.
25. Munday and Chettle 2011, 6.92, 189.
26. Munday and Chettle 2011, 9.96, 190.
27. Ibid., 6.112, 191.
28. Ibid., 6.156, 196.
29. See Jowett 2011, 37–41.
30. Munday and Chettle 2011, 9.93–5, 248.
31. Ibid., 8.40–1, 221.
32. Ibid.
33. See Fox 1981, 168.
34. Munday and Chettle 2011, 8.25–6, 220.
35. See Jowett 2011, 88–9.
36. Munday and Chettle 2011, 17.66, 322; see Fox 1981, 166.
37. Munday and Chettle 2011, 9.261–2, 260.
38. Ibid., 9.295, 261.
39. Fox 1981, 162–73.
40. Jowett 2011, 9.
41. See Cave 2008.
42. There is a good summary of the difficulties of tracing the influence of More's *Utopia* in Goodwin and Taylor 2009, 125.
43. Bodin 1606, 3.
44. Bodin 1606, 482.
45. Ibid., 255, 271.
46. Salmon 1996, 502.
47. Bodin 1606, 188.
48. Nelson 2004, 99.
49. We might also include Samuel von Pufendorf, who quotes frequently from *Utopia* in his 1672 *De iure naturae et gentium* (*On the Law of Nature and Nations*).
50. Quoted in Dust 1973, 32.
51. Quoted ibid., 36.
52. James I 1994, 127.
53. Quoted in Boswell 2002, 8.
54. Norbrook 1990, 11.
55. See Curtis 2006.
56. Quoted in Hibbard 1980, 211.
57. Quoted in Sabbadini 2013, 90.
58. Hobbes 2012, 574.
59. See Talaska 2013, 64, 105.
60. Somers 1688–9, 17. The same is expressed in a contemporary pamphlet by Thomas Hunt; see Hunt 1680, 35.
61. Somers 1688–9, 18.

62. Huseman 2004, 255.
63. See Deval 2004, 175–6.
64. See Houston 2014, 53–4.
65. Ibid., 55.
66. Quoted ibid., 56.
67. As Houston 2014 establishes.
68. Ibid., 66.
69. Quoted ibid., 67.
70. Salzman 2002, 28. Houston 2014, 90–1 discusses this passage in depth.
71. Colclough 2002, 61–2, 66.
72. As Houston 2014, 97 points out.
73. See Eden 2001.
74. Houston 2014, 110.
75. Quoted ibid., 115.
76. See Sargent 1996, 164–8.
77. Salzman 2002, 30.
78. McCutcheon 1998, 62.
79. Quoted ibid., 69–70.
80. Burton quoted ibid., 70.
81. Gowland 2006, 238.
82. See Nelson 2004, 105.
83. Ibid., 111–12.
84. Ibid., 114.
85. Ibid., 122: Nelson suggests that Harrington is here writing against More, but it is Hythloday who makes the statement, and More's view, as we've seen, in fact comes closer to that of Harrington.
86. Ibid., 125.
87. Hume 1983, vol. 2: 537.
88. Ibid., vol. 3: 184.
89. Ibid., 216.
90. Ibid.
91. Ibid., 197.
92. Ibid., 222.
93. Ibid., 197.
94. Ibid., 215.
95. Reid 1990, 281.
96. Ibid., 283.
97. Ibid.
98. Ibid., 287.
99. Ibid.
100. Ibid.
101. See Kumar 2003, 67. It is a thesis also advanced in Olson 1982. For other Enlightenment utopias, see Claeys 1994.
102. Claeys 2014, 897. The connections between early socialism and the French Revolution are explored in depth in Lichtheim 1969, 3–5.

103. Claeys 1997, xiv.
104. See ibid., xxiv.
105. Mill 1981, 266.
106. Taylor 1870, 132.
107. Ibid., 125, 131.
108. Ibid., 136.
109. Ibid., 133.
110. Ibid., 137.
111. See Levin 2003, 68–82.
112. Quoted in Roberts 1991, 82.
113. Vieira 2010, 13–14. See also Geoghegan 1987, 39.
114. Marx 1987, 481.
115. Marx 1996, 710, 725.
116. Harstick, Sperl and Strauss 1999, 470 claim that Engels was responsible for the annotations on two pages and Marx for those on the other sixty-five. The RGASPI archive in Moscow, where the text is housed, maintains that all annotations were contributed by Engels; however, they bear a striking resemblance to the marks left by Marx in his copy of Machiavelli's *History*, which is held in the same archive.
117. Engels 1987, 611.
118. Engels and Marx 1975, 461.
119. Engels 1989, 481.
120. Ibid., 671.
121. Marx 1991, 505.
122. Kaufmann 1879, vi.
123. Ibid., v.
124. Ibid., 3, 1.
125. Ibid., 2.
126. Ibid.
127. Ibid., 5.
128. Ibid., 9.
129. Ibid., 10.
130. Ibid., 11.
131. Ibid., 3.
132. Quoted in Kumar 1995, xvii.
133. Engels 2001a, 96.
134. Engels 2001b, 164.
135. Kautsky (1979 [1927]), 94.
136. Ibid., 3.
137. Ibid.
138. Ibid., 98.
139. Ibid., 131.
140. Ibid., 139.
141. Ibid., 108.
142. Ibid., 109.

143. Ibid., 146.
144. Ibid., 249.
145. Ibid., 250.
146. Ibid.

Conclusion

1. Hankins 2000, 2–3.

References

Ackroyd, Peter (1999). *The Life of Thomas More*. London: Vintage.

Augustine (1998). *The City of God against the Pagans*, edited by R. W. Dyson. Cambridge: Cambridge University Press.

Baker, David Weil (1996). 'Topical Utopias: Radicalizing Humanism in Sixteenth-Century England'. *Studies in English Literature, 1500–1900*, 36.1, 1–30.

Baker, David Weil (1999). *Divulging Utopia*. Amherst: University of Massachusetts Press.

Baker-House, Seymour (2008). 'More, Sir Thomas (1478–1535)', in *ODNB*, available at http://oxforddnb.com/public/index.html (accessed 16 April 2016).

Baker-Smith, Dominic (2011). 'Reading *Utopia*', in George M. Logan, ed., *Cambridge Companion to Thomas More*, Cambridge: Cambridge University Press, pp. 139–67.

Baumann, Uwe (2015). 'The Humanistic and Religious Controversies and Rivalries of Thomas More (1477/8–1535): A Typology of Literary Forms and Genres?', in David A. Lines, Marc Laureys and Jill Kraye, eds, *Forms of Conflict and Rivalries in Renaissance Europe*, Bonn: Bonn University Press, pp. 79–108.

Beier, Benjamin V. (2012). ' "Colour" That Fails "to Set": Unethical Persuasion and the Nature of Rhetoric in More's *History of King Richard III*'. *Moreana*, 49, 189–212.

Betteridge, Thomas (2004). *Literature and Politics in the English Reformation*. Manchester: Manchester University Press.

Betteridge, Thomas (2013). *Writing Faith and Telling Tales: Literature, Politics, and Religion in the Work of Thomas More*. Notre Dame, IN: University of Notre Dame Press.

Bishop, Malcolm (2005). 'Ambrosius Holbein's *memento mori* Map for Sir Thomas More's *Utopia*: The Meanings of a Masterpiece of Early Sixteenth Century Graphic Art'. *British Dental Journal*, 199.2, 107–12.

Bodin, Jean (1606). *Six Books of a Commonweal*, trans. Richard Knolles. London.

Boswell, Jackson C. (2002). 'References and Allusions to Thomas More: 1641–1700 (Part One)'. *Moreana*, 39.151/2, 5–68.

Brown, Alison (2000). 'De-masking Renaissance Republicanism', in James Hankins, ed., *Renaissance Civic Humanism: Reappraisals and Reflections*, Cambridge: Cambridge University Press, pp. 179–99.

Brown, Rawdon, ed. (1867). *Calendar of State Papers: Venice*, vol. II: *1509–1519*. London: Longmans, Green, Reader, and Dyer.

Burgess, Glenn (2009). *British Political Thought, 1500–1660: The Politics of the Post-Reformation*. Basingstoke: Palgrave Macmillan.

Burns, James H. (1991). 'Scholasticism: Survival and Revival', in James H. Burns, ed., *The Cambridge History of Political Thought 1450–1700*, Cambridge: Cambridge University Press, pp. 132–55.

Cachey, Theodore J., Jr. (2003). 'Petrarchan Cartographical Writing', in Stephen Gersh and Bert Roest, eds, *Medieval and Renaissance Humanism: Rhetoric, Representation and Reform*, Leiden: Brill, pp. 73–91.

Cameron, Euan (1991). 'The Late Renaissance and the Unfolding Reformation in Europe', in James Kirk, ed., *Humanism and Reform: The Church in Europe, England, and Scotland, 1400–1643*, Oxford: Blackwell, pp. 15–36.

Cargill Thompson, W. D. J. (1975). 'Luther and the Right of Resistance to the Emperor', in Derek Baker, ed., *Church Society and Politics*, Oxford: Basil Blackwell, pp. 159–202.

Cargill Thompson, W. D. J. (1979). 'The Two Regiments: The Continental Setting of William Tyndale's Political Thought', in Derek Baker, ed., *Reform and Reformation: England and the Continent, c. 1500–1750*, Oxford: Basil Blackwell, pp. 17–33.

Cave, Alfred A. (1991). 'Thomas More and the New World', *Albion* 23.2, 209–29.

Cave, Terence, ed. (2008). *Thomas More's* Utopia *in Early Modern Europe: Paratexts and Contexts*. Manchester: Manchester University Press.

Cavill, Paul (2014). 'Heresy, Law and the State: Forfeiture in Late Medieval and Early Modern England'. *English Historical Review*, 129, 270–95.

Chadwick, Henry (1986). *Augustine: A Very Short Introduction*. Oxford: Oxford University Press.

Cicero (1913). *De officiis*, trans. Walter Miller. Cambridge, MA: Harvard University Press.

Claeys, Gregory, ed. (1994). *Utopias of the British Enlightenment*. Cambridge: Cambridge University Press.

Claeys, Gregory (1997). 'Introduction', in Gregory Claeys, *Modern British Utopias, 1700–1850*, vol. 1, London: Pickering & Chatto, pp. xiii–xxxix.

Claeys, Gregory (2014). 'Early Socialism as Intellectual History'. *History of European Ideas*, 40.7, 893–904.

Clapham, John (1602). *Historie of England: The First Book*. London.

Colclough, David (2002). 'Ethics and Politics in the *New Atlantis*', in Bronwen Price, ed., *Francis Bacon's New Atlantis: New Interdisciplinary Essays*, Manchester: Manchester University Press, pp. 60–81.

Conrad, F. W. (1995). 'Manipulating Reputations,' in Thomas Mayer and Daniel R. Woolf, eds, *The Rhetorics of Life-Writing in Early Modern Europe: Forms of Biography from Cassandra Fedele to Louis XIV*, Ann Arbor: University of Michigan Press, pp. 133–61.

Cooper, Helen (2010). *Shakespeare and the Medieval World*. London: Bloomsbury.

Croot, Patricia A. (2004). 'Settlement and Building: Chelsea up to 1680', in Patricia A. Croot, *A History of the County of Middlesex*, vol. 12: *Chelsea*. London: Victoria County History, pp. 14–26.

Cummins, Brian (2002). *The Literary Culture of the Reformation: Grammar and Grace*. Oxford: Oxford University Press.

Curtis, Cathy (2006). '"The Best State of the Commonwealth": Thomas More and Quentin Skinner', in Holly Hamilton-Bleakley, Annabel Brett and James Tully, eds, *Rethinking the Foundations of Modern Political Thought*. Cambridge: Cambridge University Press, pp. 93–112.

Curtis, Cathy (2011). 'More's Public Life', in George Logan, ed., *The Cambridge Companion to Thomas More*, Cambridge: Cambridge University Press, pp. 69–92.

Curtright, Travis (2012). *The One Thomas More*. Washington, DC: Catholic University of America Press.

Deval, Edwin M. (2004). '*Pantagruel*', in Elizabeth Chesney Zegura, ed., *Rabelais Encyclopedia*, Westport, CT: Greenwood Press, pp. 174–6.

Duffy, Eamon (2009). *Fires of Faith: Catholic England under Mary Tudor*. New Haven, CT: Yale University Press.

Dust, Philip (1973). 'Alberico Gentili's Commentaries on Utopian War'. *Moreana*, 37, 31–40.

Eden, Kathy (1991). 'Rhetoric in the Hermeneutics of Erasmus' Later Works'. *Erasmus of Rotterdam Society Yearbook*, 11, 88–104.

Eden, Kathy (2001). *Friends Hold All Things in Common: Tradition, Intellectual Property, and the Adages of Erasmus*. New Haven, CT: Yale University Press.

Elsky, Stephanie (2013). 'Common Law and the Common Place in Thomas More's *Utopia*'. *English Literary Renaissance*, 43.2, 181–210.

Engels, Friedrich (1987). '*Preparatory Writings for Anti-Dühring*', in *Marx and Engels Collected Works*, vol. 25, London: Lawrence & Wishart, pp. 591–620.

Engels, Friedrich (1989). *Marx and Engels Collected Works*, vol. 44: *Letters*. London: Lawrence & Wishart.

Engels, Friedrich (2001a). *Marx and Engels Collected Works*, vol. 48: *Letters*. London: Lawrence & Wishart.

Engels, Friedrich (2001b). *Marx and Engels Collected Works*, vol. 49: *Letters*. London: Lawrence & Wishart.

Engels, Friedrich and Karl Marx (1975). *The German Ideology*, in *Marx and Engels Collected Works*, vol. 5: London: Lawrence & Wishart, pp. 19–539.

Erasmus, Desiderius (1982). *Adages: Ii1 to Iv100*, in *Collected Works of Erasmus*, edited by Roger A. B. Mynors, vol. 31, Toronto: University of Toronto Press.

Erasmus, Desiderius (1992). *Education of a Christian Prince*, edited by Lisa Jardine, trans. Neil M. Cheshire and Michael J. Heath. Cambridge: Cambridge University Press.

Fox, Alistair (1981). 'The Paradoxical Design of *The Book of Sir Thomas More*'. *Renaissance and Reformation*, 17.3, 162–73.

Fox, Alistair (1982). *Thomas More: History and Providence*. New Haven, CT: Yale University Press.

Fox, Alistair (1986). 'Facts and Fallacies: Interpreting English Humanism', in Alistair Fox and John Guy, eds, *Reassessing the Henrician Age: Humanism, Politics and Reform 1500–1550*, Oxford: Basil Blackwell, pp. 9–33.

Fox, Alistair (1990). 'English Humanism and the Body Politic', in Gordon J. Schochet with Patricia E. Tatspaugh and Carol Brobeck, eds, *Reformation, Humanism and 'Revolution': Papers Presented at the Folger Institute Seminar 'Political Thought in the Henrician Age, 1500–1550'*, Washington, DC: Folger Shakespeare Library, pp. 147–62.

Gatti, Hilary (2015). *Ideas of Liberty in Early Modern Europe*. Princeton, NJ: Princeton University Press.

Geoghegan, Vincent (1987). 'Maxism and Utopianism'. *Utopian Studies*, 1, 37–51.

Goodey, Brian R. (1970). 'Mapping "Utopia": A Comment on the Geography of Sir Thomas More'. *Geographical Review*, 60.1, 15–30.

Goodwin, Barbara and Keith Taylor (2009). *The Politics of Utopia: A Study in Theory and Practice*, 2nd edn. Bern: Peter Lang AG.

Gowland, Angus (2006). *The Worlds of Renaissance Melancholy*. Cambridge: Cambridge University Press.

Gransden, Antonia (1997). *Historical Writing in England II: c. 1307 to the Sixteenth Century*. Abingdon: Routledge.

Greenblatt, Stephen (1980). 'At the Table of the Great: More's Self-Fashioning and Self-Cancellation', in Stephen Greenblatt, *Renaissance Self-Fashioning: From More to Shakespeare*. Chicago, IL: University of Chicago Press, pp. 11–73.

Guy, John (1986). 'Scripture as Authority: Problems of Interpretation in the 1530s', in Alistair Fox and John Guy, eds, *Reassessing the Henrician Age: Humanism, Politics and Reform 1500–1550*, Oxford: Basil Blackwell, pp. 199–220.

Guy, John (2000). *Thomas More*. London: Arnold.

Hadfield, Andrew (1998). *Literature, Travel, and Colonial Writing in the English Renaissance, 1545–1625*. Oxford: Oxford University Press.

Hall, Edward (1548). *The Union of the Two Noble and Illustre Families of Lancastre and Yorke*. London: Richard Grafton.

Hall, Edward (1809). *Chronicle: Containing the History of England during the Reign of Henry the Fourth and the Succeeding Monarchs to the End of the Reign of Henry the Eighth, in Which Are Particularly Described the Manners and Customs of Those Periods Carefully Collated with the Editions of 1548 and 1550* [edited by Henry Ellis], London: J. Johnson, F. C. and J. Rivington.

Hallett, Charles A. and Elaine S. Hallett (2011). *The Artistic Links between William Shakespeare and Sir Thomas More: Radically Different Richards*. New York: Palgrave Macmillan.

Hanham, Alison (2007). 'The Texts of Thomas More's *Richard III*'. *Renaissance Studies*, 21.1, 62–84.

Hankins, James (2000). 'Introduction', in James Hankins, ed., *Renaissance Civic Humanism: Reappraisals and Reflections*, Cambridge: Cambridge University Press, pp. 1–13.

Harstick, Hans-Peter, Richard Sperl and Hanno Strauss, eds (1999). *Die Bibliotheken von Karl Marx und Friedrich Engels: Annotiertes Verzeichnis des ermittelten Bestandes* (Gesamtausgabe IV/32). Berlin: Akademie Verlag.

Herbrüggen, Hubertus Schulte (2011 [1967]). 'Thomas More's Fortune Verses: A Contribution to the Solution of a Few Problems', trans. Amon Johannes Hunt. *Moreana*, 48.185/6, 121–48.

Hibbard, George R. (1980). 'Sequestration "into Atlantick and Eutopian polities": Milton on More', *Renaissance and Reformation*, 16.2, 209–25.

Hobbes, Thomas (2012). *Leviathan*, vol. 1, edited by Noel Malcolm. Oxford: Oxford University Press.

Hosington, Brenda (2003). 'Thomas More's Views on Language and Translation and Their Place in the Classical and Humanist Tradition'. *Moreana*, 40.153/4, 69–98.

Houston, Chloë (2014). *The Renaissance Utopia: Dialogue, Travel and the Ideal Society*. Farnham: Ashgate.

Hume, David (1983). *The History of England from the Invasion of Julius Caesar to the Revolution in 1688*, 6 vols. Indianapolis, IN: Liberty Fund.

Hunt, Thomas (1680). *The Great and Weighty Considerations Relating to the Duke of York*. London.

Huseman, William H. (2004). '*Utopia*', in Elizabeth Chesney Zegura, ed., *Rabelais Encyclopedia*, Westport: Greenwood Press, pp. 255–6.

James I (1994). *Triplici nodo, triplex cuneus: Or an Apology for the Oath of Allegiance*, in Johann P. Sommerville (ed.), *King James VI and I Political Writings*. Cambridge: Cambridge University Press, pp. 85–131.

Jowett, John (2011). 'Introduction', in Anthony Munday and Henry Chettle, *Sir Thomas More*, edited by John Jowett, London: Bloomsbury, pp. 1–131.

Kaufmann, Moritz (1879). *Utopias; Or, Schemes of Social Improvement: From Thomas More to Karl Marx*. London: C. Kegan Paul & Co.

Kautsky, Karl (1979 [1927]). *Thomas More and His Utopia*, trans. Henry James Stenning. London: Lawrence & Wishart.

Kelly, Henry Ansgar, Louis W. Karlin and Gerard B. Wegemer, eds (2011). *Thomas More's Trial by Jury*. Woodbridge: Boydell & Brewer.

Kempshall, Matthew (2011). *Rhetoric and the Writing of History*. Manchester: Manchester University Press.

Kenny, Anthony (1983). *Thomas More*. Oxford: Oxford University Press.

Kilroy, Gerard (2009). 'The Pleasant Learned Poet', in *The Epigrams of Sir John Harington*, edited by Gerard Kilroy, Farnham: Ashgate, pp. 1–90.

Kincaid, Arthur Noel (1977 [1972]). 'The Dramatic Structure of Sir Thomas More's History of King Richard III', in Richard S. Sylvester and Germain P. Marc'hadour, eds, *Essential Articles for the Study of Thomas More*, Hamden, CT: Archon Books, pp. 375–87.

Kinney, Arthur F. and David W. Swain, eds (2001). *Tudor England: An Encyclopedia*. New York: Garland.

Kinney, Daniel (1986). 'Introduction', in *Complete Works of St Thomas More*, vol. 15: *In Defense of Humanism: Letter to Martin Dorp, Letter to the University of Oxford, Letter to Edward Lee, Letter to a Monk, with a New Text and Translation of Historia Richardi Tertii*, edited by D. Kinney, New Haven, CT: Yale University Press, pp. xix–xxviii.

Kristeller, Paul Oskar (1980). 'Thomas More as a Renaissance Humanist'. *Moreana*, 65/6, 5–22.

Kumar, Krishan (1995). 'Introduction', in William Morris, *News from Nowhere, or an Epoch of Rest: Being Some Chapters of a Utopian Romance*, edited by Krishan Kumar, Cambridge: Cambridge University Press, pp. vii–xxiii.

Kumar, Krishan (2003). 'Aspects of the Western Utopian Tradition'. *History of the Human Sciences*, 16.1, 61–75.

Lanham, Richard A. (1991). 'Decorum', in Richard A. Lanham, *A Handlist of Rhetorical Terms*, 2nd edn, Berkeley: University of California Press, pp. 45–6.

Lederman, Cary J. (2000). 'Rhetoric, Reason, and Republic: Republicanisms – Ancient, Medieval, and Modern', in James Hankins, ed., *Renaissance Civic Humanism: Reappraisals and Reflections*, Cambridge: Cambridge University Press, pp. 247–69.

Lemon, Rebecca (2006). *Treason by Words: Literature, Law, and Rebellion in Shakespeare's England*. Ithaca, NY: Cornell University Press.

Levin, Michael (2003). 'A Liberal Looks at Utopian Socialism in the Years of Revolution 1848–9'. *Utopian Studies*, 14.2, 68–82.

Lichtheim, George (1969). *The Origins of Socialism*. London: Weidenfeld & Nicolson.

Logan, George M. (2007). 'Thomas More on Tyranny', *Thomas More Studies*, 2, 19–32.

Logan, George M. and Robert M. Adams (2011). 'Note on the Translation', in Thomas More, *Utopia*, edited by George M. Logan and Robert M. Adams, Cambridge: Cambridge University Press, pp. xxx–xxxi.

Lucian (1959). 'How to Write History', in Lucian, *Works*, vol. 6 (Loeb Classical Library), trans. K. Kilburn, Cambridge, MA: Harvard University Press, pp. 2–73.

Luther, Martin (1991). 'On Secular Authority', in Harro Höpfl, ed., *Luther and Calvin on Secular Authority*, Cambridge: Cambridge University Press, pp. 3–43

MacCulloch, Diarmaid (2002). *Tudor Church Militant: Edward VI and the Protestant Reformation*. Berkeley: University of California Press.

MacCulloch, Diarmaid (2003). *Reformation: Europe's House Divided, 1490–1700*. London: Viking.

Manley, Lawrence (1980). *Convention, 1500–1750*. Cambridge, MA: Harvard University Press.

Marc'hadour, Germain (2009). 'Latin Lives of Thomas More', in Anthony D. Cousins and Damian Grace, eds, *A Companion to Thomas More*. Cranbury, NJ: Associated University Presses, pp. 21–38.

Marius, Richard (1978). 'Henry VIII, Thomas More, and the Bishop of Rome'. *Albion: A Quarterly Journal Concerned with British Studies*, 10, 89–107.

Marius, Richard (1990). 'Community, Consent, and Coercion', in Gordon J. Schochet with Patricia E. Tatspaugh and Carol Brobeck, eds, *Reformation, Humanism, and 'Revolution': Papers Presented at the Folger Institute Seminar 'Political Thought in the Henrician Age, 1500–1550'*, Washington, DC: Folger Shakespeare Library, pp. 17–38.

Marsh, David (1998). *Lucian and the Latins: Humor and Humanism in the Early Renaissance*. Ann Arbor, MI: University of Michigan Press.

Marshall, Peter (2002). 'Evangelical Conversion in the Reign of Henry VIII', in Peter Marshall and Alec Ryrie, eds, *The Beginnings of English Protestantism*. Cambridge: Cambridge University Press, pp. 14–37.

Martz, Louis L. (1990). *Thomas More: The Search for the Inner Man*. New Haven, CT: Yale University Press.

Marx, Karl (1987). *A Contribution to the Critique of Political Economy* and 'From the Preparatory Materials: Original text of Second and beginning of Third chapter of Contribution to Critique of Political Economy', in *Marx and Engels Collected Works*, vol. 29, London: Lawrence & Wishart, pp. 257–417 and 430–507.

Marx, Karl (1991). *Marx and Engels Collected Works*, vol. 45: *Letters*. London: Lawrence & Wishart.

Marx, Karl (1996). *Marx and Engels Collected Works*, vol. 35: *Capital*. London: Lawrence & Wishart.

McConica, James Kelsey (1963). 'The Recusant Reputation of Thomas More'. *CCHA Report*, 30, 47–61.

McConica, James Kelsey (1965). *English Humanists and Reformation Politics*. Oxford: Oxford University Press.

McConica, James Kelsey (2011). 'Thomas More as Humanist', in George M. Logan, ed., *The Cambridge Companion to Thomas More*, Cambridge: Cambridge University Press, pp. 22–45.

McCutcheon, Elizabeth (1998). 'Robert Burton/Democritus Junior and Thomas More'. *Moreana*, 35.135/6, 55–74.

McCutcheon, Elizabeth (2011). 'More's Rhetoric', in George Logan, ed., *The Cambridge Companion to Thomas More*, Cambridge: Cambridge University Press, pp. 46–68.

McSheffrey, Shannon and Norman Tanner (2003). 'Introduction', in *Lollards of Coventry, 1486–1522*, edited and trans. by Shannon McSheffrey and Norman Tanner, Cambridge: Cambridge University Press, pp. 1–56.

Mill, John Stuart (1981). *Autobiography*, in John M. Robson and Jack Stillinger, eds, *Collected Works of John Stuart Mill*, vol. 1, Abingdon: Routledge, pp. 1–290.

Miller, Clarence H. (2005). 'A Man for All Seasons'. Address to the Thomas More Studies Conference, 5 November 2005, available at http://www.thomasmorestudies.org/docs/Miller_on_man_for_all_seasons.pdf (accessed 16 April 2016).

Milward, Peter (1990). 'The Morean Counsellor in Shakespeare's Last Plays'. *Moreana*, 27.103, 25–32.

Mitjans, Frank (2012). 'Reviewing and Correcting the Article on the Date of Birth of Thomas More'. *Moreana*, 49.189/90, 251–62.

More, Cresacre (1828 [1630]). *The Life of Sir Thomas More*. London: W. Pickering.

More, Thomas (1551). *Utopia*, trans. Ralph Robinson. London: Henry Frowde.

Munday, Anthony and Henry Chettle (2011). *Sir Thomas More*, censored by Edmund Tilney, revised by Henry Chettle, Thomas Dekker, Thomas Heywood and William Shakespeare; edited by John Jowett. London: Bloomsbury Publishing.

Murphy, Clare M. (2005). 'Thomas More in the Subtext of Shakespeare and Fletcher's *Henry VIII*'. *Moreana*, 42.163, 105–18.

Nauta, Lodi (2007). 'Lorenzo Valla and the Rise of Humanist Dialectic', in James Hankins, ed., *The Cambridge Companion to Renaissance Philosophy*, Cambridge: Cambridge University Press, pp. 193–210.

Nauta, Lodi (2009). *In Defense of Common Sense: Lorenzo Valla's Humanist Critique of Scholastic Philosophy*. Cambridge, MA: Harvard University Press.

Nelson, Eric (2004). *The Greek Tradition in Republican Thought*. Cambridge: Cambridge University Press.

Nelson, William (1977 [1943]). 'Thomas More, Grammarian and Orator', in Richard S. Sylvester and Germain P. Marc'hadour, eds, *Essential Articles for the Study of Thomas More*, Hamden, CT: Archon Books, pp. 150–60.

Norbrook, David (1990). 'The Monarchy of Wit and the Republic of Letters: Donne's Politics', in Elizabeth D. Harvey and Katharine Eisaman Maus, eds, *Soliciting Interpretation: Literary Theory and Seventeenth-Century English Poetry*, Chicago, IL: University of Chicago Press, pp. 3–36.

Oakley, Francis (1981). 'Natural Law, the *Corpus mysticum*, and Consent in Conciliar Thought from John of Paris to Matthias Ugonius'. *Speculum*, 56.4, 786–810.

Oakley, Francis (2008). *The Conciliarist Tradition: Constitutionalism in the Catholic Church 1300–1870*. Oxford: Oxford University Press.

Olson, Theodore (1982). *Millennialism, Utopianism, and Progress*. Toronto: University of Toronto Press.

Parker, Patricia (2002). 'What's in a Name: And More', in Pilar Cuder Dominquez, ed., special issue of *SEDERI, Revista de la Sociedad Espanola de Estudio Renacentistas Ingleses*, 11, 101–50.

Paul, Joanne (2014). 'The Uses of *kairos* in Renaissance Political Philosophy'. *Renaissance Quarterly*, 67.1, 43–78.

Perreiah, Alan R. (2004). *Renaissance Truths: Humanism, Scholasticism and the Search for the Perfect Language*. Farnham: Ashgate.

Plato (1926). *Laws*, trans. R. G. Bury. Cambridge, MA: Harvard University Press.

Prescott, Anne Lake (1994). 'Introduction', in Jackson Campbell Boswell, *Sir Thomas More in the English Renaissance: An Annotated Catalogue*, Binghamton, NY: Medieval and Renaissance Texts and Studies, pp. xi–xxxiv.

Rappaport, Steve (2002 [1989]). *Worlds within Worlds: Structures of Life in Sixteenth-Century London*. Cambridge: Cambridge University Press.

Reid, Thomas (1990). 'Some Thoughts on the Utopian System', in Knud Haakonssen, ed., *Practical Ethics: Being Lectures and Papers on Natural Religion, Self-Government, Natural Jurisprudence, and the Law of Nations*, Princeton, NJ: Princeton University Press, pp. 277–99.

Rex, Richard (2011). 'Thomas More and the Heretics: Statesman or Fanatic?', in George Logan, ed., *The Cambridge Companion to Thomas More*, Cambridge: Cambridge University Press, pp. 93–115.

Roberts, Leslie J. (1991). 'Etienne Cabet and His *Voyage en Icarie*, 1840'. *Utopian Studies*, 2.1/2, 77–94.

Roper, William (1932). *The Life of Thomas Moore, Knight*, edited by Elsie Vaughan Hitchcock. Oxford: Oxford University Press.

Rummel, Erika (2004). *Desiderius Erasmus*. London: Continuum.

Runciman, David and Monica Brito Vieira (2008). *Representation*. Cambridge: Polity.

Sabbadini, Lorenzo (2013). *Property, Liberty and Self-Ownership in the English Revolution*. PhD thesis, Queen Mary, University of London.

Salmon, John H. M. (1996). 'The Legacy of Jean Bodin: Absolutism, Populism or Constitutionalism'. *History of Political Thought*, 17.4, 500–22.

Salzman, Paul (2002). 'Narrative Contexts for Bacon's *New Atlantis*', in Bronwen Price, ed., *Francis Bacon's* New Atlantis: *New Interdisciplinary Essays*, Manchester: Manchester University Press, pp. 28–47.

Sargent, Rose-Mary (1996). 'Bacon as an Advocate for Cooperative Scientific Research', in Markku Peltonen, ed., *The Cambridge Companion to Bacon*, Cambridge: Cambridge University Press, pp. 146–71.

Schuster, Louis A. (1973). 'Thomas More's Polemical Career, 1523–1533', in *CTA*, pp. 1137–268.

Shakespeare, William and John Fletcher (2002). *King Henry VIII (All Is True)*, edited by Gordon McMullan. London: Bloomsbury.

Sieman, James R. (2009). 'Introduction', in William Shakespeare, *King Richard III*, edited by James R. Sieman, London: Bloomsbury, pp. 1–123.

Skinner, Quentin (2002). 'Thomas More's *Utopia* and the Virtue of True Nobility', in Quentin Skinner, *Visions of Politics*, vol. 2: *Renaissance Virtues*, Cambridge: Cambridge University Press, pp. 213–44.

Skinner, Quentin (2007). '*Paradiastole*: Redescribing the Vices as Virtues', in Sylvia Adamson, Gavin Alexander and Katrina Ettenhuber, eds, *Renaissance Figures of Speech*, Cambridge: Cambridge University Press, pp. 148–63.

Somers, John (1688–9). *A Brief History of the Succession of the Crown of England*. London.

Surtz, Edward (1977). 'Richard Pace's Sketch of Thomas More', in Richard S. Sylvester and Germain P. Marc'hadour, eds, *Essential Articles for the Study of Thomas More*, Hamden, CT: Archon Books, pp. 180–8 and 611–14.

Sylvester, Richard S. (1963). 'The "Man for All Seasons" Again'. *Huntington Library Quarterly*, 26, 147–54.

Talaska, Richard (2013). *The Hardwick Library and Hobbes's Early Intellectual Development*. Charlottesville, VA: Philosophy Documentation Center.

Taylor, Helen (1870). 'Sir Thomas More on the Politics of To-Day'. *The Fortnightly Review*, pp. 125–37.

Trapp, Joseph Burney and Hubertus Schulte Herbrüggen (1997). *'The King's Good Servant': Sir Thomas More, 1477/8–1535*. London: National Portrait Gallery.

Vieira, Fátima (2010). 'The Concept of Utopia', in Gregory Claeys, ed., *The Cambridge Companion to Utopian Literature*, Cambridge: Cambridge University Press, pp. 3–27.

Wagner, John A. and Susan Walters Schmid, eds (2012). 'Heresy Law', in John A. Wagner and Susan Walters Schmid, eds, *Encyclopedia of Tudor England*, vol. 2. Santa Barbara, CA: ABC-CLIO, pp. 591–3.

Wannenwetsch, Bernd (2003). 'Luther's Moral Theology', in Donald McKim, ed., *The Cambridge Companion to Martin Luther*, Cambridge: Cambridge University Press, pp. 120–35.

Wegemer, Gerard (1993). 'The Political Philosophy of Sir Thomas More', in Robert A. Herrera, ed., *Saints, Sovereigns, and Scholars*, New York: Peter Lang, pp. 135–45.

Wegemer, Gerard (2007). 'Thomas More's *History of King Richard III*: Educating Citizens for Self-Government'. *Thomas More Studies*, 2, 38–48.

Wegemer, Gerald and Stephen Smith, eds (2004). *A Thomas More Source Book*. Washington, DC: CUA Press.

White, Thomas I. (1982). 'Pride and the Public Good: Thomas More's Use of Plato in *Utopia*'. *Journal of the History of Philosophy*, 20.4, 329–54.

Whitford, David M. (2003). 'Luther's Political Encounters', in Donald McKim, ed., *The Cambridge Companion to Martin Luther*, Cambridge: Cambridge University Press, pp. 179–91.

Williams, Raymond (1983). *Keywords*. London: Fontana Paperbacks.

Wilson, Nigel (1992). 'The Name Hythlodaeus'. *Moreana*, 29.110, 33.

Wilson, Thomas (1560). *The Arte of Rhetorique*. London: John Kingston.

Wooden, Warren W. (1982). 'Thomas More in Hostile Hands: The English Image of More in Protestant Literature of the Renaissance'. *Moreana*, 19.75/6, 77–87.

Wooding, Lucy E. (2000). *Rethinking Catholicism in Reformation England*. Oxford: Oxford University Press.

Wreidt, Markus (2003). 'Luther's Theology', trans. Katharina Gustav, in Donald McKim, ed., *The Cambridge Companion to Martin Luther*, Cambridge: Cambridge University Press, pp. 86–119.

Yoran, Hanan (2010). *Between Utopia and Dystopia: Erasmus, Thomas More, and the Humanist Republic of Letters*. Lanham, MD: Lexington Books.

Recommended Reading

Note   In addition to those sources listed below, the introductions to the Yale *Complete Works of Thomas More* are essential reading and were instrumental to this study.

Online Resources

Baker-House, Seymour (2008). 'More, Sir Thomas (1478–1535)', in *ODNB*, available at http://oxforddnb.com/public/index.html (accessed 16 April 2016).

Baker-Smith, Dominic (2014). 'Thomas More', in *Stanford Encyclopedia of Philosophy*, available at http://plato.stanford.edu/archives/spr2014/entries/thomas-more (accessed 16 April 2016).

The Center for Thomas More Studies, available at http://thomasmorestudies.org (accessed 19 April 2016).

John Foxe's The Acts and Monuments Online, available at www.JohnFoxe.org (accessed 19 April 2016).

Silva Rhetoricae: The Forest of Rhetoric, available at http://rhetoric.byu.edu/default.htm (accessed 19 April 2016).

Tudor England

Brigden, Susan (2000). *New Worlds, Lost Worlds: The Rule of the Tudors 1485–1603*. London: Penguin Books.

Gunn, Steven (1995). *Early Tudor Government, 1485–1558*. Basingstoke: Palgrave Macmillan.

Guy, John (1988). *Tudor England*. Oxford: Oxford University Press.

Kinney, Arthur F. and David W. Swain, eds (2001). *Tudor England: An Encyclopedia*. New York: Garland.

Rappaport, Steve (2002). *Worlds within Worlds: Structures of Life in Sixteenth-Century London*. Cambridge: Cambridge University Press.

Withington, Phil (2009). *The Politics of Commonwealth: Citizens and Freemen in Early Modern England*. Cambridge: Cambridge University Press.

Early Modern Europe

Cameron, Euan, ed. (2001). *Early Modern Europe*. Oxford: Oxford University Press.

Kamen, Henry (2000). *Early Modern European Society*. Abingdon: Routledge.

Kümin, Beat (2009). *The European World, 1500–1800: An Introduction to Early Modern European History*. Abingdon: Routledge.

The Church and the Reformation

Beckwith, Sarah (1993). *Christ's Body: Identity, Culture and Society in Late Medieval Writings*. London: Routledge.

Bossy, John (1985). *Christianity in the West, 1400–1700*. Oxford: Oxford University Press.

Cameron, Euan (1991). *The European Reformation*, 2nd edn. Oxford: Oxford University Press.

Chroust, Anton-Hermann (1947). 'The Corporate Idea and the Body Politic in the Middle Ages'. *The Review of Politics*, 9.4, 423–52.

Duffy, Eamon (1992). *The Stripping of the Altars: Traditional Religion in England, 1400–1580*. New Haven, CT: Yale University Press.

Guy, John (1990). 'Perceptions of Heresy, 1200–1500', in Gordon J. Schochet with Patricia E. Tatspaugh and Carol Brobeck, eds, *Reformation, Humanism and 'Revolution': Papers Presented at the Folger Institute Seminar 'Political Thought in the Henrician Age, 1500–1550'*. Washington, DC: Folger Shakespeare Library, pp. 39–61.

Haigh, Christopher (1993). *English Reformations: Religion, Politics and Society under the Tudors*. Oxford: Oxford University Press.

MacCulloch, Diarmaid (2003). *Reformation: Europe's House Divided, 1490–1700*. London: Viking.

Oakley, Francis (1981). 'Natural Law, the *Corpus mysticum*, and Consent in Conciliar Thought from John of Paris to Matthias Ugonius'. *Speculum*, 56.4, 786–810.

Oakley, Francis (2008). *The Conciliarist Tradition: Constitutionalism in the Catholic Church 1300–1870*. Oxford: Oxford University Press.

Rex, Richard (1993). *Henry VIII and the English Reformation*. Basingstoke: Palgrave Macmillan.

Rex, Richard (2002). *The Lollards*. Basingstoke: Palgrave Macmillan.

Humanism

Eden, Kathy (2001). *Friends Hold All Things in Common: Tradition, Intellectual Property, and the* Adages *of Erasmus*. New Haven, CT: Yale University Press.

Hankins, James, ed. (2000). *Renaissance Civic Humanism: Reappraisals and Reflections*. Cambridge: Cambridge University Press.

Hosington, Brenda (2003). 'Thomas More's Views on Language and Translation and Their Place in the Classical and Humanist Tradition'. *Moreana*, 40.153/4, 69–98.

Jardine, Lisa (1993). *Erasmus, Man of Letters*. Princeton, NJ: Princeton University Press.

Kristeller, Paul Oskar (1980). 'Thomas More as a Renaissance Humanist'. *Moreana*, 65/6, 5–22.

Nauert, Charles G. (2006). *Humanism and the Culture of Renaissance Europe*. Cambridge: Cambridge University Press.

Nauta, Lodi (2007). 'Lorenzo Valla and the Rise of Humanist Dialectic', in James Hankins, ed., *The Cambridge Companion to Renaissance Philosophy*, Cambridge: Cambridge University Press, pp. 193–210.

Rummel, Erika (1995). *The Humanist–Scholastic Debate in the Renaissance and Reformation*. Cambridge, MA: Harvard University Press.

Skinner, Quentin (1978). *The Foundations of Modern Political Thought*, vol. 1: *The Renaissance*. Cambridge: Cambridge University Press.

Yoran, Hanan (2010). *Between Utopia and Dystopia: Erasmus, Thomas More, and the Humanist Republic of Letters*. Lanham, MD: Lexington Books.

General Studies: Thomas More

Cousins, Anthony D. and Damian Grace, eds (2011). *A Companion to Thomas More*. Cranbury, NJ: Associated University Presses.

Curtright, Travis (2012). *The One Thomas More*. Washington, DC: Catholic University of America Press.

Fox, Alistair (1982). *Thomas More: History and Providence*. New Haven, CT: Yale University Press.

Greenblatt, Stephen (1980). 'At the Table of the Great: More's Self-Fashioning and Self-Cancellation', in Stephen Greenblatt, *Renaissance Self-Fashioning: From More to Shakespeare*, Chicago, IL: University of Chicago Press, pp. 11–73.

Kenny, Anthony (1983). *Thomas More*. Oxford: Oxford University Press.

Logan, George M., ed. (2011). *The Cambridge Companion to Thomas More*. Cambridge: Cambridge University Press.

Sylvester, Richard S. and Germain P. Marc'hadour, eds (1977). *Essential Articles for the Study of Thomas More*. Hamden, CT: Archon Books.

Wegemer, Gerard B. (2011). *Young Thomas More and the Arts of Liberty*. Cambridge: Cambridge University Press.

Biographies

Ackroyd, Peter (1999). *The Life of Thomas More*. London: Vintage.
Guy, John (2000). *Thomas More*. London: Arnold.
Marius, Richard (1999). *Thomas More: A Biography*. Cambridge, MA: Harvard University Press.

Early Works

Cousins, A. D. (2010). *Pleasure and Gender in the Writings of Thomas More: Pursuing the Common Weal*. Pittsburgh, PA: Duquesne University Press.
Grace, Damian. (1988). 'Subjects or Citizens? *People* and *gives* in More's *Epigrammata*'. *Moreana*, 97, 133–6.

Utopia

Baker-Smith, Dominic (2000). *More's* Utopia. Toronto: University of Toronto Press.
Goodey, Brian R. (1970). 'Mapping "Utopia": A Comment on the Geography of Sir Thomas More'. *Geographical Review*, 60.1, 15–30.
Headley, John M. (2003). 'The Problem of Counsel Revisited: More, Castiglione and the Resignation of Office in the Sixteenth Century'. *Moreana*, 40.153/4, 99–119.
Hexter, Jack H. (1952). *More's* Utopia: *The Biography of an Idea*. Princeton, NJ: Princeton University Press.
Logan, George M. (1983). *The Meaning of More's* Utopia. Princeton, NJ: Princeton University Press.
Logan, George M. (1994). 'Utopia and Deliberative Rhetoric'. *Moreana*, 31.118/19, 103–20.
Nelson, Eric (2004). 'Greek Nonsense in More's Utopia', in Eric Nelson, *The Greek Tradition in Republican Thought*, Cambridge: Cambridge University Press, pp. 19–48.
Skinner, Quentin (2002). 'Thomas More's *Utopia* and the Virtue of True Nobility', in Quentin Skinner, *Visions of Politics*, vol. 2: *Renaissance Virtues*. Cambridge: Cambridge University Press, pp. 213–44.

History of Richard the Third

Beier, Benjamin V. (2012). ' "Colour" That Fails "to Set": Unethical Persuasion and the Nature of Rhetoric in More's *History of King Richard III*'. *Moreana*, 49, 189–212.

Hanham, Alison (2007). 'The Texts of Thomas More's *Richard III*'. *Renaissance Studies*, 21.1, 62–84.

Wegemar, Gerard (2007). 'Thomas More's *History of King Richard III*: Educating Citizens for Self-Government'. *Thomas More Studies*, 2, 38–48.

Yoran, Hanan (2001). 'Thomas More's *Richard III*: Probing the limits of humanism'. *Renaissance Studies*, 15.4, 514–37.

Polemics and Religious Works

Gogan, Brian (1982). *The Common Corps of Christendom: Ecclesiological Themes in the Writings of Sir Thomas More*. Leiden: Brill.

Oakley, Francis (1980). 'Headley, Marius and the Matter of More's "Conciliarism"'. *Moreana*, 64, 82–8.

Sheldrake, Philip (1977). 'Thomas More and Authority'. *The Month: A Review of Christian Thought and World Affairs*, 10.4, 122–5, 134.

Legacy

Boswell, Jackson Campbell (1994). *Sir Thomas More in the English Renaissance: An Annotated Catalogue*. Binghamton, NY: Medieval and Renaissance Texts and Studies.

Cave, Terence, ed. (2008). *Thomas More's* Utopia *in Early Modern Europe: Paratexts and Contexts*. Manchester: Manchester University Press.

Claeys, Gregory, ed. (2010). *The Cambridge Companion to Utopian Literature*. Cambridge: Cambridge University Press.

Duffy, Eamon (2009). *Fires of Faith: Catholic England under Mary Tudor*. New Haven, CT: Yale University Press.

Houston, Chloë (2014). *The Renaissance Utopia: Dialogue, Travel and the Ideal Society*. Farnham: Ashgate.

Kautsky, Karl (1979 [1927]). *Thomas More and His Utopia*. London: Lawrence & Wishart.

McConica, James Kelsey (1963). 'The Recusant Reputation of Thomas More'. *CCHA Report*, 30, 47–61.

Nelson, Eric (2006). '*Utopia* through Italian Eyes: Thomas More and the Critics of Civic Humanism'. *Renaissance Quarterly*, 59.4, 1029–57.

Wooden, Warren W. (1982). 'Thomas More in Hostile Hands: The English Image of More in Protestant Literature of the Renaissance'. *Moreana*, 19.75/6, 77–87.

Index